Bases of Adult Attachment

Vivian Zayas • Cindy Hazan
Editors

Bases of Adult Attachment

Linking Brain, Mind and Behavior

Springer

Editors
Vivian Zayas
Department of Psychology
Cornell University
Ithaca
NY
USA

Cindy Hazan
Department of Human Development
Cornell University
Ithaca
NY
USA

ISBN 978-1-4614-9621-2 ISBN 978-1-4614-9622-9 (eBook)
DOI 10.1007/978-1-4614-9622-9
Springer New York Heidelberg Dordrecht London

Library of Congress Control Number: 2014947239

Printed on acid-free paper

Springer is part of Springer Science+Business Media (www.springer.com)

Contents

Contributors

Bianca P. Acevedo Department of Public Health, Weill Cornell Medical College, NY, NY, USA

Mark W. Baldwin McGill University, Montreal, Quebec, Canada

Jennifer A. Bartz McGill University, Montreal, Quebec, Canada

Lane Beckes Department of Psychology, Bradley University, Peoria, IL, USA

James A. Coan Department of Psychology, University of Virginia, Charlottesville, VA, USA

W. Andrew Collins University of Minnesota, Minneapolis, USA

Lisa M. Diamond University of Utah, Salt Lake City, USA

Allison K. Farrell University of Minnesota, Minneapolis, USA

R. Chris Fraley University of Illinois at Urbana-Champaign, Champaign, USA

Omri Gillath Department of Psychology, University of Kansas, Lawrence, KS, USA

Gül Günaydin Department of Psychology, Bilkent University, Ankara, Turkey

Cindy Hazan Department of Human Development, Cornell University, Ithaca, NY, U.S.A

Marie E. Heffernan University of Illinois at Urbana-Champaign, Champaign, USA

Gery Karantzas Deakin University, Burwood, Australia

John E. Lydon McGill University, Montreal, Quebec, Canada

K. Lee Raby University of Minnesota, Minneapolis, USA

Emre Selcuk Department of Psychology, Middle East Technical University, Ankara, Turkey

Yuichi Shoda Department of Psychology, University of Washington, Seattle, USA

Jeffry A. Simpson University of Minnesota, Minneapolis, USA

Vivian Zayas Department of Psychology, Cornell University, Ithaca, NY, USA

About the Authors

Bianca Acevedo holds a B.A. in Psychology from New York University and a Ph.D. in Social/Health Psychology from the State University of New York at Stony Brook. Dr. Acevedo is currently a research scientist at the University of California, Santa Barbara with expertise in Interpersonal Relationships, Neuroscience and Public Health research. She was formerly at Weill Cornell's Dept of Public Health and at Albert Einstein College of Medicine. She has published several widely recognized articles on the neural underpinnings of love and attachment in humans which earned her the 2012 International Woman in Science Award and several invitations to national and international scientific conferences.

Mark W. Baldwin is currently a Professor in the Department of Psychology at McGill University in Montreal Canada. He completed his Ph.D. at the University of Waterloo, held postdoctoral fellowships at the University of Michigan and the Clarke Institute of Psychiatry, and held a faculty position at the University of Winnipeg before moving to McGill. His research interests broadly involve interpersonal cognition, and specifically focus on the sense of self-with-other that arises from the activation of interpersonal representations. In recent work he and his students are examining the possibility of using repetitive computer tasks to train people's associative and attentional processes, to facilitate an increased sense of security.

Jennifer A. Bartz is currently an Assistant Professor in the Department of Psychology at McGill University in Montreal Canada. She completed her Ph.D. at McGill and then was a post-doctoral fellow in the Department of Psychiatry at the Mount Sinai School of Medicine in New York City. She remained at Mount Sinai as an Assistant Professor (academic track) for four years before joining the faculty at McGill. Her research focuses broadly on the communal behaviors (e.g., cooperation, trust, empathy) that are vital to forming and maintaining close attachment relationships, and how attachment facilitates or hinders such behaviors. To address this question, she uses an interdisciplinary approach involving methods from experimental social psychology, cognitive psychology and neuroscience (e.g., pharmacological challenge, functional imaging, genetics), and studies both healthy and clinical populations (e.g., borderline personality disorder). A major focus of her current work is aimed at understanding the role of biological factors and, in particular, the oxytocin and opioid systems in regulating attachment, social motivation, and prosocial behavior in humans.

Lane Beckes' research focuses on emotional, attachment, and prosocial processes in interpersonal relationships. His approach is cross-disciplinary employing theory and methods from social psychology, social cognitive and affective neuroscience, and evolutionary theory. He has published in a variety of journals with diverse specializations such as *Psychological Science, Social Cognitive and Affective Neuroscience, Social and Personality Psychology Compass, The Journal of Social and Personal Relationships, Psychophysiology, Behavioral and Brain Sciences, Frontiers in Human Neuroscience, and NeuroImage.* He received his PhD from the University of Minnesota in Social Psychology and conducted post-doctoral research in the University of Virginia's Affective Neuroscience Laboratory. Currently he is an Assistant Professor at Bradley University where he is continuing to study the neurobiological and social processes involved in the social regulation of emotion and bonding.

James Coan is Associate Professor of Clinical Psychology and Director of the Virginia Affective Neuroscience Laboratory at the University of Virginia, in Charlottesville.

W. Andrew Collins Professor of Child Development. *Research areas:* Social development, interpersonal relationships, adolescence, attachment processes.

Lisa M. Diamond is Professor of Psychology and Gender Studies at the University of Utah. She received her doctorate in Human Development from Cornell University in 1999. Dr. Diamond's research focuses on adolescent and young adult social and sexual development, and on the psychobiological mechanisms through which intimate relationships influence physical and mental health over the life course. Dr. Diamond is particularly interested in the longitudinal course of sexual identity development, and in the multiple environmental and psychosocial factors that influence the emergence and expression of sexual and affectional feelings for same-sex and other-sex partners at different stages of life. Dr. Diamond has been awarded grants in support of her research from the National Institute for Mental Health, The W.T. Grant Foundation, the American Psychological Foundation, the Gay and Lesbian Medical Association, the American Institute for Bisexuality, and the Templeton Foundation.

Allison K. Farrell Graduate student in Psychology. *Research areas:* Interpersonal relationships, power and influence, attachment processes.

R. Chris Fraley is a professor of psychology at the University of Illinois at Urbana-Champaign. His research focuses on attachment theory and close relationships, personality dynamics and development, and research methods.

Omri Gillath, PhD is an associate professor in the Department of Psychology and the Hoglund Brain Imaging Center at the University of Kansas. His work focuses on human pair-bonding and the effects of personality on cognition and behavior. He uses diverse methodologies including neuroimaging, gene mapping, and advanced cognitive techniques to explore the associations between attachment style and cognitive performance, sexual motivation and behavior, mating strategies, and caregiving behavior. He has published extensively on the topics of interpersonal relationships and relationship neuroscience and is currently an associate editor of *Personal Relationships*, and a member of the editorial board *of Journal of Personality and Social Psychology, Journal of Social and Personal Relationships, and Journal of Research in Personality*. He is a fellow of the Society for Experimental Psychology. He won the 2012 IARR Gerald R. Miller Award for Early Career Achievement, the 2011 Caryl Rusbult Close Relationships Early Career Award, the Sage 2010 Young Scholar Award, and the J. Michael Young academic advisor award at the University of Kansas.

Gul Gunaydin received her B.S. in business from Middle East Technical University, Turkey. Before starting her graduate training at Cornell University, she spent a year at the University of California, Berkeley as a Fulbright Fellow conducting research on interpersonal relationships. She completed her Ph. D. in Social and Personality Psychology at Cornell, with a minor in Cognitive Science. Gul currently works at Bilkent University, Turkey as an Assistant Professor of Psychology. In her program of research, she studies interpersonal relationships from a multidisciplinary approach that draws on research and theory from social and cognitive psychology. Her current work focuses on how others from unknown individuals to romantic partners are mentally represented and the consequences of these representations for impression formation, interpersonal behavior, and emotion regulation.

Marie E. Heffernan is a graduate student at the University of Illinois at Urbana-Champaign. Her research focuses on close relationships, the development of attachment bonds in adult romantic relationships, and understanding the factors that influence romantic attraction.

Gery Karantzas is a Senior Lecturer in the School of Psychology at Deakin University. He is currently the convenor the Australian Psychological Society (APS) Psychology of Relationships Interest Group. He has published numerous studies in the area of close personal relationships with a specific interest in investigating couple and family relationships during transitions and in adult attachment. His research activities have been funded by grants from the Australian Research Council, the Academy of Social Sciences in Australia and beyondblue.

John E. Lydon is currently a Professor in the Department of Psychology at McGill University in Montreal, Canada. He completed his Ph.D. at the University of Waterloo and was a post-doctoral fellow at UCLA. He has been a visiting fellow at Radboud University (NL), UC-Berkeley, Louvain-la-neuve (BE), Concordia University (CA), and Universite du Quebec a Montreal. His research focuses on intimate social bonds and has examined (1) how attachment bonds regulate stress and well-being; (2) how relationship commitment motivates an individual to expend effort to overcome relationship adversities, and (3) how the social environment impacts on maternal well-being in ways that affect the maternal–infant bond and child development. His current focus is on how a close relationship becomes internalized and a core part of one's identity.

K. Lee Raby Graduate student in Child Development. *Research areas:* Social development, parenting, attachment processes.

Emre Selcuk received his Ph.D. degree from Cornell University. His research focuses on the formation, maintenance, and functions of attachment relationships across the lifespan, and the individual difference factors (e.g., perceived partner responsiveness, attachment style, relationship quality) moderating these processes. He is currently an assistant professor at the Department of Psychology at Middle East Technical University, Turkey.

Yuichi Shoda is a Professor of Psychology at the University of Washington. His research is centered on the notion that the ever changing stream of an individual's social cognition, affects, and behaviors can be understood as a function of her "cognitive-affective processing system" (CAPS), and that individual differences in behavior are a result of each individual's distinctive associative network of thoughts and feelings in such a system. Most relevant for the work presented in this volume, this approach has been applied to understanding the dynamics and the emergent properties of dyadic systems (Zayas et al. 2002; Shoda and LeeTiernan 2002; Zayas and Shoda 2005, 2008). This approach has also led to the development of the Highly Repeated Within Person approach for detecting individual differences in the effects of specific situations without relying on moderator variables (Whitsett and Shoda 2014), which can also be used to enhance clinical interventions through "quantitative idiography" of each client's CAPS system. Together, these new approaches suggest reconceptualizing the scientific paradigm used in psychology research (Shoda et al. 2014). Currently, he also serves as an associate editor of *Social Psychological and Personality Science.*

Jeffry A. Simpson Professor of Psychology. Research areas: Interpersonal relationships, social development, evolution and social behavior, attachment processes.

Editor Biographies

Vivian Zayas is an Associate Professor of Psychology and Director of the Personality, Attachment, and Control Laboratory at Cornell University. Her research examines the cognitive and affective processes that regulate behaviors within close relationships. She approaches the study of the individual and his or her relationships from a multi-level, interdisciplinary perspective that bridges the study of attachment processes with research on executive control and self-regulation and blurs traditionally defined boundaries between social and personality psychology and cognitive and cognitive neuroscience. Her research appears in journals such as *Psychological Science, Journal of Personality and Social Psychology, Proceedings of the National Academy of Sciences. Personality and Social Psychology Bulletin, Child Development, Nature Neuroscience, and Journal of Personality.* She has received funding from National Science Foundation and National Institutes of Health.

Cindy Hazan is an Associate Professor of Human Development and the Director of the Adult Attachment Laboratory at Cornell University. Her current research focus is pair-bond formation which she investigates at multiple levels of analysis using a wide variety of methods. The primary goal of present projects is to identify "markers" of attachment at the levels of brain, mind, and behavior. A recipient of the Scientific Impact Award from the Society of Experimental Social Psychology, she is an internationally recognized scholar whose seminal work on affectional bonds helped define a new field of study in social and personality psychology. Her 1987 article (coauthored with Phillip R. Shaver) "Romantic Love Conceptualized as an Attachment Process" is one of the ten most cited articles ever published in the *Journal of Personality and Social Psychology.*

Part I
Introduction

Chapter 1
Normative Processes in Romantic Attachment: Introduction and Overview

Cindy Hazan and Emre Selcuk

In 1987 Hazan and Shaver published an article entitled "Romantic Love Conceptualized as an Attachment Process." In the years since, adult romantic attachment has been the focus of more than a dozen books and edited volumes. An additional three dozen books and edited volumes have included extensive coverage of adult attachment theory and research. The present volume has something unique to add to this discourse. It addresses the phenomena of adult romantic attachment from perspectives that have heretofore been missing and that promise to move the field forward in both significant and exciting ways.

When asked about their familiarity with attachment theory it is not unusual for anyone outside the field to say something along the lines of, "…that theory about the three different ways that babies attach to their mothers?" The reference is to the groundbreaking research by Mary Ainsworth et al. (1978) showing that human infants tend to form either a secure or one of two forms of insecure attachment to their primary caregivers. This common (mis)understanding of Bowlby's (1982) theory is due in large part to Ainsworth et al.'s brilliant experimental paradigm—the "strange situation"—and the associated landmark findings which revolutionized developmental psychology. Hazan and Shaver (1987) unintentionally perpetuated this narrow focus by offering a new measure of three similar ways that adults attach to their romantic partners. As a consequence of these two parallel lines of inquiry, attachment research diverged from attachment theory by focusing not on why or how bonds of attachment are formed and maintained but rather on differences in the ways individuals relate to attachment figures.

Bowlby's original theory was very explicitly a normative one. It was developed to explain why all normal human infants, who as members of an highly altricial species born in a state of extreme immaturity and helplessness, are evolutionarily predisposed to develop strong and enduring emotional ties to adult caregivers. If

C. Hazan (✉)
Department of Human Development, Cornell University, Ithaca, NY, U.S.A
e-mail: ch34@cornell.edu

E. Selcuk
Department of Psychology, Middle East Technical University, Ankara, Turkey

V. Zayas, C. Hazan (eds.), *Bases of Adult Attachment*,
DOI 10.1007/978-1-4614-9622-9_1

our young did not form attachment bonds with their adult caregivers they simply would not survive. Two central postulates of the theory are (1) an innate attachment behavioral system evolved to regulate proximity to an attachment figure, and (2) the attachment behavioral system is operative across the entire lifespan.

The functioning of the attachment behavioral system is readily observable in the behavior of a typical 1-year-old infant in relation to his or her attachment figure. She/he maintains proximity to the attachment figure, resists and is distressed by separations from the attachment figure, retreats to the attachment figure for comfort and protection, and explores confidently in the presence of the attachment figure. Attachment bonds are qualitatively different from other types of social ties, and the dynamics of the attachment system highlight the defining and differentiating features: proximity maintenance, safe haven, separation distress, secure base. This dynamic also underscores a core feature of attachment bonds—i.e., emotion regulation. If the infant is confident that the attachment figure is available and responsive and the situation is relatively safe, she/he feels content and secure. If, however, the infant senses either that the situation is threatening or the attachment figure is unavailable or unresponsive, she/he feels anxious and insecure. In essence, whether an infant feels content and secure or anxious and insecure depends primarily on whether she/he perceives that an attachment figure is able and willing to provide protection and care as needed.

In Bowlby's words, attachment is integral to human behavior "from the cradle to the grave." However, infant–caregiver attachments differ from adult romantic attachments in at least two fundamental respects. First, pair bond attachments are typically reciprocal; partners not only seek care from but also provide care to each other. Second, pair bonds are inherently sexual in nature. Romantic attachments thus involve not only the attachment behavioral system, but also the parental/caregiving and sexual mating systems as well. Despite these normative developmental changes, emotion regulation continues to be a central function of attachment bonds. Growing evidence convincingly demonstrates that simply holding a romantic attachment figure's hand (Beckes and Coan, this volume) or merely viewing her/his photograph (Selcuk et al. 2012) alleviates negative emotions in times of stress. It is this ability of attached pairs to regulate each other's affective states that determines well-being in adulthood. Again, to quote Bowlby (1988), people of all ages are "happiest when life is organized around a series of excursions, long or short, from the secure base provided by our attachment figures." (p. 62).

While the attachment system itself is innate, attachment bonds between infant and caregiver—like any close interpersonal relationship—take time to form. Bowlby proposed four phases in the ontogeny of attachment bonding. In the *pre-attachment* phase (0 to 2 months) infants are inherently interested in social interaction and open to care from virtually anyone. In the *attachment-in-the-making* phase (2 to 6 months), infants will typically still accept care from anyone but begin to show preferences among caregivers, such as smiling at some more than others or being more readily soothed by some versus others. In the *clear-cut attachment* phase (6 to 8 months), a few important developments coincide. Just as infants become capable of self-produced locomotion and thus able to venture into potentially dangerous situations they simultaneously and quite suddenly express wariness of strangers and also distress at being separated from attachment figures. In the final phase, *goal-corrected partnership* (around 2 years of age), children have less immediate needs for physical proximity thanks to their increasing ability to mentally represent their attachment figures, and, importantly, to derive comfort from the representations.

Whether a similar, four-phase model applies to romantic attachments (in whole or in part) will require considerable further investigation (see Zayas, Gunaydin, and Shoda, this volume, for a discussion). At the level of observable behavior, however, the similarities are quite striking (Zeifman and Hazan 1997). In a preattachment phase, attraction draws potential partners together into flirtatious and physiologically arousing interactions. If mutual interest continues it may evolve into an attachment-in-the-making phase characterized by more intimate physical and psychological exchanges. Eventually, if a clear-cut attachment bond is established it might be revealed not so much in the pleasure and comfort of the partner's presence as the distress and disorganization experienced during separations. In the final, goal-corrected-partnership phase, the establishment of a base of security—along with a comforting mental representation that can be conjured when needed—frees the partners to refocus their attention on more exploratory-type activities.

Although much more research is needed it is highly probable that a veridical model of romantic attachment formation will be more complex, first due to the lasting effects of early attachment experiences, second due to the advanced social cognitive abilities and a larger social network in adulthood (vs. infancy), and finally because romantic attachments involve reciprocal emotion regulation and sexual mating. The central foci of the present volume are these processes of attachment formation and maintenance between adult romantic partners. Each of the chapters in the first section addresses a process that promotes the formation of romantic attachment bonds—i.e., the development of physiological coregulation and the development of expectancy-value working models. Chapters in the second section identify possible mechanisms by which attachment experiences in infancy and childhood might affect the formation and maintenance of attachment relationships in adulthood. This includes specifying which aspects of early relationships have lasting influence, detailing how early attachment experiences shape the functioning of stress-reactivity systems, and modeling the psychological transference processes by which attraction to mates is facilitated by caregiver-based template matching. Chapters in the third section cover development and change in the course of adult pair bonding, specifically, how parental figures serve as bases of security from which to explore peer attachments, the development of "coupled" cognitive systems that both mark the formation of and help maintain romantic attachments, and the engagement of the dopamine-reward neural system as one of the core features of adult romantic attachment.

Processes that Promote Adult Attachment Formation

In Chap. 1, authors Lane Beckes and James Coan propose that physiological coregulation is a hallmark of adult attachment. They define coregulation as the conditioning of the hypothalamic–pituitary–adrenal (HPA) axis to the stimulus of a specific romantic partner. They begin with evidence that threat promotes social affiliation and responsive interpersonal contact reduces threat-induced stress. Over time, the combination of threat and a comforting social response leads to the development of a secure attachment bond. Thus, the process of adult attachment formation relies heavily on negative reinforcement conditioning. Adult romantic relationships are also characterized by positive reinforcement in the form of sexual and/or playful interactions, but only negative reinforcement influences the security of the bond. Oxytocin and endogenous opioids are critical to these processes. Oxytocin motivates social approach whereas opioids down regulate stress. It is the conditioning of both systems to the stimulus of a specific romantic partner that results in coregulation. In their view, this distress-relief dynamic is critical for adult attachment formation.

In Chap. 2, authors Jennifer Bartz, John Lydon and Mark Baldwin argue that people's expectations regarding whether an interpersonal goal is achievable or not should be as central to attachment theory as the value they attach to the said goal. Attachment researchers and theorists have traditionally emphasized the importance of expectancies in working models of the interpersonal world. These traditional perspectives translate attachment requirements into emotional reactions and plans for action. But attachment working models depend not only on commitment to and motivation for but also on the subjective value of achieving attachment goals. In the authors' view, expectancy-value calculations influence whether and how people initiate new relationships, move from casual to committed relationships, and persevere in the face of conflict within long-term relationships.

Effects of Previous Experience on Adult Attachment Formation

In Chap. 3, authors Jeffry Simpson, Andrew Collins, Allison Farrell and Lee Raby posit that specific aspects of early attachment experiences will be predictive of individual and relationship functioning in adulthood. Their organizational-developmental model is based on findings from the Minnesota Longitudinal Study of Risk and Adaptation. The focus of their chapter is on why and how certain types of early interpersonal experience can have profound and lasting effects on later interpersonal functioning.

In Chap. 4, Lisa Diamond presents a model of how early attachment experiences can shape not only later attachment-related affect, behavior, and cognition but also a range of basic physiological systems involved in stress reactivity and stress regulation. Specifically, she proposes that (1) the quality of early caregiving and overall stress exposure calibrate an individual's basic stress-regulatory systems—i.e., autonomic nervous system (ANS) and HPA; (2) the profile of ANS and HPA reactivity shapes individual capacity for emotion regulation and interpersonal skills; and (3) such skills affect individuals' ability to form and maintain romantic attachments. In other words, an individual's ANS and HPA reactivity is influenced by early attachment experience and, in turn, influences later attachment experiences via the pathway of impacting interpersonal skills and especially the ability to serve as a haven of safety and base of security for a romantic partner.

In Chap. 5, authors Marie Heffernan and Chris Fraley address the question of how early attachment experiences shape adult mate preferences. People sometimes fall in love with individuals who bear a striking resemblance to their parents. Indeed, there is evidence that early experiences with parental caregivers contribute to the construction of a mate template, and that adult pair bonding is facilitated by template matching. The authors propose that psychological transference—and specifically the activation of a mate template—may be the underlying mechanism that explains the connections between and similarities of childhood caregivers and adult romantic partners.

Development and Change in Adult Attachment Bonds

In Chap. 6, authors Omri Gillath and Gery Karantzas explain how by serving as bases of security, childhood attachment figures potentiate not only exploration but also social affiliation. The resulting social network of peers provides opportunities for adult attachment and pair bonding. A major normative development is the formation of attachment bonds outside one's initial hierarchy of (mostly) familial attachment figures. A central focus of the chapter is how factors such as social network density (i.e., how close members of a social network are to each other) and multiplexity (i.e., the number of social functions fulfilled by each member of a network) play important roles in bridging the gap between infant and adult attachment.

In Chap. 7, authors Vivian Zayas, Gul Gunaydin and Yuichi Shoda tackle the question of how an individual moves from the status of unknown other to attachment figure, and specifically how the corresponding mental representation evolves from stranger to beloved. They propose that a "coupled" cognitive system develops as a result of multiple factors but most especially aspects of partners' proximity and exposure to each other. Further, such a "coupled" cognitive system is hypothesized to be evident in a wide variety of social-cognitive processes, including elaboration, accessibility, automaticity, and interconnectedness of self-other representations.

In Chap. 8, author Bianca Acevedo cites findings from fMRI studies identifying the neural correlates of human attachments. The dopamine reward system appears to play a central role in attachment formation. Romantic partners, and even their mere images, can trigger the circuitry underlying neural reward processing systems. In addition, it is proposed that the ventral palladium may play an important role in distinguishing pair bonds from other types of close, rewarding social ties. Evidence is mounting that attachment formation, whether between infants and caregivers or adult romantic partners, is based on common neurobiological systems.

As emphasized in several of the chapters in this volume, the neurobiological systems underlying pair bonds play a fundamental role in virtually every aspect of human social cognition. Recent work suggests that even the development of our relatively large brains compared to those of other species is likely a response to the complexities of pair bond formation and maintenance (Dunbar and Shultz 2007). The ability to form and maintain these bonds is a central process characterizing adult development and affects future happiness, mental and physical health, and even longevity. Examining this process at multiple levels from neural and physiological activity to cognition and behavior, and to social networks, the present volume provides a unique perspective and a novel research agenda for understanding why and how we form and maintain attachment bonds.

References

Ainsworth, M. D. S., Blehar, M. C., Waters, E., & Wall, S. (1978). *Patterns of attachment: Assessed in the strange situation and at home*. Hillsdale: Erlbaum.

Bowlby, J. (1982). *Attachment and loss: Vol. 1. Attachment* (2nd ed.). New York: Basic Books.

Bowlby, J. (1988). *A secure base: Clinical applications of attachment theory*. London: Routledge.

Dunbar, R. I., & Shultz, S. (2007). Evolution in the social brain. *Science, 317,* 1344–1347. doi:10.1126/science.1145463.

Hazan, C., & Shaver, P. R. (1987). Romantic love conceptualized as an attachment process. *Journal of Personality and Social Psychology, 52,* 511–524. doi:10.1037/0022-3514.52.3.511.

Selcuk, E., Zayas, V., Günaydin, G., Hazan, C., & Kross. E. (2012). Mental representations of attachment figures facilitate recovery following upsetting autobiographical memory recall. *Journal of Personality and Social Psychology, 103,* 362–378. doi:10.1037/a0028125.

Zeifman, D., & Hazan, C. (1997). A process model of adult attachment formation. In S. Duck (Ed.), *Handbook of personal relationships: Theory, research, and interventions* (2nd ed., pp. 179–195). Chichester: Wiley.

Part II
The Processes that Promote Adult Attachment Formation

Chapter 2
The Distress-Relief Dynamic in Attachment Bonding

Lane Beckes and James A. Coan

The Distress-Relief Dynamic in Attachment Bonding

Human beings need other human beings for their general health and well-being (c.f., Baumeister and Leary 1995; Holt-Lunstad et al. 2010). Awareness of the importance of interpersonal bonds grew rapidly in the mid-twentieth century due to the work of psychological pioneers like John Bowlby (e.g., 1969/1982) and Harry Harlow (1958). Their work demonstrated that for infant monkeys and humans, physical touch, sensitive care, and a consistent primary relationship are fundamental to healthy development.

Bowlby's (e.g., 1969/1982) attachment theory continues to have a tremendous impact on the field of psychology. His theory predicted both normative and individual differences in the functioning of a putative attachment system. For many years the field focused largely on the individual differences in attachment first documented by Mary Ainsworth and her colleagues (Ainsworth et al. 1978). Despite this focus, as the branches of attachment theory have expanded into areas such as attachment in adults (c.f., Hazan and Shaver 1987; Mikulincer and Shaver 2007), renewed efforts to understand the normative processes that form attachment bonds are receiving attention. Further, insights concerning normative processes are beginning to shed light on the formation of attachment bonds and individual differences in them.

In this chapter we explore some of the normative processes that lead to social bonding and the development of attachment styles. First, we explore the distress-relief dynamic as a fundamental process in the formation of feelings of security in adults. Second, we tackle the issue of how and why attachment bonds form, how different styles emerge, and how the distress-relief dynamic contributes to these

L. Beckes (✉)
Department of Psychology, Bradley University,
1501 W. Bradley Ave. Peoria, IL 61625, USA
e-mail: lanebeckes@gmail.com

J. A. Coan
Department of Psychology, University of Virginia, 102 Gilmer Hall,
PO Box 400400, Charlottesville, VA 22904, USA

V. Zayas, C. Hazan (eds.), *Bases of Adult Attachment*,
DOI 10.1007/978-1-4614-9622-9_2

processes. Third, we discuss how our work and the work of other social affective neuroscientists influences the depth and breadth of our understanding of distress-relief processes.

In this review, we address several key issues regarding the development of attachment bonds and attachment security. The first issue is how security develops through a distress-relief dynamic in which interpersonal responsiveness plays a crucial role. The central argument of this chapter is that attachment security develops through repeated iterations of a sequence of distress followed by seeking proximity to another person. If that other is responsive to the distressed individual's state, a sense of relief or felt security arises (c.f., Mikulincer and Shaver 2003). This form of negative reinforcement conditioning, we argue, produces over time a secure attachment bond, which buffers an individual from the stressors of daily life. This is the process that we refer to as the distress-relief dynamic. Moreover, we argue that alterations in the variability of this negative reinforcement sequence can lead to insecure bonds. For example, inconsistent responsiveness may lead to extinction resistance and hyperactive support-seeking behavior.

We should emphasize at the outset that this is not the only process through which attachment bonds form. The normative formation of attachment quality is not the same as the normative formation of an attachment bond, although the two are intimately linked, and the formation of a secure bond necessarily implies the formation of an attachment bond. This leads to the second set of issues we address here, namely how attachment bonds form, and what processes lead to the development of different qualities of attachment. Here we argue that the distress-relief dynamic is critical in determining the type of bond, although other kinds of social contact may foster attachment bonds in addition to the distress-relief dynamic. Specifically, sex, play, caregiving, and general familiarity may all play a role in bond formation, but they may have little influence on the quality of that bond, secure or insecure. Throughout this chapter it is important to keep in mind that attachment quality and attachment bonds are not the same.

Threat and Responsiveness in the Development of Attachment Security

Feelings of attachment security provide a person with a number of advantages. Priming the availability of attachment figures elevates mood (e.g., Mikulincer et al. 2001b), diminishes trauma-related cognition (Mikulincer et al. 2006), and enhances helping behavior (Mikulincer et al. 2001a; Mikulincer et al. 2003a). Further, secure attachment in adulthood is associated with greater relationship satisfaction and more positive means of conflict resolution (e.g., Selcuk et al. 2010; Carnelley et al. 1994; Rholes et al. 2006). Despite this, the process by which secure bonds are formed in the initial stages of a relationship remains relatively unexplored.

Expanding on Bowlby (e.g., 1969/1982), Mikulincer and Shaver (2003; Mikulincer et al. 2003b) argue that attachment styles develop after repeated iterations of a threat-response sequence. According to this perspective, the attachment system is activated by signs of threat, which motivate the seeking of proximity to an external or internalized attachment figure. If the attachment figure is available, attentive, and responsive, then the threatened individual experiences relief and stress reduction, which contributes to an overall sense of felt security (Sroufe and Waters 1977). Alternatively, if attachment figures are not available, attentive, or responsive, individuals will engage in alternative strategies to meet their attachment needs—strategies associated with attachment insecurity. A relatively stable style of attachment emerges as a function of repeated iterations of one of these processes, leading individuals to respond more frequently and automatically with whichever strategy has been most commonly used.

Threat and Social Affiliation

Abundant evidence for a connection between threat and the desire to affiliate exists in the psychological literature. Despite varied nuances and interpretations, the body of social psychological research points to one salient fact: Threats of all kinds increase affiliative motivation.

Social Psychological Evidence

Schachter (1959), for example, found that individuals were more likely to affiliate with similar others when under the threat of electric shock. He argued that this occurs because affiliation with similar others provides an opportunity for social comparison, allowing a person to determine the appropriateness of his or her emotional state. In apparent contradiction, others have found that anxious individuals, as opposed to fearful ones, are less likely to affiliate with similar others and more likely to affiliate with dissimilar others (Sarnoff and Zimbardo 1961; Firestone et al. 1973; see Shaver and Klinnert 1982, for a review). In the attraction literature, many studies have noted that people find potential mates more attractive after experiencing a negatively arousing event such as crossing a shaky bridge or exposure to electric shock or aversive noises (e.g., Allen et al. 1989; Brehm et al. 1978; Dutton and Aron 1974; Jacobs et al. 1971; Kenrick and Johnson 1979; Riordan and Tedeschi 1983). As with the social comparison literature, such studies have inspired several alternative explanations for the link between negative arousal and attraction (e.g., misattribution of arousal, response facilitation, and negative reinforcement). Each perspective has been challenged by others, yet the persistent fact that negative arousal often promotes affiliation remains.

Similarly, threatening and painful events can motivate increased group identification (e.g., Aronson and Mills 1959), even when the pain and threat find their source within the very group with which one identifies. Harsh treatment related to hazing during initiation to collegiate groups of various kinds is associated with increased social identification and social dependence (Keating et al. 2005). Alternatively, external threats to groups, such as the 9/11 attacks in the USA, are known to increase group identification, bolstering nationalistic or patriotic identities (Li and Brewer 2004). Thus, threat-affiliation dynamics exist at multiple levels of social organization.

Attachment Evidence

In the adult attachment and social support literature, numerous studies have indicated a link between threat and affiliation. Greater stress and problem severity have been associated with increased support seeking in people who possess positive schemas of others (Lopez et al. 1998), more support seeking generally (Kobak and Duemmler 1994; Lazarus and Folkman 1984), and more direct support seeking in interactions between romantic partners (Collins and Feeney 2000). Experimentally presented acute stressors also induce support seeking in securely attached romantic couples (e.g., Simpson et al. 1992), and separations induce proximity seeking (e.g., Fraley and Shaver 1998). Moreover, experimentally induced threat primes increase the accessibility of social representations (Mikulincer et al. 2000), the accessibility of attachment figure's names (Mikulincer et al. 2002), and recall, by adults, of positive interactions with parents (Cox et al. 2008). Despite decades of interest in this subject, the precise mechanisms remain debatable. Recently, however, social neuroscientists have begun to provide some possible mechanisms that may shed light on higher-level social and psychological mechanisms.

Neurobiological Evidence

Recent theory and empirical findings are suggestive of the hypothesis that the neuropeptide oxytocin is released in response to threatening stimuli in order to prepare individuals to seek out and/or provide social support. Taylor's (2006; Taylor et al. 2000) "tend and befriend" model argues that people have increased affiliative motivations when under threat because of a link between environmental threats and oxytocin release that evolved because of the importance of finding allies and defending offspring. Supporting the "tend and befriend" hypothesis, oxytocin has been linked to affiliative motivation and behavior (Insel 1997) such as social grooming and maternal care in nonhuman animals (Panksepp et al. 1999). In humans, women who experience laboratory challenges have higher cortisol stress responses if they also have higher plasma oxytocin levels (Taylor et al. 2006), and elevated plasma oxytocin has been associated with relationship distress (Grewen et al. 2005; Turner et al. 1999). Similarly, indicators of trust, such as generosity in economic games, have been linked to experimentally administered oxytocin (e.g., Kosfeld et al. 2005; Zak et al. 2007), plasma oxytocin levels (Zak et al. 2005), and polymorphisms in the oxytocin receptor gene (Israel et al. 2009).

Oxytocin is likely involved in organizing perception and behavior in ways that increase social approach and inhibit social withdrawal (Kemp and Guastella 2011). It inhibits amygdala activity (implicated in avoidance motivation) in relation to negative social targets (Baumgartner et al. 2008; Domes et al. 2007a), increases the assessment of attractiveness and trustworthiness of target faces (Theodoridou et al. 2009), and improves performance on tasks that require accurate identification of emotional facial expressions (Domes et al. 2007b). Further, recent evidence suggests that methylation of the oxytocin receptor gene (methylation diminishes the expression of a gene) is associated with neural responses to animacy displays (e.g., Jack et al. 2012), indicating a role for oxytocin in social perception more broadly. Thus, one critical reason for the link between threat and affiliation may be evolved mechanisms involving oxytocin (and the highly similar peptide vasopressin; see Carter et al. 2008, for a review and a discussion of sex differences) that promote social approach during stressful experiences.

This explanation fits well with the seemingly disparate findings that oxytocin is, on the one hand, associated with relationship distress and, on the other hand, with trust, social approach, and attraction. If oxytocin motivates social approach, it may do so in both negative and positive contexts. For example, if one's primary romantic relationship is in distress, the adaptive response is usually to attempt to repair it. This requires social approach, which is enhanced by oxytocin. This motivation for social approach, however, may not always be positively valenced. Indeed, Kemp and Guastella (2011) argue that oxytocin should be associated with darker aspects of social approach as well, such as anger or aggression. From this perspective aggressive mate-guarding behavior, jealousy, and other negative social approach behaviors may be motivated partly by oxytocin.

Responsiveness and Felt Security

There is now considerable evidence for the second part of the distress-relief dynamic: the sense of safety that emerges from social contact with responsive others. The concept of responsiveness is operationalized differently depending on the methods and traditions of a particular subfield. In studies of communication, the relevance of verbal and nonverbal communication by a responder to a person's distress communication is highlighted (e.g., Davis 1982). In social psychological studies, the focus is often on whether each party perceives the other to be providing "validation" (Reis et al. 2004). In observational studies, responsiveness can be gauged by coders in terms of engagement and understanding (e.g., Allen et al. 2007; Coan et al. 2013). And from a behavioral perspective, nonverbal behaviors such as physical touch, physical warmth, eye contact, facial expressions, and licking and grooming are often used as indicators of responsiveness (e.g., Coan et al. 2006; Coan et al. 2013; Harlow 1958; Hofer 2006; Beckes et al. 2010; Champagne et al. 2003).

Social Psychological Evidence

Much of the social psychological work on responsiveness has been summarized by Reis et al. (2004), who focus on the construct *perceived partner responsiveness*. They argue that perceived responsiveness is the *core construct* in interpersonal relationships, which, while broad in scope, has tremendous organizing power. For example, mutual validation is associated with low levels of marital distress (Gottman 1979), interpersonal synchrony between mothers and infants is associated with infant security (Reddy et al. 1997), and perceived social support is a strong predictor of stress and health outcomes (e.g., Cohen 1991). Although this literature is complex (e.g., expectations have been found to interact with enacted support to determine whether a partner is responsive, with higher expectations being placed on close others; e.g., Clark and Mills 1993), the gist is clear: Perceived responsiveness matters to health, well-being, and relationship functioning.

Attachment and Social Support Evidence

The attachment literature has advanced some significant evidence for the link between responsiveness and felt security (see Sbarra and Hazan 2008). For example, the presence of a romantic partner has been associated with a diminished stress response in physiological measures (Feeney and Kirkpatrick 1996), and individuals who have responsive partners report a greater sense of being cared for and a more elevated mood after a supportive interaction (Collins and Feeney 2000). Further, thoughts of attachment figures reduce the accessibility of thoughts of death after a mortality salience manipulation (Cox et al. 2008) and facilitate recovery after thinking about an upsetting personal experience (Selcuk et al. 2012) indicating a reduction in negative rumination following access to representations of attachment figures. Similar inferences can be derived from the social support literature (see Uchino 2006, or Uchino et al. 1996, for a review). This literature contains evidence that social support reduces autonomic nervous system load and boosts immune function during stressful tasks and over time. For example, studies have found links between social support and lower blood pressure (e.g., Kamarck et al. 1990), decreased cortisol (e.g., Turner-Cobb et al. 2000), and improved immune functioning (e.g., Lutgendorf et al. 2005). Indeed, this extensive literature highlights the powerful effect that high quality social support has on individual health and longevity (see Holt-Lunstad et al. 2010, for a meta-analysis and review).

Neurobiological Evidence

In neuroscience, responsiveness has rarely been studied. Despite this lack, many basic behavioral measures, manipulations, and conceptualizations that are likely to be affected by perceived responsiveness have been studied. Beginning with Harlow's

(1958) seminal work with infant monkeys, it has been understood that certain types of social cues and physical contact have intrinsically rewarding properties. In his studies, Harlow examined how infant monkeys preferred soft cloth surrogate mothers to wire mothers who fed them with milk. Over the years researchers, including Hofer, have examined these processes in great detail. For example, infant rats prefer smells associated with strokes from an artist's brush (Sullivan et al. 1986), warmth stimulates pups' activity levels (Hofer 1995), and milk appears to regulate pups' heart rates. Hofer has concluded that many physiological, behavioral, and affective systems are sensitive to particular stimulus properties of physical contact during development. These *hidden regulators* tone the physiology and behavior of the pups in ways that extend into the future. For example, licking and grooming, high-arched back nursing, and time in contact are associated with blood pressure throughout the life span. Female rats raised by dams with high levels of licking and grooming behavior are quicker to instigate maternal behavior in the presence of pups, and pups whose dams engage in higher levels of licking and grooming tend to be less fearful and have healthier stress profiles (Francis and Meaney 1999). Furthermore, those individuals also have greater numbers of oxytocin receptors in the medial preoptic area of the brain and in the lateral septum, amygdala, and hypothalamus (Champagne et al. 2001).

One important set of neuropeptides that have been somewhat overlooked in the literature on attachment are the endogenous opioids (Machin and Dunbar 2011). The brain opioid theory of social attachment (c.f., Panksepp 1998; Liebowitz 1983) comes from the observation that opiate addicts have strong similarities to people who are in love. Opioids are involved in the consummatory or termination phase of basic motivated behaviors (Bowlby 1969/1982; reviewed by Beckes and Coan 2013). During this phase, opioids reach peak levels, producing feelings of euphoria, satiation, and well-being (Nelson and Panksepp 1998). Further, opioids are known to be powerful analgesics, reducing physical and social pain rapidly, and they are believed to mediate the effects of pain reduction through social contact (e.g., Cohen et al. 2010; D'Amato and Pavone 1993). Thus they may be the best candidate mechanisms for brain mediation of the relationship between responsiveness and felt security.

In humans, the neuropeptides supporting the link between social contact and felt security are less well established, but social contact is known to decrease stress, threat response, and pain perception (Beckes and Coan 2011; Cohen et al. 2010; Coan et al. 2006; Eisenberger et al. 2011; Master et al. 2009) similar to what one would be predicted from the opioid theory. Liebowitz (1983) argued that relationships have three stages that are highly similar to those experienced by opiate addicts. The first stage is associated with euphoria and subsequent addiction, which parallels early-stage romantic love. The second is characterized by tolerance-habituation in which the intense feelings of euphoria are replaced by a baseline maintaining dependence. Similarly, young love gets replaced with a calmer attachment and greater interdependence. Finally, when the drug is no longer used or available, addicts experience withdrawal symptoms that mirror the grief process.

Although compelling, this hypothesis has yet to be definitively supported in humans. Still, some human studies have shown a clear connection between social contact and downregulation of threat and stress. In a study that directly tested the stress reducing benefits of social contact, Coan et al. (2006) scanned married women to see if holding hands with their spouse, or a stranger, would reduce their threat responses to a possible shock, relative to when they were threatened alone. There was a clear reduction in threat response in conditions in which the women held someone's hand. Moreover, that effect was larger in the spousal hand-holding condition than the stranger condition, and the effect was most pronounced in women with the highest quality relationships. Similarly, Eisenberger and colleagues (e.g., Eisenberger et al. 2011; Master et al. 2009) have found that participants have decreased neural pain responses when viewing photos of attachment figures. Thus, social contact does appear to lead to less threat response, supporting the notion that responsiveness-related behaviors can reduce threat and instill a sense of felt security.

The Combination of Threat and Responsiveness—A Security Cocktail

Thus far we have shown evidence for each individual piece of the argument that threat and responsiveness facilitate secure attachments. There is sparse but growing evidence that feelings of attachment security can be fostered through this mix of stimuli. Perhaps the most direct evidence comes from a set of studies by Beckes et al. (2010) who conducted a conditioning experiment to test this hypothesis directly. These studies involved implicitly backward pairing a negative unconditioned stimulus (US), either a photo of a striking snake or a mutilation scene, or a neutral US, such as a rolling pin or picnic basket, with conditioned stimuli (CS) in the form of faces with either neutral or warm, smiling expressions. After repeated iterations of the pairing of US followed by CS these researchers tested the effects of the pairings using the CS faces as primes in a lexical decision task for words associated with attachment security and insecurity. They found that warm, smiling faces paired with negative unconditioned stimuli routinely facilitated recognition of secure words and interfered with recognition of insecure words, whereas no such effects were found for neutral faces, or faces paired with neutral unconditioned stimuli. They concluded that both the negative stimuli and the cues of social responsiveness in the faces were necessary to increase associations between the novel faces and security concepts.

Recently, Beckes et al. (2013) found evidence that an early event-related potential component, the P1 component, which has been associated with approach-motivated attentional bias to ingroup members (Cunningham et al. 2012) is increased to smiling faces that were previously paired with striking snake images. Further, the difference in the P1 to snake-paired and rolling pin-paired faces predicted the inhibition of response times to insecure words in a lexical decision task. Other studies support this hypothesis as well, either through marital interventions (Johnson et al. 2013) or developmental associations with the social regulation of emotion (Coan et al. 2013). For example, Coan et al. found fMRI evidence that maternal supportiveness in mid-adolescence predicted the threat reduction benefit received from holding a friend's hand 8 years later. Specifically, maternal engagement during a supportive behavior task in which the adolescent discussed a problem with which they were struggling predicted the adolescent's ability to receive the benefits of social contact with friends under threat in adulthood. This points to the likelihood that their mother's supportiveness in times of distress led to greater ability to capitalize on social support later in life, providing naturalistic and longitudinal support for the idea that security grows out of a distress-relief sequence. Johnson and colleagues (Johnson et al. 2013) demonstrated that emotionally focused therapy, based on attachment concepts, changed the neural profile of threat responding during hand-holding in distressed couples. This therapeutic intervention involves the primary components of threat and responsiveness by opening the emotional wounds of one member of the couple, and teaching the other to be responsive to that pain. Functional imaging before and after the intervention indicated that hand-holding before therapy was associated with greater threat response, whereas hand-holding after therapy was associated with a marked decrease in threat response, relative to threat response in the alone condition.

Taken as a whole, the evidence is strong that attachment security is sensitive to the distress-relief dynamic, and consistent responsiveness to distressing situations promotes a sense of security in a close relationship. Further, we have good leads on the neurochemistry that supports this dynamic, with evidence that oxytocin promotes affiliative motivation and is stimulated by stressful circumstances, and evidence that endogenous opioids are stimulated by social contact and downregulate the stress response.

From the Absence to the Presence of an Attachment Bond

A clear difficulty in understanding the nature and formation of attachment bonds is the slow developmental progression that such bonds undergo. Although evidence for an association between secure attachment associations and the distress-relief dynamic (e.g., Beckes et al. 2010, 2013) is useful and informative, such associations do not demonstrate the formation of a true attachment bond. Whereas feelings of security may be important in the formation of attachment bonds, they are not the same as an attachment bond. Further, ascribing a bond to such feelings in the absence of other indicators would ignore qualitative differences in relationships and the important fact that many people have insecure bonds, suggesting that bonds can occur between individuals in which contact after a stressor is not associated with easy relief.

Given these challenges it is important to understand what features of adult attachment relationships are capable of distinguishing between a general attraction to, fondness for, or sense of comfort with another, and a true attachment bond. Bowlby (1969/1982) described four primary behavioral features of attachment relationships: proximity seeking, secure base behaviors, safe haven activities, and separation distress. By necessity, the best feature to use as a measure of an attachment bond is one that is relatively unique to attachment relationships. Proximity seeking, or the degree to which an individual seeks out physical proximity to a specific other, is difficult to use as a discriminative behavior because adults seek proximity to others for many reasons including general attraction. Secure base behavior, or the degree to which the individual regulates his or her exploratory behavior, also becomes problematic in adults given the relatively greater degree of independence and potentially long latencies adults may use when returning to their secure base. Safe haven activities, or the degree to which individuals seek out a specific other when in distress, may be similarly difficult to use as a measure because of adult independence and a greater tendency to seek support from more specialized sources as a function of a particular friend, partner, or acquaintances' skills and affordances. Separation distress, however, may be particularly useful in this regard, and it has frequently been identified as the strongest indicator of an attachment bond (e.g., Bowlby 1980; Fraley and Shaver 1999). Separation distress in infants is commonly measured as protests and cries when separation from an attachment figure occurs. In adults, however, such protests are less likely unless the separation is thought to be permanent or of considerable duration. Another way of measuring separation distress is via biological signatures related to the coregulation of physiological systems (Sbarra and Hazan 2008) that become dysregulated after separation due to the removal of "hidden regulators" (Hofer 1995).

Coregulation and Bond Formation

The concept of coregulation may be the key to identifying whether a relationship constitutes a true attachment bond. Coregulation refers to the manner in which relationship partners' physiology becomes conditioned to the presence of the other. Sbarra and Hazan (2008, p. 143) define coregulation as "the reciprocal maintenance of psychophysiological homeostasis within a relationship." In humans there is a relatively sparse literature regarding the mechanisms that produce coregulation in relationships. Sbarra and Hazan (2008) have presented a coherent theoretical framework that relies on a combination of literatures across human and animal investigations. According to this model, attachment bonds emerge from reinforcement learning via various types of social interaction. The distress-relief dynamic refers specifically to the negative reinforcement side of this learning in which the attachment figure becomes associated with the reduction of distress and removal of painful, fearful, or otherwise threatening stimuli. Other types of learning, such as positive reinforcement, may support bond formation in addition to negative reinforcement. For example, sex, play, and other positive interactions lacking the component of distress may serve to form an attachment bond by conditioning physiological coregulation with the partner. Over time, the consistent presence of the partner, regular social and sexual contact, and physical touch may tone various physiological systems, such as the stress system, to the presence of the partner. Separation from the partner can then lead to changes in those systems, manifesting psychologically as separation distress.

Neurobiological Processes in Bond Formation.

Oxytocin and endogenous opioids are likely important neural mechanisms involved in bond-formation reinforcement processes. As discussed above, they may be critical in the distress-relief dynamic, but their properties make it reasonable to assume that their action is central to bond formation as well. Oxytocin is associated with a variety of social behaviors including maternal behaviors, sexual behaviors, and social bonding (e.g., Lim and Young 2006). Central administration of oxytocin in animal models is sufficient to affect maternal behavior and pair-bonding (e.g., Keverne and Kendrick 1994; Pederson et al. 1982; Williams et al. 1994), and in humans oxytocin is associated with maternal behaviors following childbirth (Feldman et al. 2007). Opioids are strongly associated with reinforcement across social and nonsocial domains (see, Panksepp 1998). During sexual behavior, opioids are known to increase (e.g., Szechtman et al. 1981). Opioid antagonists prevent the development of partner and place preferences (Pfaus 2009). Critically, opioids diminish stress and pain responses (e.g., D'Amato and Pavone 1993), providing a potentially direct mechanism through which physiological systems become conditioned to an attachment figure and through which coregulatory processes develop.

One way in which various reinforcement processes could lead to an attachment bond is through the conditioned inhibition of stress in response to the partner's perceptual characteristics. In prairie voles, stress hormones such as corticotropin-releasing hormone (CRH), involved in the stress cascade via the hypothalamic pituitary adrenal axis (HPA-axis), are associated with facilitated pair-bonding (e.g., DeVries et al. 2002). Other stress indicators, such as corticosterone levels, tend to increase upon separation and diminish upon reunification (Carter 1998). This finding, that HPA activity is greater upon separation from a partner, is consistent across various social mammals, hinting that social proximity to an attachment figure conditions diminished HPA-axis activity (Hennesy 1997; Mendoza and Mason 1997). Similarly, social support may desensitize brain regions involved in the detection and appraisal of threat, such as the dorsal anterior cingulate cortex (dACC), via the regular release of opioids (e.g., Eisenberger et al. 2007), offering another pathway through which social contact inhibits and conditions diminished stress response. Critically these features of attachment bonds are present even in insecure relationships. A history of sex, play, physical touch, and consistent proximity is probably sufficient to condition oxytocinergic and opioid systems to the presence of the partner. These systems diminish threat reactivity and stress systems broadly, so separation from an attachment partner is likely to increase the individual's threat and stress responses to negative events.

Reinforcement Schedules and the Development of Attachment Styles

An important observation about the role of oxytocin and opioids in social bonding is that they are involved not only in negative-reinforcement occurring as part of the distress-relief dynamic, but also in positive reinforcement during a variety of other social behaviors such as sex, rough and tumble play, and caregiving (see Panksepp 1998, for a review). Thus, if they are involved in both the development of attachment bonds *and* attachment styles, the type of reinforcement that occurs, its frequency, and its predictability may be critical for which style emerges, explaining why insecure bonds develop. From our perspective the negative reinforcement aspect of the distress-relief dynamic may be central to determining attachment style in a manner in which positive reinforcement processes may not. Differences in the variability and predictability of the distress-relief negative reinforcement process may lead to distinct attachment qualities, leaving open the possibility that bonding and attachment style emerge from many of the same neural substrates acted upon via different stimuli or degrees of consistency.

Emergence of Insecurity in Attachment Bonds

Attachment anxiety may emerge out of inconsistent responsiveness in which the responder only sometimes responds, or responds only after persistent proximity and reassurance seeking (Mikulincer and Shaver 2003). Mikulincer and Shaver argue that when responders are not available, attentive, or responsive, but proximity seeking is a viable strategy, individuals will turn to a "hyperactivating" strategy associated with attachment anxiety. Hyperactivation is characterized by excessive reassurance seeking and needy behavior. Interestingly this hyperactive seeking for the negative reinforcement properties of the responder may be a function of random or variable reinforcement schedules. Because the partner sometimes responds effectively, and at other times does not, the reward becomes unpredictable. As Skinner (1956) discovered, consistent reward can lead to the extinction of the rewarded behavior, in this case proximity seeking, because of satiation. However, when reinforcement follows a variable schedule in which reinforcement is unpredictable, a behavior can become resistant to extinction, and in some cases can increase in frequency. Thus, security may be associated with a sense of reward predictability and the seeking behavior becomes contingent on need, circumstance, and internal state.

Alternatively, anxiety may be associated with unpredictability in the reinforcement schedule, producing hyperactivated behaviors toward the attachment figure.

Avoidant attachment is thought to emerge in response to consistently unavailable and unresponsive partners (Mikulincer and Shaver 2003). Mikulincer and Shaver argue that a strategy of "hypoactivation" develops in this case. Hypoactivation involves distancing oneself from threat, relying on self-regulation to cope with stressors, and ignoring or avoiding attachment-related cues. It is unlikely that any attachment bonds form completely absent of the distress-relief dynamic. Avoidant attachment likely emerges in the presence of an indirect form of distress-relief in which the individual learns to maintain proximity to the attachment figure, but also learns not to directly seek out support, maintaining an optimal proximity to the caregiver that provides relief, but does not trigger the punishment associated with rejection and inadequate responsiveness (Simpson et al. 2007). Moreover, after such a bond has been established, and the partners are actively coregulating each other, the distress-relief dynamic necessarily applies to these relationships. If separation leads to physiological dysregulation and reunification reestablishes normal regulatory function, then the mere presence of the attachment figure will provide distress relief. Thus, even in highly avoidant individuals, negative reinforcement is likely part of the attachment process.

Notably, however, the reinforcement of support seeking behavior will be absent due to punishing or never reinforcing direct support-seeking behaviors. Thus proximity in a more general sense is reinforced, but direct support seeking is not. This, however, does not require that the initial bonding process is largely driven by the distress-relief dynamic. This is highly speculative, but a possibility given animal models of pair-bonding (Carter 1998).

Sexual contact may produce a type of intimacy that at first is both stressful and rewarding, as is indicated by increases in stress hormone output during sexual encounters in prairie voles (DeVries et al. 2002). Because sex usually requires intimate contact, vulnerability could be an integral part of sexual contact for many individuals. In this sense, sexual encounters may be composed of a form of distress-relief dynamic when normatively experienced. Thus, avoidant individuals may form bonds with sexual partners despite either never directly seeking the partner out for support in stressful situations, or learning not to directly seek support because of the punishment associated with an unresponsive partner.

A Neurobiologically Based Model of Security Development

Of importance for those who wish to improve the quality of relationships through insights from attachment literature, the processes that promote security are of particular interest. From current evidence and logic, one can hypothesize a model of the neurobiological processes that promote the development of a secure attachment bond to a specific partner (see Fig. 2.1). Further, the model also can be used to

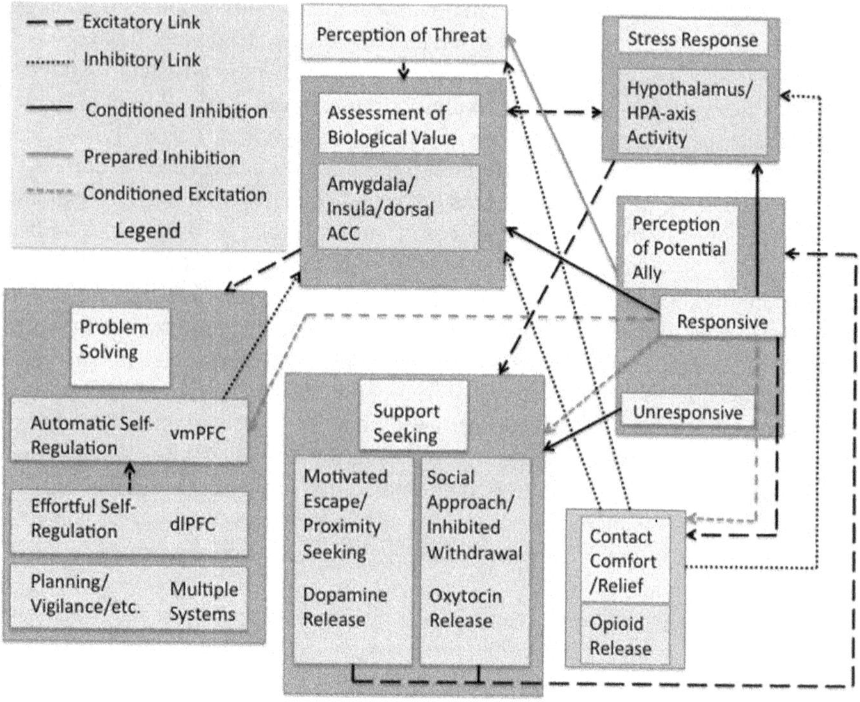

Fig. 2.1 Model of the distress-relief dynamic with psychological processes mapped onto neurobiological substrates and their linkages. The process begins with perception of threat, which activates threat responsive brain regions. From there a stress cascade is initiated in the hypothalamus and brainstem, along with the engagement of prefrontal systems for problem solving. These, in turn, initiate oxytocin and dopamine release to promote support seeking, which will lead to diminished distress via endogenous opioids if the individual perceives a responsive ally

predict both quantitative and qualitative differences in the degree to which close others regulate stress relative to less well known others.

It is clear from numerous studies of threat responding that the perception of threat leads to a cascade of activity in a network of brain regions (Coan et al. 2006, 2013). It is likely that the perceptual information first activates areas such as the amygdala and dACC, which begin to process the biological value of the stimulus and act as a neural alarm bell for other regions of the brain (Adolphs 2010; Bush et al. 2000). The amygdala immediately engages the HPA-axis via projections to the hypothalamus, initiating a cascading stress response (e.g., Gray et al. 1989).

Various regions of the cortex, such as the ventromedial prefrontal cortex (vmPFC) and dorsolateral prefrontal cortex (dlPFC) are activated in an effort to solve various problems associated with the emerging threat, such as the need to self-regulate (Poldrack et al. 2008). Additional activations occur as a way of monitoring the evaluative meaning of the stimulus in regions such as the orbitofrontal cortex (OFC; Damasio 1996), and actual and anticipated changes in the body via regions such as the insula (Craig 2009).

There is now some evidence that activation of the HPA axis will elicit both oxytocin release (Onaka 2004), potentiating social receptivity, and dopaminergic activity in the ventral striatum (e.g., Wanat et al. 2008), possibly potentiating motivated escape and/or social proximity seeking. In particular, oxytocinergic activity is thought to improve social perception (e.g., Jack et al. 2012), diminish social fear (e.g., Domes et al. 2007a), benefit "mind-reading" (e.g., Domes et al. 2007b), and motivate social approach (e.g., Kemp and Guastella 2011). This potentiation of social receptivity then heightens the perception of social others as responsive to the person's needs, instigating opioid release to responsive social contact (Machin and Dunbar 2011). Opioids inhibit threat responsiveness by downregulating activity in regions such as the dACC and HPA-axis (Nelson and Panksepp 1998). The consistent association of perceptual characteristics of the partner with downregulation of threat response and HPA-axis activity then conditions an inhibitory link between the partner's perceptual characteristics and threat responsive brain regions.

These inhibitory links could be supported through multiple pathways, including (a) excitatory associations between the perceptual characteristics of the partner and the vmPFC, which can downregulate threat-responsive brain regions (Eisenberger et al. 2011); (b) conditioned facilitation of the links between perception of the partner and opioid systems; (c) conditioned facilitation of the link between perception of the partner and oxytocin systems; and (d) conditioned links between the perception of the partner and threat response through the facilitation of relatively direct linkages. Additionally, support-seeking behavior is reinforced, increasing the association between the partner and social receptivity. Consistent responsiveness leads to a well formed association that is dependent on physiological homeostasis, whereas variable responsiveness may create stronger associations leading to constant reassurance-seeking through a form of chronic social deprivation. Nonresponsiveness, alternatively, may weaken this link, leading to greater reliance of self-regulation and avoidance of direct support seeking.

This model has several implications if correct. First it predicts quantitatively greater threat reduction in the presence of a consistently responsive partner. Indeed evidence from Coan and colleagues (e.g., Coan et al. 2006; see also Coan et al. 2013) supports this contention through findings that spouses are associated with less threat responding than strangers, and the degree to which that is the case is moderated by relationship quality. Further, the model implies a qualitative difference in threat and stress responding for individuals with consistently responsive partners. First, consistent positive social contact should potentiate greater opioid activity in general, an idea Nelson and Panksepp (1998) refer to as opioid tone. Greater opioid tone should lead to generally less threat responding as long as opioid tone is maintained. Additionally, the conditioning of the partner to reduced HPA-axis and threat response activity should not only strengthen the link between perception of the partner and diminished stress response, but could, over time, condition the individual's stress response to the partner, leading to coregulation of this system. In this case, separation distress becomes more likely. From this, one might predict increased HPA activity in situations in which the partner is known to be unavailable for support. Indeed, this facet of the model is what most clearly separates attachment relationships from nonattachment relationships in that it indicates a dependence on the other person for regulation of the individual's stress system.

Conclusion

Many components of the psychological literature suggest that distress and responsiveness are intimately linked with bond formation, stress reduction, and a sense of security in relationships. A small but growing body of evidence suggests that the distress-relief dynamic is critical in the development of secure attachments through negative reinforcement conditioning. Importantly, attachment security and its associated feelings are not the same as an attachment bond. Bonds may be formed via positive social interactions such as sex or play through positive reinforcement processes. Yet, positive reinforcement may lead to little information regarding the availability, attentiveness, and responsiveness of a given relationship partner. Without this information a sense of security cannot develop. Thus, various reinforcement processes may help to create a bond, but it is likely that only negative reinforcement strongly influences the security of that bond. Further, as a bond develops, even one that is built largely on positive reinforcement processes will eventually yield to the distress-relief dynamic and negative reinforcement processes as members of a relationship begin to coregulate each other.

This argument provides some possible directions to explore how and why particular attachment styles develop. For example, we argue that inconsistent responsiveness may lead to anxious attachment strategies through resistance to extinction of the proximity-seeking response. Variable reward schedules may intensify and maintain proximity seeking even in the presence of an acute reward; thus predictability may be critical for the extinction of proximity seeking and a sense of security that the attachment figure will be there when needed. Alternatively, avoidance may emerge out of a relative lack of negative reinforcement or even the presence of punishment when seeking out direct support. This is not to imply that negative reinforcement is not critical to these relationships, but rather direct support-seeking strategies for achieving that negative reinforcement are not sustained (or in adulthood they may never be adequately attempted in light of previous learning). Thus, proximity may be soothing for an avoidant person, but support may be sought in a less direct manner.

Additionally, oxytocin and endogenous opioids may be critical neurobiological substrates for these processes. We argue that oxytocin is most likely involved in the organization of proximity-seeking motivation and behavior by motivating social approach and sensitizing social perception processes. Opioids are likely involved in the reinforcing properties of social context, and when they are paired with social contact and physiological arousal due to distress, the perceptual characteristics of the partner become linked with downregulation of stress systems. Over time the stress system becomes conditioned to the presence of a partner resulting in coregulation, which we argue is the hallmark of an attachment relationship. Many of the health and well-being benefits commonly associated with close relationships may be supported through coregulation, which moderates the stress system. This chapter provides a detailed model of how this process might occur, providing the necessary connections and predictions to guide further investigation of the neurobiological and psychological foundations of attachment and security.

Future investigations should further explore several key aspects of the model presented here. First, more evidence concerning the links between stress, oxytocin, and support seeking is needed to fully validate the idea that stressors often promote oxytocin release and in turn support proximity-seeking behavior. Second, the links between feelings of security, stress reduction, positive social contact, and opioid release need to be further explored, particularly in humans. For example, investigations should determine whether opioids are necessary for the stress-reducing benefits of social contact. Third, research should explore whether a history of security and responsiveness in an attachment relationship leads to decreased threat perception in the presence of that attachment figure, and whether that process occurs in a bottom-up perceptual manner and/or through cortically mediated processes. Fourth, the degree to which negative reinforcement is necessary for security should be further explored. Such investigations could, for example, determine whether proximity-seeking behavior is heightened in the context of a variable reinforcement schedule, and whether security is associated with extinction due to consistent and predictable responsiveness. Fifth, more research on the establishment of coregulatory patterns in relationships over time and the impact of separation should be top priorities for the field.

Exploring these questions further and sharpening our models at multiple levels of analysis will lead to increasingly well honed abilities to predict outcomes for attachment relationships and develop potential interventions. Due to the benefits of close personal relationships for health and well-being, a better understanding of both the normative psychological and neurobiological processes supporting attachment bond formation and attachment quality formation would be a great boon to both science and society.

References

Adolphs, R. (2010). What does the amygdala contribute to social cognition? *Annals of the New York Academy of Sciences, 1191*(1), 42–42.

Ainsworth, M. D. S., Blehar, M. C., Waters, E., & Wall, S. (1978). *Patterns of attachment: A psychological study of the strange situation*. Hillsdale: Erlbaum.

Allen, J. B., Kenrick, D. T., Linder, D. E., & McCall, M. A. (1989). Arousal and attraction: A response-facilitation alternative to misattribution and negative-reinforcement models. *The Journal of Personality and Social Psychology, 57,* 261–270.

Allen, J. P., Porter, M., McFarland, C., McElhaney, K. B., & Marsh, P. (2007). The relation of attachment security to adolescents' paternal and peer relationships, depression, and externalizing behavior. *Child Development, 78,* 1222–1239.

Aronson, E., & Mills, J. (1959). The effect of severity of initiation on liking for a group. *Journal of Abnormal and Social Psychology, 59,* 177–181.

Baumeister, R. F., & Leary, M. R. (1995). The need to belong: Desire for interpersonal attachments as a fundamental human motivation. *Psychological Bulletin, 117,* 497–529.

Baumgartner, T., Heinrichs, M., Vonlanthen, A., Fischbacher, U., & Fehr, E. (2008). Oxytocin shapes the neural circuitry of trust and trust adaptation in humans. *Neuron, 58*(4), 639–650. doi:10.1016/j.neuron.2008.04.009.

Beckes, L., & Coan, J. A. (2011). Social baseline theory: The role of social proximity in emotion and economy of action. *Personality and Social Psychology Compass, 5,* 976–988.

Beckes, L., & Coan, J. A. (2013). Toward an integrative neuroscience of relationships. In J. A. Simpson & L. Campbell (Eds.), *The Oxford handbook of close relationships* (pp. 684–710). New York: Oxford University Press.

Beckes, L., Simpson, J., & Erickson, A. (2010). Of snakes and succor. *Psychological Science, 21*(5), 721.

Beckes, L., Coan, J. A., & Morris, J. P. (2013). Implicit conditioning of faces via the social regulation of emotion: ERP evidence of early attentional biases for security conditioned faces. *Psychophysiology*, doi:10.1111/psyp.12056.

Bowlby, J. (1969/1982). *Attachment and loss, Vol. I: Attachment*. New York: Basic Books.

Bowlby, J. (1980). *Attachment and loss: Vol 3. Loss: Sadness and depression*. New York: Basic Books.

Brehm, J., Gatz, M., Goethals, G., McCrimmon, J., & Ward, L. (1978). Psychological arousal and interpersonal attraction. *JSAS: Catalog of Selected Documents in Psychology, 8,* 63.

Bush, G., Luu, P., & Posner, M. I. (2000). Cognitive and emotional influences on the anterior cingulate cortex. *Trends in Cognitive Neuroscience, 4,* 215–222.

Carnelley, K. B., Pietromonaco, P. R., & Jaffe, K. (1994). Depression, working models of others, and relationship functioning. *Journal of Personality and Social Psychology, 66,* 127–140.

Carter, C. S. (1998). Neuroendocrine perspective on social attachment and love. *Psychoneuroendocrinology, 23,* 779–818.

Carter, C. S., Grippo, A. J., Pournajafi-Nazarloo, H., Ruscio, M. G., & Porges, S. W. (2008). Oxytocin, vasopressin and sociality. *Progress in Brain Research, 170,* 331–336. doi:10.1016/S0079-6123(08)00427-5.

Champagne, F. A., Dorio, J., Sharma, S., & Meaney, M. J. (2001). Naturally occurring variations in maternal behavior in the rat are associated with differences in estrogen-inducible central oxytocin receptors. *Proceedings of the National Academy of Sciences, 98,* 12736–12741.

Champagne, F. A., Francis, D. D., Mar, A., & Meaney, M. J. (2003). Variations in maternal care in the rat as a mediating influence for the effects of environment on development. *Physiology and Behavior, 79,* 359–371.

Clark, M. S., & Mills, J. (1993). The difference between communal and exchange relationships: What it is and is not. *Personality and Social Psychology Bulletin, 19,* 684–691.

Coan, J. A., Beckes, L., & Allen, J. P. (2013). Childhood maternal support and neighborhood quality moderate the social regulation of neural threat responding in adulthood. *International Journal of Psychophysiology, 88,* 224–231.

Coan, J. A., Schaefer, H. S., & Davidson, R. J. (2006). Lending a hand: Social regulation of the neural response to threat. *Psychological Science, 17,* 1032–1039.

Cohen, S. (1991). Social supports and physical health: Symptoms, health behaviors and infectious disease. In A. L. Greene, M. Cummings, & K. H. Karraker (Eds.), *Life-span developmental psychology: Perspectives on stress and coping*. Hillsdale: Erlbaum.

Cohen, E., Ejsmond-Frey, R., Knight, N., & Dunbar, R. (2010). Rowers' high: Elevated endorphin release under conditions of active behavioural synchrony. *Biology Letters, 6,* 106–108.

Collins, N. L., & Feeney, B. C. (2000). A safe haven: An attachment theory perspective on support seeking and caregiving in intimate relationships. *Journal of Personality and Social Psychology, 78,* 1053–1073.

Cox, C. R., Arndt, J., Pyszczynski, T., Greenberg, J., Abdollahi, A., & Solomon, S. (2008). Terror management and adults' attachment to their parents: The safe haven hypothesis. *Journal of Personality and Social Psychology, 94,* 696–717.

Craig, A. D. B. (2009). How do you feel-now? The anterior insula and human awareness. *Nature Reviews Neuroscience, 10,* 59–70. doi:10.1038/nrn2555.

Cunningham, W. A., Van Bavel, J. J., Arbuckle, N. L., Packer, D. J., & Waggoner, A. S. (2012). Rapid social perception is flexible: Approach and avoidance motivational states shape P100 responses to other-race faces. *Frontiers in Human Neuroscience, 6*. doi:10.3389/fnhum.2012.00140.

Damasio A. R. (1996). The somatic marker hypothesis and the possible functions of the prefrontal cortex. *Proceedings of The Royal Society*, 351, 1413–1420.

D'Amato, F., & Pavone, F. (1993). Endogenous opioids: A proximate reward mechanism for kin selection? *Behavioral and Neural Biology, 60,* 79–83.

Davis, D. (1982). Determinants of responsiveness in dyadic interaction. In W. I. Ickes & E. S. Knowles (Eds.), *Personality roles and social behaviors* (pp. 85–139). New York: Springer.

DeVries, A. C., Guptaa, T., Cardillo, S., Cho, M., & Cartner, C. S. (2002). Corticotropin-releasing factor induces social preferences in male prairie voles. *Psychoneuroendocrinology, 27,* 705–714.

Domes, G., Heinrichs, M., Gläscher, J., Büchel, C., Braus, D. F., & Herpertz, S. C., et al. (2007a). Oxytocin attenuates amygdala responses to emotional faces regardless of valence. *Biological Psychiatry, 62,* 1187–1190. doi:10.1016/j.biopsych.2007.03.025.

Domes, G., Heinrichs, M., Michel, A., Berger, C., & Herpertz, S. C. (2007b). Oxytocin improves "mind-reading" in humans. *Biological Psychiatry, 61,* 731–733. doi:10.1016/j.biopsych.2006.07.015.

Dutton, D. G., & Aron, A. P. (1974). Some evidence for heightened sexual attraction under conditions of high anxiety. *Journal of Personality and Social Psychology, 23,* 510–517.

Eisenberger, N. I., Taylor, S. E., Gable, S. L., Hilmert, C. J., & Lieberman, M. D. (2007). Neural pathways link social support to attenuated neuroendocrine stress response. *Neuroimage, 35,* 1601–1612.

Eisenberger, N. I., Master, S. L., Inagaki, T. I., Taylor, S. E., Shirinyan, D., Lieberman, M. D., & Naliboff, B. (2011). Attachment figures activate a safety signal-related neural region and reduce pain experience. *Proceedings of the National Academy of Sciences, 1081,* 11721–11726.

Feeney, B. C., & Kirkpatrick, L. A. (1996). Effects of adult attachment and presence of romantic partners on physiological responses to stress. *Journal of Personality and Social Psychology, 70,* 255–270.

Feldman, R., Weller, A., Zagoory-Sharon, O., & Levine, A. (2007). Evidence for a neuroendocrinological foundation of human affiliation: Plasma oxytocin levels across pregnancy and the postpartum period predict mother-infant bonding. *Psychological Science, 18,* 965–970.

Firestone, I. J., Kaplan, K. J., & Russell, J. C. (1973). Anxiety, fear, and affiliation with similar-state versus dissimilar-state others: Misery sometimes loves nonmiserable company. *Journal of Personality and Social Psychology, 26,* 409–414.

Fraley, R. C., & Shaver, P. R. (1998). Airport separations: A naturalistic study of adult attachment dynamics in separating couples. *Journal of Personality and Social Psychology, 75,* 1198–1212.

Fraley, R. C., & Shaver, P. R. (1999). Loss and bereavement: Attachment theory and recent controversies concerning "grief work" and the nature of detachment. In J. Cassidy & P. R. Shaver (Eds.), *Handbook of attachment: Theory, research, and clinical applications* (pp. 735–759). New York: Guilford.

Francis, D. D., & Meaney, M. J. (1999). Maternal care and the development of stress responses. *Current Opionions in Neurobiology, 9,* 128–134.

Gottman, J. M. (1979). *Marital interaction: Empirical investigations*. New York: Academic.

Gray, T. S., Carney, M. E., & Magnuson, D. J. (1989). Direct projections from the central amygdaloid nucleus to the hypothalamic paraventricular nucleus: Possible role in stress induced adrenocorticotrpoin release. *Neuroendocrinology, 50,* 433–446.

Grewen, K. M., Girdler, S. S., Amico, J. A., & Light, K. C. (2005). Effects of partner support on resting oxytocin, cortisol, norepinephrine and blood pressure before and after warm partner contact. *Psychosomatic Medicine, 67,* 531–538.

Harlow, H. (1958). The nature of love. *American Psychologist, 13,* 673–685.

Hazan, C., & Shaver, P. (1987). Romantic love conceptualized as an attachment process. *Journal of Personality and Social Psychology, 5,* 511–524.

Henessy, M. B. (1997). Hypothalamic-pituitary-adrenal responses to brief social separation. *Neuroscience and Biobehavioral Reviews, 21,* 11–29.
Hofer, M. A. (1995). Hidden regulators: Implications for a new understanding of attachment, separation, and loss. In S. Goldberg, R. Muir, & J. Kerr (Eds.), *Attachment theory: Social, developmental, and clinical perspectives* (pp. 203–230). Hillsdale: Analytic Press.
Hofer, M. A. (2006). Psychobiological roots of early attachment. *Current Directions in Psychological Science, 15,* 84–88.
Holt-Lunstad, J., Smith, T. B., & Layton, J. B. (2010). Social relationships and mortality risk: A meta- review. *Plos Medicine, 7,* e1000316. doi:10.1371/journal.pmed.1000316.
Insel, T. R. (1997). A neurobiological basis of social attachment. *The American Journal of Psychiatry, 154,* 726–735.
Israel, S., Lerer, E., Shalev, I., Uzefovsky, F., Riebold, M., & Laiba, E., et al. (2009). The oxytocin receptor (OXTR) contributes to prosocial fund allocations in the dictator game and the social value orientations task. *Plos One, 4,* e5535. doi:10.1371/journal.pone.0005535.
Jack, A., Connelly, J. J., & Morris, J. P. (2012). DNA methylation of the oxytocin receptor gene predicts neural response to ambiguous social stimuli. *Frontiers in Human Neuroscience, 6,* 1–7. doi:10.3389/fnhum.2012.00280.
Jacobs, L., Berscheid, E., & Walster, E. (1971). Self-esteem and attraction. *Journal of Personality and Social Psychology, 17,* 84–91.
Johnson, S. M., Burgess Moser, M. Beckes, L., Smith, A., Dagleish, T., Halchuk, R., Hasselmo, K., Greenman, P. S., Merali, Z., & Coan, J. A. (2013). Soothing the threatened brain: Leveraging contact comfort with emotionally focused therapy. *PLoS One, 8(11),* e79314. doi: 10.1371/journal.pone.0079314.
Kamarck, T. W., Manuck, S. B., & Jennings, J. R. (1990). Social support reduces cardiovascular reactivity to psychological challenge: A laboratory model. *Psychosomatic Medicine, 52,* 42–58.
Keating, C. F., Pomerantz, J., Pommer, S. D., Ritt, S. J. H., Miller, L. M., & McCormick, J. (2005). Going to college and unpacking hazing: A functional approach to decrypting initiation practices among undergraduates. *Group Dynamics: Theory, Research, and Practice, 9,* 104–126.
Kemp, A. H., & Guastella, A. J. (2011). The role of oxytocin in human affect: A novel hypothesis. *Current Directions in Psychological Science, 20,* 222–231.
Kenrick, D. T., & Johnson, G. A. (1979). Interpersonal attraction in aversive environments: A problem for the classical conditioning paradigm. *Journal of Personality and Social Psychology, 37,* 572–579.
Keverne, E. B., & Kendrick, K. M. (1994). Maternal behavior in sheep and its neuroendocrine regulation. *Acta Pediatrica, 397,* 47–56.
Kobak, R. R., & Duemmler, S. (1994). Attachment and conversation: Toward a discourse analysis of adolescent and adult security. In K. Bartholomew & D. Perlman (Eds.), *Attachment processes in adulthood* (pp. 121–149). London: Jessica Kingsley.
Kosfeld, M., Heinrichs, M., Zak, P. J., Fischbacher, U., & Fehr, E. (2005). Oxytocin increases trust in humans. *Nature, 435,* 673–676. doi:10.1038/nature03701.
Lazarus, R. S., & Folkman, S. (1984). *Stress, appraisal, and coping*. New York: Springer.
Li, Q., & Brewer, M. B. (2004). What does it mean to be an American? Patriotism, nationalism, and American identity after 9/11. *Political Psychology, 25,* 727–739.
Liebowitz, M. R. (1983). *Chemistry of love*. Boston: Little Brown.
Lim, M. M., & Young, L. J. (2006). Neuropeptidergic regulation of affiliative behavior and social bonding in animals. *Hormones and Behavior, 50,* 506–517.
Lopez, F. G., Melendez, M. C., Sauer, E. M., Berger, E., & Wyssman, J. (1998). Internal working models, self-reported problems, and help-seeking attitudes among college students. *Journal of Counseling Psychology, 45,* 79–83.
Lutgendorf, S. K., Sood, A. K., Anderson, B., McGinn, S., Maiseri, H., Dao, M., Sorosky, J. I., DeGeest, K., & Lubaroff, D. M. (2005). Social support, distress, and natural killer cell activity in ovarian cancer patients. *Journal of Clinical Oncology, 23,* 7106–7113.
Machin, A. J., & Dunbar, R. I. M. (2011). The brain opioid theory of social attachment: A review of the evidence. *Behaviour, 148,* 985–1025.

Master, S. L., Eisenberger, N. I., Taylor, S. E., Naliboff, B. D., Shirinyan, D., & Lieberman, M. D. (2009). A picture's worth: Partner photographs reduce experimentally induced pain. *Psychological Science, 20,* 1316–1318.

Mendoza, S. P., & Mason, W. A. (1997). Attachment relationships in new world primates. In C. S. Carter, I. I. Lederhendler & B. Kirkpatrick (Eds.), *The Integartive Neurobiology of Affiliation* (pp. 203–209). New York: New York Academy of Sciences.

Mikulincer, M., & Shaver, P. R. (2003). The attachment behavioral system in adulthood: Activation, psychodynamics, and interpersonal processes. In M. P. Zanna (Ed.), *Advances in experimental social psychology* (Vol. 35, pp. 53–152). New York: Academic.

Mikulincer, M., & Shaver, P. R. (2007). *Attachment in adulthood: Structure, dynamics, and change.* New York: Guilford Press.

Mikulincer, M., Birnbaum, G., Woddis, D., & Nachmias, O. (2000). Stress and accessibility of proximity-related thoughts: Exploring the normative and intraindividual components of attachment theory. *Journal of Social and Personality Psychology, 78,* 509–523.

Mikulincer, M., Gillath, O., Halevy, V., Avihou, N., Avidan, S., & Eshkoli, N. (2001a). Attachment theory and reactions to others' needs: Evidence that activation of the sense of attachment security promotes empathic responses. *Journal of Personality and Social Psychology, 81,* 1205–1224.

Mikulincer, M., Hirschberger, G., Nachmias, O., & Gillath, O. (2001b). The affective component of the secure base schema: Affective priming with representations of attachment security. *Journal of Personality and Social Psychology, 81,* 305–321.

Mikulincer, M., Gillath, O., & Shaver, P. R. (2002). Activation of the attachment system in adulthood: Threat-related primes increase the accessibility of mental representations of attachment figures. *Journal of Personality and Social Psychology, 83,* 881–895.

Mikulincer, M., Gillath, O., Sapir-Lavid, Y., Yaakobi, E., Arias, K., Tal-Aloni, L., & Bor, G. (2003a). Attachment theory and concern for others' welfare: Evidence that activation of the sense of secure base promotes endorsement of self-transcendence values. *Basic and Applied Social Psychology, 25,* 299–312.

Mikulincer, M., Shaver, P. R., & Pereg, D. (2003b). Attachment theory and affect regulation: The dynamics, development, and cognitive consequences of attachment-related strategies. *Motivation and Emotion, 27,* 77–102.

Mikulincer, M., Shaver, P. R., & Horesh, N. (2006). Attachment bases of emotion regulation and posttraumatic adjustment. In D. K. Snyder, J. A. Simpson, & J. N. Hughes (Eds.), *Emotion regulation in families: Pathways to dysfunction and health.* Washington, DC: American Psychological Association.

Nelson, E. E., & Panksepp, J. (1998). Brain substrates of infant-mother attachment: Contributions of opioids, oxytocin, and norepinephrine. *Neuroscience and Biobehavioral Reviews, 22,* 437–452.

Onaka, T. (2004). Neural pathways controlling central and peripheral oxytocin release during stress. *Journal of Neuroendocrinology, 16,* 308–312.

Panksepp, J. (1998). *Affective neuroscience.* New York: Oxford University Press.

Panksepp, J., Nelson, E., & Bekkedal, M. (1999). Brain systems for the mediation of social separation distress and social reward: Evolutionary antecedents and neuropeptide intermediaries. In C. S. Carter, I. I. Lederhendler, & B. Kirkpatrick (Eds.), *The integrative neurobiology of affiliation* (pp. 221–244). Cambridge: MIT Press.

Pfaus, J. (2009). Pathways of sexual desire. *The Journal of Sexual Medicine, 6,* 1506–1533.

Poldrack, R. A., Wagner, A. D., Ochsner, K. N., & Gross, J. J. (2008). Cognitive emotion regulation: Insights from social cognitive and affective neuroscience. *Current Directions in Psychological Science, 17,* 153–158.

Reddy, V., Hay, D., Murray, L., & Trevarthen, C. (1997). Communication in infancy: Mutual regulation of affect and attention. In G. Bremner, A. Slater, et al. (Eds.), *Infant development: Recent advances* (pp. 247–273). Hove: Psychology Press.

Reis, H., Clark, M., & Holmes, J. (2004). Perceived partner responsiveness as an organizing construct in the study of intimacy and closeness. In D. J. Masek & A. Aron (Eds.), *Handbook of closeness and intimacy* (pp. 201–201). Mahwah: Erlbaum.

Rholes, W. S., Simpson, J. A., & Friedman, M. (2006). Avoidant attachment and the experience of parenting. *Personality and Social Psychology Bulletin, 32,* 275–285.

Riordan, C. A., & Tedeschi, J. T. (1983). Attraction in aversive environments: Some evidence for classical and negative reinforcement. *Journal of Personality and Social Psychology, 44,* 683–692.

Sarnoff, I., & Zimbardo, P. G. (1961). Anxiety, fear and social affiliation. *Journal of Abnormal and Social Psychology, 62,*356–363.

Sbarra, D. A., & Hazan, C. (2008). Coregulation, dysregulation, self-regulation: An integrative analysis and empirical agenda for understanding adult attachment, separation, loss, and recovery. *Personality and Social Psychology Review, 12,* 141–167.

Schachter, S. (1959). *The psychology of affiliation: Studies of the sources of gregariousness.* Stanford: Stanford University Press.

Selcuk, E., Zayas, V., & Hazan, C. (2010). Beyond satisfaction: The role of attachment in marital functioning. *Journal of Family Theory and Review, 2,* 258–279.

Selcuk, E., & Zayas, V., Gunaydin, G., Hazan, C., & Kross, E. (2012). Mental representations of attachment figures facilitate recovery following upsetting autobiographical recall. *Journal of Personality and Social Psychology, 103,* 362–378.

Shaver, P. R., & Klinnert, M. (1982). Schachter's theories of affiliation and emotion: Implications of developmental research. In L. Wheeler (Ed.), *Review of personality and social psychology* (Vol. 3, pp. 37–72). Beverly Hills, CA: Sage Publications.

Simpson, J. A., Rholes, W. S., & Nelligan, J. S. (1992). Support seeking and support giving within couples in an anxiety-provoking situation: The role of attachment styles. *Journal of Personality and Social Psychology, 62,* 434–446.

Simpson, J. A., Beckes, L., & Weisberg, Y. J. (2007). Evolutionary accounts of individual differences in adult attachment orientations. In J. V. Wood, A. Tesser, & J. G. Holmes (Eds.), *The self and social relationships* (pp. 183–206). New York: Psychology Press.

Skinner, B. F. (1956). A case history in scientific method. *American Psychologist, 11,* 221–233.

Sroufe, L. A., & Waters, E. (1977). Attachment as an organizational construct. *Child Development, 48,* 1184–1199.

Sullivan, R. M., Hofer, M. A., & Brake, S. C. (1986). Olfactory-guided orientation in neonatal rats is enhanced by a conditional change in behavior state. *Developmental Psychobiology, 19,* 615–623.

Szechtman, H., Hershkowitz, M., & Simantov, R. (1981). Sexual behavior decreases pain sensitivity and stimulated endogenous opioids in male rats. *European Journal of Pharmacology, 70,* 279–285.

Taylor, S. E. (2006). Tend and befriend: Biobehavioral bases of affiliation under stress. *Current Directions in Psychological Science, 15,* 273–277.

Taylor, S. E., Klein, L. C., Lewis, B. P., Gruenewald, T. L., Gurung, R. A., & Updegraff, J. A. (2000). Biobehavioral responses to stress in females: Tend-and-befriend, not fight-or-flight. *Psychological Review, 107,* 411–429.

Taylor, S. E., Gonzaga, G. C., Klein, L. C., Hu, P., Greendale, G. A., & Seeman, T. E. (2006). Relation of oxytocin to psychological stress responses and hypothalamic-pituitary-adrenocortical axis activity in older women. *Psychosomatic Medicine, 68,* 238–245.

Theodoridou, A., Rowe, A. C., Penton-Voak, I. S., & Rogers, P. J. (2009). Oxytocin and social perception: Oxytocin increases perceived facial trustworthiness and attractiveness. *Hormones and Behavior, 56,* 128–132. doi:10.1016/j.yhbeh.2009.03.019.

Turner, R. A., Altemus, M., Enos, T., Cooper, B., & McGuinness, T. (1999). Preliminary research on plasma oxytocin in normal cycling women: Investigating emotion and interpersonal distress. *Psychiatry, 62,* 97–113.

Turner-Cobb, J. M., Sephton, S. E., Koopman, C., Blake-Mortimer, J., & Spiegel, D. (2000). Social support and salivary cortisol in women with metastatic breast cancer. *Psychosomatic Medicine, 62,* 337–345.

Uchino, B. N. (2006). Social support and health: A review of physiological processes potentially underlying links to disease outcomes. *Journal of Behavioral Medicine, 29,* 377–387.

Uchino, B. N., Cacioppo, J. T., & Kiecolt-Glaser, J. K. (1996). The relationship between social support and physiological processes: A review with emphasis on underlying mechanisms and implications for health. *Psychological Bulletin, 119,* 488–531.

Wanat, M. J., Hopf, F. W., Stuber, G. D., Phillips, P. E., & Bonci, A. (2008). Corticotrpin-releasing factor increase mouse ventral tegmental area dopamine neuron firing through protein kinase C-dependent enhancement of lh. *Journal of Physiology, 586,* 2157–2170.

Williams, J. R., Insel, T. R., Harbaugh, C. R., & Carter, C. S. (1994). Oxytocin administered centrally facilitates formation of a partner preference in female prairie voles (Microtus ochrogaster). *Journal of Neuroendocrinology, 6,* 247–250.

Zak, P. J., Kurzban, R., & Matzner, W. T. (2005). Oxytocin is associated with human trustworthiness. *Hormones and Behavior, 48,* 522–527. doi:10.1016/j.yhbeh.2005.07.009.

Zak, P. J., Stanton, A. A., & Ahmadi, S. (2007). Oxytocin increases generosity in humans. *Plos One, 2,* e1128. doi:10.1371/journal.pone.0001128.

Chapter 3
An Expectancy-Value Approach to Attachment

Jennifer A. Bartz, Mark W. Baldwin and John E. Lydon

Working models of how the interpersonal world functions translate attachment requirements into emotional reactions and plans for action, from the initiation stage throughout the duration of a close relationship. These working models can be effective in allowing a person to satisfy attachment needs and desires, in which case they may operate without being noticed, but in some circumstances, or for some individuals, they can also produce unforeseen, unwanted, and even contrary outcomes. For example, people who are highly motivated to be close to others, like the anxiously attached, often think and behave in ways that undermine their chances for closeness. Intriguingly, such ironic effects often occur precisely when these individuals are *most* highly motivated to connect. *Why does attachment goal pursuit sometimes become derailed even under relatively favorable circumstances?*

In this chapter we address such questions as this by exploring an approach broadly based on *expectancy-value* theory, which was originally proposed as a framework for understanding attitude formation and change but has since been applied to a number of domains including theories of motivation. Simply put, goal

"…a child is busy constructing working models of how the physical world may be expected to behave, how his mother and other significant persons may be expected to behave, how he himself may be expected to behave, and how each interacts with all the others. Within the framework of these working models he evaluates his situation and makes his plans… How these models are built up and thenceforward bias perception and evaluation, how adequate and effective for planning they become, how valid or distorted as representations they are, and what conditions help or hinder their development, all these are matters of great consequence for understanding the different ways in which attachment behavior becomes organized as children grow older." (Bowlby 1982, p. 354; Man and Hamid 1998)

J. A. Bartz (✉) · M. W. Baldwin · J. E. Lydon
McGill University, Montreal, Quebec, Canada
e-mail: jennifer.bartz@mcgill.ca

M. W. Baldwin
e-mail: mark.baldwin@mcgill.ca

J. E. Lydon
e-mail: john.lydon@mcgill.ca

V. Zayas, C. Hazan (eds.), *Bases of Adult Attachment*,
DOI 10.1007/978-1-4614-9622-9_3

commitment—and motivation more generally—is a function of people's expectancies about whether they can achieve the goal (which is based on assessments of self-efficacy and environmental contingencies) and the value they attach to the goal. We believe this perspective can be useful in furthering our understanding of attachment dynamics and especially those related to the formation and maintenance of attachment bonds. In particular, expectancy-value calculations likely influence many processes related to attachment including whether (and how) people initiate new relationships, move from casual to more committed relationships, and persevere in the face of conflict. Moreover, we think this perspective—and the value component in particular—can be useful in unraveling the kinds of paradoxical observations described above.

Although the notion of expectancy-value may be new to attachment, the notion of expectancies is not. In terms of *expectancies* we submit that, as Bowlby indicated in the quotation above, expectancies are at the core of attachment working models. Thinking is for doing, as James (1983/1890) pointed out, and the attachment behavioral system is guided by expectancies about whether attachment needs are likely to be satisfied, and in particular about how various behaviors one might perform are likely to produce satisfying—or unsatisfying—outcomes. Main et al. (1985; Main 1981) emphasized that attachment behavior is goal-directed behavior and from childhood onward we learn the types of behaviors that work—as well as those that do not work—in achieving our goals. In this way, although the content of expectancies may differ from person to person, expectancies function in a normative way to guide attachment goal pursuit.

In our opinion, less attention has been paid to the *value* side of the equation. Certainly, attachment researchers have identified a range of goals, hopes and fears with particular relevance to attachment (e.g., Gillath et al. 2006) including maintaining proximity or closeness to another, seeking emotional or instrumental support, seeking approval, maintaining an affective state of felt security, as well as autonomy, privacy, safety, and control (e.g., Mikulincer 1998). Although we touch on several of these domains, our primary focus in this chapter concerns the more basic valuing of communal goals, broadly stated as seeking closeness, acceptance, and emotional responsiveness from a valued other rather than rejection, abandonment, or poor treatment. Importantly, the point about value that we wish to emphasize is not so much the specific goal, but rather the subjective value associated with the goal, and how subjective value either alone or in interactions with expectancies influence attachment dynamics.

We begin the chapter with an examination of expectancies in the context of attachment working models. As noted, considerable work has been conducted in this area and, for this reason, much of this portion of the chapter is a review and synthesis of this work. Specifically, we discuss people's self-reports of their explicit interpersonal expectancies as well as work looking at cognitive activation patterns that reveal implicit expectancies. We also examine differences in expectances between individuals characterized by different chronic attachment orientations but, consistent with the theme of this volume on normative attachment processes, we highlight work showing variability in expectancies within individuals across their different relationships, as these patterns of variability reveal much about the nature of working models. In the second half of this chapter, we turn our focus to *value* and how value alone, or in interactions with expectancies, influence attachment goal pursuit. Here, we highlight studies that involve heightened valuing of interpersonal connection (due to the influence of situational factors or physiological factors that increase the incentive salience of the goal object), and discuss how such changes in subjective value interact with expectancies to influence people's willingness to initiate a relationship and persevere in the face of the uncertainty that occurs at the outset of a relationship. Because less work has focused on the notion of subjective value in the context of attachment dynamics, this section will necessarily be more speculative but we hope helpful in laying out an agenda for future work on this topic.

Expectancies and Working Models

We begin with an examination of the expectancy element of attachment working models (we will hold the valuing component constant by assuming, for the time being, that there is a normative and consistent motive for communal relations with others, an assumption we will revisit later in the chapter). Expectancy is a representation or judgment of what is likely to happen. People can evaluate the likelihood of any number of potential interpersonal events, from being loved and supported, to being hurt, let down, or abandoned, and these judgments can be guided by all manner of information as represented in internal working models.

From a social cognitive perspective—and certainly Bowlby was one of the first great social cognitive theorists—an attachment working model can be thought of as an associative network of mental representations relating to the pursuit of attachment needs. Baldwin (1992) discussed attachment working models as a special type of *relational schema*, or integrated knowledge structure representing self, an interaction partner, and an interpersonal script for typical patterns of interaction between self and other. Collins and Read (1994) elaborated on this approach, identifying four central components of attachment working models: (1) autobiographical memories; (2) generalized expectancies and beliefs; (3) attachment-relevant goals and needs; and, finally, (4) procedural knowledge contributing to strategies and plans. Other researchers (e.g., Shaver et al. 1996; Dykas and Cassidy 2011; Mikulincer et al. 2011) have taken the understanding of working models to new levels, specifying in greater detail the mechanisms whereby models can influence selective attention, attribution, memory, affect, and a host of other attachment-related processes.

Expectancies have long been understood as central to working models. Main et al. (1985) described the process whereby the child builds representations of different attempts to achieve goals, along with the results of those attempts: "If the child's knowledge of relationships is organized by actions and action outcomes, then the internal working model of the infant-parent relationship will be formed out of a history of the infants' actions, infant-parent interactions, and the fate of the infant's 'attempts and outcomes'" (Main et al. 1985, p. 75). In an important contribution to our understanding of working models, Bretherton (1985, 1990) emphasized the significance of generalized expectancies as scripts for such typical attachment patterns as "When I hurt myself, my mommy always comes to comfort and help me." Other researchers (e.g., Mikulincer et al. 2009; Waters and Waters 2006) have elaborated on this view to propose that the core of security-giving attachment models is the secure base script—that is, of being in distress and reaching out to the attachment figure. It is thought that such secure base scripts are normative, in that we all possess such scripts, but that the content of these scripts differ. More securely attached individuals expect that the attachment figure will respond to such bids with help and comfort, whereas more insecurely attached individuals expect that bids for closeness, dependency or trust will lead to negative outcomes.

One way to conceptualize the interpersonal script is as a chain of smaller cognitive units; specifically, *if…then* behavior-outcome expectancies (e.g., Mischel 1973) that structure a person's experience and behavior. These if…then expectancies essentially reflect conditional probabilities: If I reach out to a loved one (or for that matter to merely a potential relationship partner), then what do I anticipate will happen? Can I trust that the other person will respond positively, with acceptance and caring, or is there a significant risk that the other will be rejecting, abandoning, or hurtful? People are keenly attuned to such learning contingencies: Actions have consequences, and people readily make this connection and store the association for future use. The *if* is normative—we all ask the question—but the *then* can be thought of as reflecting the unique expectancies that a specific person develops over the course of experience.

As Bowlby stated, these working models are subsequently used to guide behavior and emotion, as the person conducts "small scale experiments within the head" (Bowlby 1969, p. 81). If the expectancy is the satisfaction of a valued goal, this produces positive affect, motivation, and behavior to enact the script; if the expectancy is negative, however, this can produce negative affect and avoidance of the unsatisfying script. In line with this, Collins and Read (1994) proposed that an important component of attachment cognition is the appraisal of events for the degree to which they facilitate or thwart the achievement of attachment goals. In a study with particular relevance to this chapter, Collins and Allard (1999) found that when young adults were asked to imagine several types of negative behaviors that their partner might perform, their affective response showed an expectancy-value pattern: Participants' emotional distress was proportional to the importance of the goal being thwarted by the partner.

Before turning to a more detailed examination of expectancies, we would like to draw attention to the issue of stability and variability. One message that has emerged clearly from the broader social cognition literature, and from the study of attachment cognition in particular, is that working models should not be thought of as fixed templates that get imposed holus-bolus on all manner of ongoing experience. Rather, the associative network responds dynamically to a variety of inputs to activate the subset of representations that are: (i) relevant to the affordances in the situation, (ii) associated with currently salient goals, and/or (iii) cued by other sources (e.g., Collins and Allard 1999). Of relevance to the key issues being addressed in this book, relationship stage may be a particularly important variable in determining the kinds of expectancies that get activated. For example, during the formation stage of an attachment bond, a default representation may be activated, or a representation that is congruent with features of the current situation, because less is known about the partner. By contrast, during the maintenance stage there is likely a wealth of attachment experiences with the partner so that a variety of relationship-specific scripts are available and can be activated depending upon the particular inputs of the situation. This theory explains how both general- and relationship-specific models are reinforced over time but also why one model type might be more relevant during a particular phase of the relationship life-cycle. We return shortly to the interplay between general and relationship-specific models.

Individual Differences in Expectancies

Explicit Expectancies

Although expectancies function in a normative way to guide attachment related behavior, people's self-reports of what they tend to expect in relationships (i.e., the content of their expectancies) reveal attachment style differences. In some studies people are explicitly asked to report their expectancies in attachment-relevant situations, for example: when seeking closeness from a relationship partner (e.g., "You reach out to hug or kiss your partner"), depending on a relationship partner ("You are in an emergency situation and you need your partner's help"), or trusting a relationship partner ("You share secrets of your past with your partner"). When asked to rate the likelihood of various outcomes, insecurely attached individuals are significantly more likely to anticipate negative behaviors from the partner (e.g., rejection or abandonment) than are securely attached individuals (Baldwin et al. 1993, 1996). Avoidantly attached individuals, for example, are particularly likely to anticipate being hurt after trusting a relationship partner, whereas anxiously attached individuals report particularly negative expectancies in the domain of closeness seeking (e.g., "If I try to get closer to my partner, my partner will reject me" Baldwin et al. 1996; see also Rowe and Carnelley 2003).

In our focus on communal motives, we are particularly interested in expectancies of acceptance versus rejection as these are vital to the central attachment goal of maintaining proximity to the other. Bowlby (1973, p. 23) described a child's experience of the mother's emotional unavailability and rejection as akin to separation. He also noted that parents sometimes use threats to abandon the child as a means of discipline. Bowlby (1973, pp. 208–209) described how such experiences can give rise to expectancies in the form of if…then contingencies: "Some may have learnt that an attachment figure responds in a comforting way only when coaxed to do so. They grow up supposing that all such figures have to be coaxed. Others may have learnt during childhood that the wished-for response can be expected only if certain rules are kept."

Expectancies relating to rejection are particularly relevant to connections between the kinds of interpersonal concerns and behaviors in the attachment domain, and those in related domains such as social support, self-esteem, and emotion regulation. For example, anxiously attached individuals score lower on measures of self-esteem (Mickelson et al. 1997), and diary data reveal that the daily experience of self-esteem of anxiously attached individuals is highly influenced by rejection feedback from others (Hepper and Carnelley 2012). Similarly, the link between anxious attachment and workplace stress and burnout is mediated by the self-reported tendency to anticipate and focus attention on rejection, as revealed by such items as "When interacting with other people, I pay close attention to any signs that they might dislike me" (Ronen and Baldwin 2010). These findings raise intriguing questions about the nature of the relationship between attachment and the experience of the self and more precisely what happens to one's sense of self when attachment goals are not met, a point to which we will return at the end of the chapter.

Implicit Expectancies

Individual differences in working models are thought to manifest at the implicit level as well. However, Baldwin et al. (2010) have observed that the measurement of implicit processes in the interpersonal context poses significant challenges. Here, the construct of interest involves interpersonal expectancies rather than, for example, the simple attitudinal valence that is the focus of many other implicit measures. So, how to assess implicit interpersonal expectancies?

Our view is that expectancies are rooted in patterns of cognitive activation. As demonstrated by research on the simulation and availability heuristics (Tversky and Kahneman 1974), people readily judge the probability of a future event based on how easily or fluently they can imagine that event. In essence, when people perform the kinds of "small scale experiments in the head" that Bowlby wrote about, the expectancy is revealed by the extent to which the person feels that "I can easily imagine that happening."

Drawing upon the notion that the ease with which we can imagine something influences its cognitive accessibility, response time measures might be a viable way to capture how readily people perceive target stimuli as relating to a particular social outcome. For example, a person who has a stable predisposition to anticipate rejection would be expected to show increased cognitive accessibility for rejection-related themes. In support of this, Baldwin and Kay (2003) found that anxiously attached individuals were quicker to recognize words relating to social rejection in a lexical decision task (which involves identifying letter strings as either words or nonwords). Similarly, Zayas et al. (2009) found that anxiously attached women were quick, although avoidantly attached women were slow, to identify rejection target words.

Beyond this kind of general orientation of anticipating particular interpersonal outcomes, we should expect variability in anticipated outcomes depending on, among other things, the if…then structure of an interpersonal script. As mentioned, a behavior-outcome expectancy is essentially a conditional probability (e.g., Watson 2001). That is, it is an expectancy that a certain outcome will occur, conditional or contingent on a certain behavior by oneself. In terms of working models, an expectancy can be conceptualized as an associative link between nodes representing a behavior by self and an expected response by the other person. This if…then, behavior-outcome expectancy produces a pattern of cognitive activation such that enacting (or even just thinking about enacting) the behavior in question results, via spreading activation, in making the interpersonal outcome more accessible. The anticipated outcome comes readily and fluently to mind, often producing the phenomenal experience that "If I do X…I can easily imagine that Y will happen."

At the implicit level, if…then expectancies about relational outcomes can be examined with sequential priming tasks. When this task has been used in cognitive psychology studies, results showed that people are faster to recognize targets (e.g., the word *nurse*) in a lexical decision task if they are first briefly shown a word that is associated with it (e.g., the word *doctor*) or a sentence fragment for which the word is an expected completion (e.g., "He gave the blood sample to the…"). In research on interpersonal cognition, a word or sentence fragment is first presented to the participant to get them thinking about a certain interpersonal context (the *if*) and this is followed by a lexical decision trial where the participant must make a word/nonword decision about letter strings, some of which represent the social outcome of interest (the *then*). If the *if* makes it easier for the person to identify the *then* as a word, this is thought to indicate that this association reflects the person's expectancy. For example, Baldwin and Sinclair (1996) examined the phenomenon of conditional acceptance, and found that individuals with low self-esteem were particularly quick to recognize words related to *rejection* on trials where they first were led to think about *failure*.

Adopting this paradigm, Baldwin et al. (1993) had participants read sentence stems relating to attachment, such as "If I trust my partner, then my partner will…", and then make lexical decision judgments of positive and negative outcomes. They found that avoidantly attached adults were quicker to recognize the word "hurt" rather than "care" in the context of trusting their partner—revealing an implicit expectancy about the dangers of trusting others. Zayas et al. (2009) extended the Baldwin et al. (1993) findings by collecting event related potential (ERP) data during the lexical decision task, and found that preoccupied women (i.e., high anxious/low avoidant) showed strong ERP reactions to rejection stimuli, within 400 ms of exposure, on trials where attachment issues were made salient.

In sum, the cognitive activation of possible outcomes such as *hurt*, *rejection*, or *abandonment* which is the basis of an implicit expectancy, arises dynamically due to multiple factors including internal representations and contextual cues. Although individual differences in attachment are clearly revealed in expectancies—indeed, much of the research in this area has progressed by comparing between people with different attachment orientations—significant variability also exists within individuals and between relationships and it is to this issue that we now turn.

Multiple Models

Expectancies arise from a dynamic interplay between a person's memories of past experiences, various cognitive representations, and the internal and external cues and affordances of the moment. In a famous passage, Bowlby stated that people can have multiple models, either of multiple attachment figures or even as multiple models of a single relationship, observing "it is not uncommon for an individual to operate, simultaneously, with two (or more) working models of his attachment figure(s) and two (or more) working models of himself" (1973, p. 205). In order to understand the creation of expectancies, then, as well as their impact on attachment dynamics, we need to examine the relative influence of multiple representations.

Bowlby's observation gives rise to at least two general issues: First, although it is sometimes convenient to assume that people have a single working model that is used across all significant attachment experiences—and certainly we agree that people tend to gravitate toward a chronically accessible model (Baldwin et al. 1996)—it is far more likely that people have multiple models that are recruited for social cognition depending on situational factors, internal influences, and so on. Second, as we know from the larger social cognitive literature, it is possible to increase the accessibility of specific models via priming as a way to reveal the mechanisms of attachment-related information processing and to understand real-world fluctuations in attachment orientations. Taken together these observations support an examination of the normative, in addition to the individual-difference, aspects of attachment working models.

An early inkling of this diversity within a person's relational world was demonstrated by Baldwin et al. (1996) when they showed that most people in their samples had relationships representing at least two different attachment orientations. Moreover, even people who described themselves as generally anxious or generally avoidant reported that more than half of their ten closest relationships elicited security rather than insecurity. If…then expectancies were also evident at the relationship-specific level: For example, concerns about closeness seeking (e.g., "If I try to be close to this person, he/she will reject me") were most strongly linked to relationships characterized as anxious-ambivalent regardless of people's "chronic" level of anxious ambivalence.

The obvious question raised by finding such as these concerns the association between dispositional and relationship-specific attachment. A cluster of papers (e.g., Cook 2000; Cozzarelli et al. 2000; La Guardia et al. 2000; Pierce and Lydon 2001) have examined this question in slightly different ways but the consistent finding is that one's chronic or dispositional attachment orientation does not represent a simple composite or synthesis of all of one's attachment relationships. Moreover, relationship-specific models appear to regulate relationship experiences (e.g., intimacy, quality of interactions) in specific relationships to a greater extent than do dispositional attachment models. In one of the most impressive demonstrations of attachment dynamics at the relational level, Cook (2000) examined attachment in families by assessing each family member's attachment to each other family member using the round robin design of the Social Relations Model (Kenny and La Voie 1984). In this way, Cook was able to assess how much an individual's attachment orientation was due to: (i) the actor's internal working model, (ii) the attachment style that the partner typically elicits from other family members, and (iii) the unique relationship between the actor and the partner. This design revealed reliable effects for actors' internal working models as evidenced by the fact that actor attachment accounted for unique variance in well-being (similar to Cozzarelli et al.); critically, however, Cook et al. also observed additional, and equally powerful, effects for the unique relationship between the actor and partner.

The ability to form distinct attachment relationships indicates that we are sensitive to attachment dynamics and informed by specific relational experiences. Moreover, findings by Cook (2000) and by Pierce and Lydon (2001) indicate that there is a "feedback loop" whereby relationship specific experiences inform and alter generalized expectancies. These observations are consistent with the notion that expectancies are updated in response to expectancy-violation experiences—be they negative *or positive*—even in adulthood.

The notion of multiple models raises questions about stability and environmental affordances. For example, if the experience of at least some attachment security is available to most individuals, why is not everyone secure? Attachment needs and their concomitant goals are so basic and potent in human experience that individuals are motivated to regulate these needs as best they can in extant situations. In infancy, attachment dynamics typically unfold in relation to a primary caregiver who serves as an attachment figure. A mental representation of that relationship is theorized to form and regulate stress and threats to security and to create expectancies that are projected onto new interpersonal relationships. However, just as the behavior of the caregiver impacts on the working model of attachment that develops, so too may the behavior of others later in life shape the specific expectancies that inform working models in relation to such specific others. Moreover, some of these specific expectancies and models that develop may be applied to new relationships and new contexts rather than being applied to the attachment model with the primary caregiver. In other words, having one secure attachment figure may not help across all interpersonal situations since suboptimal attachment relationships may be activated depending upon contextual cues.

To summarize, expectancies about closeness, dependency and security appear to exist at a general, global level as reflected in individual differences in attachment, and at the relationship-specific level. More recent theory (Chen et al. 2006) and research (Overall et al. 2003) suggests that a middle level may even exist, consisting of, e.g., a set of attachment expectancies for friends, another set for siblings, and another set for parents. In a novel interpersonal situation, one might apply a global model of attachment, a middle level model, or, possibly, even a relationship-specific model because of distinct similarities between the new person and a prior significant other, a phenomenon known as *Transference* (Andersen and Baum 1994; Andersen and Chen 2002; Andersen et al. 1996). Again, the factors that influence which level model will be activated in such novel situations are, to date, unclear but likely depend on features of the situation as described above and upon value as discussed below.

Before concluding this section on multiple models, we would like to turn to the specific question of which attachment representation is brought to mind when attachment security is threatened. We raise this point because in any given situation, a person may not have a great deal of control over the other people physically or mentally present to them—and yet their attachment goals (e.g., for felt-security) may be strong at the moment. Thus, as a backdrop to an examination of attachment dynamics it is worth appreciating the diversity of social relations that may be activated during these times. Indeed, we suspect that it is precisely because of the immense power of attachment needs that an individual may latch onto the interpersonal figure most accessible to them in that particular situation even if that person does not provide optimal attachment security (i.e., satisfy attachment functions of secure base, safe haven and proximity seeking). In support of this, Trinke and Bartholomew (1997) showed that individuals may have significant others that they ideally would seek out for attachment even though those individuals do not meet attachment needs and are not regarded as strong attachment figures. More recently, Milyavskaya and Lydon (2013) found that even figures nominated as strong attachment figures may not necessarily provide attachment security. Specifically, more than a quarter of their participants nominated attachment figures whom they seek to meet attachment functions despite the insecurity elicited by the attachment figure; moreover, they found that strong but insecure figures were turned to for as many attachment functions as strong secure figures. Finally, they found that, not surprisingly, individuals with strong insecure figures were lower in subjective well being than individuals with strong secure figures. These results are a reminder that attachment goals and strivings are regulated within the boundaries of situational affordances. Moreover, they may partly answer the question raised earlier about why, if we all have at least some experiences with attachment security, we are not all secure. Perhaps it is a person's ability to draw upon security conferring others specifically during times of need that produces a more generalized sense of security.

In sum, work on multiple models has greatly advanced our understanding of the functioning attachment behavior system, and how it shapes relationship experience and maintenance. This work has refined our predictions about what to expect from specific individuals in specific situations. What is interesting to consider in the context of the present work, is how the availability of multiple models feeds into more normative processes. More specifically, because of the availability of multiple attachment models, even someone who is "chronically secure" can display anxious or avoidant profiles in certain social contexts. So while we often think of secure, anxious, and avoidant attachment styles as reflecting individual differences that arise as a function of repeated experiences with, for example, an unresponsive or inconsistently responsive mother, in fact, the notion of multiple models reinforces the idea that these "styles" are normative.

Priming

We end our discussion of expectancies with the topic of priming. Numerous researchers have utilized experimental priming as a way to carefully delineate the dynamics of the attachment expectancies that regulate the formation and maintenance of attachment bonds. The reasoning behind this methodological approach is that if multiple models of attachment are available in memory then it should be possible to prime specific models and observe their effects on associated expectancies, affect, motivation, and so on. The attachment priming literature has grown exponentially and we will not attempt to review it here, apart from mentioning a few particularly relevant examples. In an early illustration of this idea, Baldwin et al. (1996) primed participants with relationships in which they felt secure, anxious, or avoidant, and found that this manipulation influenced dating choices, with people being drawn to potential dating partners who "matched" their primed orientation. Pierce and Lydon (2001) tested the stress buffering effects of specific attachment models and found that subliminally priming words reflecting a warm-accepting versus a cold-critical attachment model influenced women's affective and coping responses to the visualization of an unplanned pregnancy. Importantly, they ruled out mood as an alternative explanation, thus highlighting the potency of the attachment model priming effect. In a third paper, Rowe and Carnelley (2003) found that participants who had been primed with a secure relationship were more likely to recall positive attachment-related words than those primed to feel avoidant. Moreover, when they reported their interpersonal expectations, secure-primed individuals reported more positive expectancies than the other groups, and anxious-primed individuals reported more negative expectancies. Finally, Bartz and Lydon (2008) used a priming procedure to look at the use of communal and exchange norms in specific attachment relationships. They found that, not surprisingly, those in secure and anxious relationships were more likely to be communal (e.g., make a personal sacrifice to help a friend). However, they also found that those in anxious (and avoidant) relationships 1) felt that their partner's reciprocation (of a communal overture) was important and 2) were quicker to reciprocate favors received, both of which are violations of the communal script. Thus, although those in anxious relationships want to be communal, they simultaneously adopt an exchange orientation, presumably to confirm the other's commitment. What is noteworthy about these findings is that the effects were not a function of people's chronic attachment style; rather, the effects were a function of the attachment quality of the specific relationship but nonetheless the findings replicate the effects of chronic attachment on communal and exchange norms (Bartz and Lydon 2006).

These and other such data indicate that through priming we can gain valuable insights into the nature of the associative network underlying the attachment system, and test the causal effects of activating specific attachment models (see, e.g., Mikulincer and Shaver's extensive work on security priming as reviewed in Mikulincer and Shaver 2007). The simple rule of thumb seems to be that priming a relationship characterized by a certain attachment orientation tends to lead a person to activate expectancies that subsequent attachment experiences will unfold in a similar manner. That having been said, priming does not always lead to such straightforward assimilation effects (see, e.g., Baldwin 2007 for discussion) and it has been some of the anomalies in cognitive-accessibility studies that have led us to consider the influence of values, as well as expectancies, in the context of attachment cognition. For example, if a prime activates an orientation that is highly incongruent with a person's chronic attachment orientation or desired self-concept, this might under some circumstances provoke a kind of contrast effect in the types of information that becomes activated (see, e.g., Bartz and Lydon 2004), perhaps as a way of defending or supporting the validity of the valued model. Similarly, in some lexical decision tasks (e.g., Zayas et al. 2009) it has been found that whereas anxiously attached individuals do show an activation of negative expectancy content, avoidantly attached individuals actually show a reduced activation: Is this because they do not hold a negative expectancy, or because they simply do not value the communal outcome as much? These are the kinds of questions we turn to next.

Value

We now turn to the topic of value. Here, our focus is on the subjective value associated with communal goals—i.e., seeking closeness, acceptance, and emotional responsiveness from a valued other. Drawing upon expectancy-value theory, we believe that both expectancies and value are important, and that gaining a better understanding of value, and on how value interacts with expectancies, can shed new light on attachment dynamics.

It is generally understood that insecure attachment is grounded in negative expectancies about relational experiences, but that whereas attachment anxiety is characterized by heightened attachment striving, avoidance involves a (actual or merely attempted) reduction in the valuing of attachment goals. Thus, starting from theory we are led to consider valuing as well as expectancies. Our appreciation for the importance of value is also empirically based. In examining topics in the attachment domain we have been struck by how experimental manipulations of valuing can lead to outcomes that are surprising, and even paradoxical (at least for some individuals, or in some situations). In our opinion these findings cannot easily be interpreted based solely on an analysis of expectancies; rather, a consideration of value is required.

In the following section we provide a more detailed examination of subjective value, alone or as it combines with expectancies, to influence affect, behavior, and relationship satisfaction. In several different paradigms, we have attempted to manipulate relational valuing—e.g., by increasing it through situational as well as, in some cases, physiological means—and then observing the effects of such heightened valuing on affect, cognition, and behavior. In our discussion, we focus on the phenomenon of anxious attachment, which we see as arising from a combination of strong relational desire plus uncertainty (or conflict) in expectancies. Importantly, although we focus on "anxious individuals," we believe that many of the findings that we discuss reflect the normative functioning of the attachment system and thus would apply to most individuals who are thrust into a situation in which there is a strong desire for closeness but concerns that close others do not (or may not) sufficiently share that desire. As noted at the outset of this chapter, from a straightforward goals analysis, it is somewhat perplexing why anxious individuals have such difficulties achieving and maintaining closeness with others given their intense desire for closeness. In an attempt to understand this disconnect between motivation and achievement, prior work has focused largely on the role of anxious expectancies. We believe that this disconnect may also stem from the value anxious individuals' attach to the goal of closeness and, more precisely, their excessive valuing of and consequent preoccupation with attachment goals in certain circumstances, which, we suspect may amplify their conflicting expectancies.

Relationship Initiation Under Heightened Valuing: Interacting with a "Potential Close Other" in the Lab and Field

We now turn to a series of studies in which we have manipulated the momentary valuing of attachment goals by situationally altering the desire and opportunity for closeness with another person, or have investigated participants' behavior in naturalistic situations involving heightened communal value (i.e., speed dating).

It is widely held that close relationships are associated with communal norms (responsiveness to need), whereas more casual relationships are associated with exchange norms (e.g., tit-for-tat; Clark 1986). However, as Lydon et al. (1997) observed, when people *desire* a close relationship with another person, they face an "interdependence dilemma" in which they must weigh the risks and rewards of communal behavior. People want to follow the communal script to signal interest but behaving communally can create anxiety because there is uncertainty about whether the interest is mutual. To reduce anxiety, people look for evidence of caring in patterns of social exchange, but this micro-level perspective (tabulating each tit-for-tat) can—paradoxically and unfortunately—further fuel feelings of vulnerability because it undermines a sense of confident trust in the positive motives of the partner.

In a series of studies, Bartz and Lydon (2006) investigated how individual differences in attachment influence this interdependence dilemma. We highlight this research because these studies manipulated people's desire for a communal relationship with another person—in effect, increasing the incentive value and salience of closeness. They built on work by Clark (1986), in which people's choices to emphasize versus downplay individual contributions in a joint activity were taken as indicators of exchange versus communal norms, respectively. Participants were brought into the lab and told they would be working on some group tasks with another participant. In one condition, participants' desire for a communal relationship with their partner was manipulated by having them interact with an attractive, opposite-sex partner (a confederate), whom they were surreptitiously informed was single and had recently transferred from another University; in this way instilling the desire and opportunity/probability for a communal relationship. Participants' use of, and reaction to the other's use of, communal norms were then measured. In Study 1, communal behavior was operationalized by a seemingly trivial indicator: the choice to use the same color pen as used by the other person for a group task, rather than selecting a different color pen, and thereby making apparent individual contributions. Anxiously attached individuals overwhelmingly (93 %) chose to work with the same color pen as their partner, indicating their desire to follow the communal script and, more precisely, their desire to *avoid* appearing exchange oriented. These data, we think, illustrate anxious individuals' strong desire for closeness—indeed, the proportion of anxious participants who chose to use the same color pen was significantly higher than that of secure participants (whose pen choice was at chance, indicating that they were following the communal script, but not actively avoiding to appear exchange oriented).

Interestingly though, in a condition in which the potential close other used communal norms, a paradoxical finding emerged amongst the anxious: rather than uniformly stimulating feelings of warmth and fulfillment, this communal overture instead increased their interpersonal anxiety (e.g., feeling self-conscious). Although anxiously attached individuals went out of their way to signal to an attractive new work partner that they were acting in a communal fashion, when they received evidence that their partner was acting in this same communal fashion (vs. not), their interpersonal anxiety spiked—a somewhat ironic response considering their desire for connection since the other's communal behavior should, if anything, signal mutual interest. This finding suggests that it is not solely expectancies of rejection that fuel anxious individuals' anxiety; if anything, our situational manipulation should have increased their expectancies of acceptance. We believe that it is the subjective value and meaning that they ascribe to these situations (possibly in combination with expectancies) that is driving their interpersonal anxiety. Indeed, a third study confirmed that the anxious were more likely to ascribe importance, meaning and relational significance to even relatively mundane communal overtures. The question then is, does—or how does—this (over)valuing lead them astray?

Data from their fourth study indicate that opportunities for closeness may lead to inhibition. In this study, participants again interacted with a potential close other, who signaled interest by acting communally or not (this time by smiling and suggesting to work together on the group task). Prior to the "group task" participants completed, among other things, a mental concentration task. Whereas secure individuals benefitted from the communal-acting other and excelled on this task, anxious individuals did not. Moreover, lexical decision data revealed that it was implicit thoughts about closeness—not rejection—that undermined anxious individuals' concentration, supporting the hypothesis that it is the value they attach to the goal and not (or not solely) a negative expectancy that is problematic.

Thus the ambivalence of the anxiously attached is reflected in the paradox that they exhibit communal strivings but are upset (or at the very least startled) by communal overtures. In a further investigation of this topic, two of us, along with Joy

McClure, examined ambivalent behavior among anxiously attached individuals (McClure et al. 2013). Participants came into the lab and played two "one-shot" social dilemma games with four different partners—specifically, the prisoner's dilemma (PD) and the assurance game (AG). As expected, compared to more secure individuals, the anxiously attached oscillated between cooperation and defection strategies in the social dilemma games. What is important here however is nature of the two games played. Specifically, oscillation is understandable in the PD because the payoff structure pits individual self-interest against relational interest. However, oscillation is not optimal in the AG because the payoff structure is designed so that individual participants are rewarded for consistent cooperative behavior—indeed, such oscillation would likely signal distrust because there is no reason (from a purely rational perspective) for not cooperating in the AG. It was precisely in this context (i.e., the AG) that the anxiously attached exhibited conflict and ambivalence. Moreover, as a further indication of their ambivalence (and possible inhibition), the anxious were slower to select a behavior in the seemingly "easier" AG game, regardless of whether they chose cooperation or defection. These findings are reminiscent of Bartz and Lydon's (2006) findings, and suggest that even if communal situations do not stimulate expectancies of rejection, there may be other competing goals (e.g., self-protection) that are raised for anxiously attached. Importantly, however, consistent with our view of attachment dynamics, priming attachment security overrode the chronic ambivalence of the anxiously attached and they exhibited less oscillation in their behavior and less hesitation in their choices when they thought about a secure attachment relationship prior to the social dilemma games, possibly because the goal of self-protection was less relevant. This priming effect reinforces the "normativity" of the attachment related cognitions and behaviors associated with specific attachment styles—that is, anxious individuals can and do act secure when they feel secure.

In another series of field studies two of us utilized speed dating to look at the effects of attachment in a situation in which the motivation for connection is high. These data shed light on how anxious individuals are perceived by others. Specifically, McClure et al. (2010) found that the anxiously attached are indeed seen as less appealing and less dateable in these zero-acquaintance situations. Moreover, McClure and Lydon (2014) found that in face-to-face interactions in the lab and in the field (at speed dating) the anxiously attached emit unfavorable interpersonal displays of social disengagement and manifest anxiety and, critically, these negative interpersonal displays mediated the negative impressions formed by observers.

Taking together data from the lab (interacting with a potential close other), and field (speed dating), a picture emerges of the anxiously attached in which their strong desire for closeness combined with ambivalent expectancies results in behavioral inhibition and/or oscillation that is then detected, and seen as undesirable, by potential close others. Again, it is not simply negative expectancies but ambivalent expectancies *combined with* desire and opportunity in the communal domain that undermines their behavior. Indeed, it appears that it is precisely in situations in which the desire and opportunity for closeness are high that the anxious experience conflict. We think an important direction for future work is to identify the specific expectancies that come online for anxiously attached individuals during these moments of heightened salience and valuing of attachment, to provoke displays of submission and withdrawal. As we discuss in the next section, it may be that for the anxious these communal opportunities a believed to require a form of self-subbordination that more secure and avoidant individuals do not experience.

In conclusion, we draw upon work on the anxiously attached—an orientation defined by a strong desire for closeness—to illustrate the role of heightened valuing of attachment goals, and how such valuing can interact with expectancies, to influence attachment dynamics. Again though, as noted at the outset of this section, we believe that anyone who is faced with an intense desire for closeness, in a context of interpersonal uncertainty, could grapple with similar issues; the chronically anxious may just have a lower threshold for displaying what is fundamentally a normative coping mechanism for the interdependence dilemma we all face at one time or another in our relational lives. We suggest the process could be the same for anyone if the subjective value attached to closeness is high enough (cf. Lydon et al. 1997) and/or the uncertainty of what to expect is acute enough.

Biological Correlates of the Subjective Value of Attachment Goals: Oxytocin

Another surprising finding regarding the anxiously attached, which we think also speaks to the issue of relational valuing, has emerged from recent work looking into the social effects of the neurohormone oxytocin in humans. Given the vital importance of attachment in humans (and some other animals), it is believed that biological mechanisms have evolved to promote the formation and maintenance of these bonds. Although there are a number of candidates, one of the most widely studied is the neurohormone oxytocin. Oxytocin is a nine-amino-acid peptide hormone that is synthesized in the paraventricular nucleus and supraoptic nucleus of the hypothalamus and released into peripheral circulation via the posterior pituitary gland. In the periphery, oxytocin has a number of actions but was first identified (and probably best known) for its role facilitating delivery during childbirth and milk-ejection during lactation (Burbach et al. 2006). In addition to its peripheral effects, oxytocin is also released into the central nervous system where it acts as a neuromodulator. Over four decades of research in non-human animals has shown that oxytocin plays a critical role regulating the formation and maintenance of attachment bonds. Specifically, oxytocin has been shown to be central to a suite of processes required for both mother–infant and adult–adult pair bonds, including: memory for and recognition of familiar others, preference of partners over other conspecifics, and motivated caregiving behavior, e.g., such maternal behaviors as retrieving and crouching over pups (for review, see Ross and Young 2009). Interestingly, and of particular relevance to this chapter, research has shown that these "prosocial" effects of oxytocin are due largely to the density of oxytocin receptors in regions of the brain associated with reward and reinforcement (e.g., the nucleus accumbens), which is thought to have the effect of making social interactions more pleasurable and rewarding.

Although much less is known about the role that oxytocin plays in human attachment, recent work suggests intriguing parallels with the animal literature. For example, increasing the availability of central oxytocin (via nasal spray administration) was shown to increase trust behavior in an economic exchange game (Kosfeld et al. 2005), cooperation (De Dreu et al. 2010; Declerck et al. 2010), the perceived approachability (Rimmele et al. 2009) and attractiveness (Theodoridou et al. 2009) of faces, and numerous other indices of prosocial cognition and behavior. Indeed, such findings have led to the conceptualization of oxytocin as a "love hormone" that promises to foster warm feelings and strong emotional bonds.

We introduce the topic of oxytocin here because, in our view, oxytocin (either alone or in combination with other neurochemicals) may be a biological correlate of the subjective value people ascribe to communal goals and attachment bonding more generally. Moreover, intriguingly, in the same way that situationally increasing the opportunity and desire for closeness can produce "ironic" effects in the anxiously attached, so too does increasing the availability of oxytocin.

In an early demonstration of this effect, Bartz et al. (2011b) administered intranasal oxytocin or placebo to healthy adults and adults with borderline personality disorder (BPD, a disorder characterized by preoccupation with being abandoned by significant others, interpersonal insecurity/instability and emotional reactivity). Participants then played the aforementioned AG with a partner (actually a research confederate). Results showed no main effect of oxytocin but rather a significant oxytocin by group interaction; however, in contrast to the popular view, oxytocin significantly *decreased* trust and the likelihood of cooperation in BPD/anxiously attached participants. These data showed, for the first time, that far from being a social panacea, oxytocin might impede trust and prosocial behavior depending on the presence of interpersonal insecurities and nature of working models (these effects held whether groups were characterized by diagnostic status or individual differences in attachment anxiety).

In another study, Bartz et al. (2010b) investigated whether oxytocin is involved in the mental representations associated with attachment given its role in attachment and social memory in animals. To address this question, they administered intranasal oxytocin versus placebo (within subject, across two testing sessions separated by several weeks) to participants and then measured recollections of maternal care and closeness in childhood—two key features of the attachment bond. Again, there was no main effect of oxytocin but rather a significant oxytocin by attachment anxiety interaction, with securely attached individuals remembering their mother as more caring and close in childhood when they received oxytocin compared to when they received placebo, but anxiously attached individuals showed the opposite pattern—that is, they remembered their mother as *less* caring and close in childhood when they received oxytocin. In terms of expectancy-value, we might hypothesize that by increasing the subjective value of closeness/close relationships, this might also bring to mind the memories and expectations cognitively associated with that value. Thus, a person with an insecure working model might be particularly likely to recall disappointments at precisely the moment when the desire for attachment is highest.

Such paradoxical effects of oxytocin in interpersonally vulnerable individuals have now been replicated by others (Bakermans-Kranenburg et al. 2012; Meinlschmidt and Heim 2007; Norman et al. 2011; Rockliff et al. 2011) and raise questions about the normative processes that oxytocin impacts to facilitate attachment bond formation in humans. How can oxytocin be helpful—socially—to some individuals but not others? Drawing upon work in animals, Bartz et al. (2011b) suggest that oxytocin may increase the desire for closeness and/or the salience of social cues in the environment (these two processes could operate in independently or in a reciprocal fashion—i.e., increasing the desire to affiliate should increase attention to social information just as increasing any other goal state increases attention to goal relevant information). If oxytocin increases affiliative motives and/or the salience of social cues, one would expect that this could heighten the effects of chronic individual differences in the relational expectancies people have and, consequently, lead to very different behavioral outputs, with oxytocin, for example, increasing trust and prosocial behavior in those who have generally positive expectations about others, but exacerbating insecurities in those who have more negative expectations. Indeed, in the aforementioned oxytocin-BPD study, it was found that those who received oxytocin initially felt more friendly than those who received placebo (unpublished data). However, as described, these pro-social inclinations were not maintained when the chronically insecure participants entered into the context of the social dilemma game, in which they had to assess the trustworthiness of the other player. These data are reminiscent of the aforementioned work on the interdependence dilemma people face in situations involving the potential for closeness and, specifically, the finding that activating closeness motives can backfire, increasing anxious individuals' interpersonal anxiety and eliciting their prosocial ambivalence.

More recent research may shed light on why activating communal motives can backfire in the anxiously attached. Although oxytocin can exacerbate interpersonal insecurities in the anxiously attached studies indicate that oxytocin can be helpful for those who are less socially engaged/motivated (Bartz et al. 2010a), or avoidantly attached (De Dreu 2012). In an attempt to explain this disparate pattern of results, Bartz et al. (under review) hypothesized that if oxytocin acts in a normative way to increase the desire to affiliate, this could shift the balance of communal and agentic motives (cf. Helgeson 1994) and result in differential effects for the anxious and avoidant. Specifically, an increase in other-oriented, communal motives should be helpful for those who are excessively focused on the self to the exclusion of others (like the avoidantly attached) but, an increase in other-oriented communal motives could be unhelpful for those who are already overly other focused and have little sense of self (like the anxiously attached) because it may further diminish the priority of the self and bring into play anxious' expectancies about a need to be submissive in order to achieve relatedness. In support of this hypothesis, Bartz et al. (under review) found that participants saw themselves as significantly more communal (e.g., "kind" and "understanding of others") following oxytocin (vs. placebo) and, consistent with prior work, this effect was especially pronounced for avoidant individuals, who are generally low in communion. With respect to agency, there was no main effect of oxytocin; however, results revealed a significant oxytocin by attachment anxiety interaction, such that highly anxious participants—who are generally low in agency—showed even further reductions following oxytocin (i.e., reporting being even less "independent" and "self-confident"). In addition to explaining anxious individuals' negative response to oxytocin, these findings may illuminate anxious individuals' ironic response to opportunities for closeness more generally—that is, closeness may be anxiety provoking for anxious individuals not (or not solely) because of expectancies of separation/abandonment but because closeness, in the mind of the anxious, requires a subordination of the self. Such feelings could make them feel even more vulnerable in interpersonal situations and even on occasion result in the kinds of "antisocial" behaviors that were observed in the BPD participants.

Although such variability in the social effects of oxytocin could at first blush be interpreted as random noise, as described, these person-specific effects may shed light on the fundamental processes oxytocin regulates across all people (cf. Mischel and Shoda 1995). In fact, other work indicates that not only do individual differences moderate the social effects of oxytocin but so can the social context (for review, see Bartz et al. 2011a). For example, in the domain of trust and cooperation, Declerck et al. (2010) found that although oxytocin increased trust when participants played a social dilemma game with someone whom they had met, oxytocin *decreased* trust when participants played with a stranger; similarly, De Dreu et al. (2010) found that oxytocin *decreased* cooperation when participants played a social dilemma game with an outgroup member (under conditions of high fear). These findings are reminiscent of the effects of oxytocin observed in BPD participants (who are chronically concerned about betrayal) and suggest that individual difference responses to oxytocin may in fact be normative for certain contexts. That is, even secure individuals will show decreased trust in response to oxytocin when put in a highly uncertain context, or when interacting with an outgroup member. Viewed in this light, the oxytocin system and how it regulates affiliation appears to be adaptive in that it does not promote closeness when closeness may be risky. Here again, expectancy and value are best understood in combination.

Conclusion

In this chapter we suggest that our understanding of attachment dynamics can benefit from an expectancy-value approach. We note that much is known about attachment expectancies and individual variation therein, the interplay between relationship-specific and general expectancies, and how, why, and when expectancies might exert their effects. However, we suggest, less is known about how the subjective value that is attached to attachment goals influences attachment dynamics. In our discussion of value, we focus on research looking at attachment anxiety in the context of the interdependence dilemma people face at the outset of a relationship, and in speed dating situations, to understand how subjective value alone, or in combination with expectancies, can influence emotion and behavior in communal goal relevant contexts. Moreover, we suggest that although situational affordances can modulate value appraisals, it appears that biological factors (e.g., oxytocin) can also modulate the valuing of social stimuli and communal goals. We conclude this chapter by calling attention to a few issues, which we think are interesting and important avenues for future work.

One question is whether and how the subjective value of communal goals, and the effects thereof, differ as a function of the extent to which such goals have been met in the past. In particular, we might speculate that the value one attaches to a chronically unmet goal may be—or may become over time—fundamentally different from the value one attaches to an important goal that has been achieved in the past. For example, we know that both secure and anxious individuals place a high value on communal goals but, as we suggested above, the value that anxious individuals attach to communal goals seems excessive. Perhaps this is due in part to the fact that such goals have been chronically unmet. This value deficit model could shed light on the agency-communion data described earlier where it was found that communal valuing impacted agency for the more anxious but not for the more secure or avoidant individuals. It may be that because communion is a chronically unmet goal for the anxious, they (i) prioritize communion over agency, or (ii) believe that communion requires a subordination of agency (possibly because suppressing agency was reinforced in the past).

Another question concerns the nature of the relationship between expectancy and value. We have discussed how value (and, more precisely, increases in subjective value) potentiates the effect of expectancies on communal goal pursuit but there are also circumstances in which the reverse is true—i.e., where expectancies impact value. Indeed, it is widely held that avoidant individuals' devalue closeness as a mechanism to cope with the experience of an unavailable and/or unresponsive significant other (or because they have learned that such unavailable significant others accept them only when they are more self-reliant). Future work should explore the factors that influence the nature of the relationship between expectancy and value.

On a related note, it is also interesting to consider the effect of the experience of achieving (or not) attachment goals on expectancies and value. We know that expectancies are updated as a function of such experiences, but does—or how does—subjective value change in response to achieving/not achieving communal goals? If uncertain/ambivalent expectancies lead anxious individuals to overvalue communal goals, might experiences of communal goal achievement lead to more moderate (less obsessive) valuing for the anxious? By contrast, might the experience of communal goals lead to an *increase* in communal goal valuing for more avoidant individuals? Data from research with oxytocin administration suggests this might be the case. As noted, avoidant individuals have a hard negative expectancy that motivates low value on communion. By increasing subjective value, oxytocin may open avoidant individuals to the kinds of positive communal experiences that can then alter their expectancies. What is interesting in regard to this last point is that, as the reader will recall, the solution is not so simple for the anxious. Because of their combination of heightened (and complex) value with ambivalent expectancies, it is not solely a matter of increasing value—in fact, increasing value tends to produce ironic effects in communal situations. Historically, and from a pure expectancy analysis, attachment anxiety has seemed to be a step closer to security than attachment avoidance, but our expectancy-value analysis suggests that this may be an oversimplification of the differences between these two forms of insecurity, whether they are the result of chronic experience or acute situations.

In conclusion, we hope this chapter sparks more interest in the notion of subjective value in the context of attachment dynamics and considerations of both expectancies and value when thinking about the effects of working models on the formation and maintenance of attachment bonds.

References

Andersen, S. M., & Baum, A. (1994). Transference in interpersonal relations: Inferences and affect based on significant-other representations. *Journal of Personality, 62*(4), 459–497.

Andersen, S. M., & Chen, S. (2002). The relational self: An interpersonal social-cognitive theory. *Psychological Review, 109*(4), 619–645.

Andersen, S. M., Reznik, I., & Manzella, L. M. (1996). Eliciting facial affect, motivation, and expectancies in transference: Significant-other representations in social relations. *Journal of Personality and Social Psychology, 71*(6), 1108–1129.

Bakermans-Kranenburg, M. J., van Ijzendoorn, M. H., Riem, M. M., Tops, M., & Alink, L. R. (2012). Oxytocin decreases handgrip force in reaction to infant crying in females without harsh parenting experiences. *Social Cognitive and Affective Neuroscience, 7*(8), 951–957. doi:10.1093/scan/nsr067.

Baldwin, M. W. (1992). Relational schemas and the processing of social information. *Psychological Bulletin, 112*(3), 461–484. doi:10.1037/0033-2909.112.3.461.

Baldwin, M. W., & Kay, A. C. (2003). Adult attachment and the inhibition of rejection. *Journal of Social and Clinical Psychology, 22*(3), 275–293. doi:10.1521/jscp.22.3.275.22890.

Baldwin, M. W., & Sinclair, L. (1996). Self-esteem and "if… then" contingencies of interpersonal acceptance. *Journal of Personality and Social Psychology, 71*(6), 1130–1141. doi:10.1037/0022-3514.71.6.1130.

Baldwin, M. W., Fehr, B., Keedian, E., Seidel, M., & Thomson, D. W. (1993). An Exploration of the relational schemata underlying attachment styles-self-report and lexical decision approaches. *Personality and Social Psychology Bulletin, 19*(6), 746–754. doi:10.1177/0146167293196010.

Baldwin, M. W., Keelan, J. P. R., Fehr, B., Enns, V., & KohRangarajoo, E. (1996). Social-cognitive conceptualization of attachment working models: Availability and accessibility effects. *Journal of Personality and Social Psychology, 71*(1), 94–109. doi:10.1037//0022-3514.71.1.94.

Baldwin, M. W., Lydon, J. E., McClure, M. J., & Etchison, S. (2010). Measuing implicit processes in close relationships. In B. Gawronski & B. K. Payne (Eds.), *Handbook of implicit social cognition: Measurement, theory, and applications* (pp. 426–444). New York: The Guilford Press.

Bartz, J. A., & Lydon, J. E. (2004). Close relationships and the working self-concept: Implicit and explicit effects of priming attachment on agency and communion. *Personality and Social Psychology Bulletin, 30*(11), 1389–1401.

Bartz, J. A., & Lydon, J. E. (2006). Navigating the interdependence dilemma: Attachment goals and the use of communal norms with potential close others. *Journal of Personality and Social Psychology, 91*(1), 77–96. doi:10.1037/0022-3514.91.1.77.

Bartz, J. A., & Lydon, J. E. (2008). Relationship-specific attachment, risk regulation, and communal norm adherence in close relationships. *Journal of Experimental Social Psychology, 44*(3), 655–663. doi:10.1016/j.jesp.2007.04.003.

Bartz, J. A., Zaki, J., Bolger, N., Hollander, E., Ludwig, N. N., Kolevzon, A., & Ochsner, K. N. (2010a). Oxytocin selectively improves empathic accuracy. *Psychological Science, 21*(10), 1426–1428. doi:10.1177/0956797610383439.

Bartz, J. A., Zaki, J., Ochsner, K. N., Bolger, N., Kolevzon, A., Ludwig, N., & Lydon, J. E. (2010b). Effects of oxytocin on recollections of maternal care and closeness. *Proceedings of the National Academy of Sciences of the United States of America, 107*(50), 21371–21375. doi:10.1073/pnas.1012669107.

Bartz, J. A., Zaki, J., Bolger, N., & Ochsner, K. N. (2011a). Social effects of oxytocin in humans: Context and person matter. *Trends in Cognitive Sciences, 15*(7), 301–309. doi:10.1016/j.tics.2011.05.002.

Bartz, J., Simeon, D., Hamilton, H., Kim, S., Crystal, S., Braun, A., & Hollander, E. (2011b). Oxytocin can hinder trust and cooperation in borderline personality disorder. *Social Cognitive and Affective Neuroscience, 6*(5), 556–563. doi:10.1093/scan/nsq085.

Bowlby, J. (1969), *Attachment and loss: Vol. 1. Attachment*. New York: Basic Books.

Bowlby, J. (1973). *Attachment and loss: Vol. 2. Separation*: Anxiety and anger. New York: Basic Books.

Bowlby, J. (1982). Attachment and loss: Retrospect and prospect. *The American Journal of Orthopsychiatry, 52*(4), 664–678.

Bretherton, I. (1985). Attachment theory—retrospect and prospect—introduction. *Monographs of the Society for Research in Child Development, 50*(1-2), 3–35. doi:10.2307/3333824.

Bretherton, I. (1990). Communication patterns, internal working models, and the intergenerational transmission of attachment relationships. *Infant Mental Health Journal, 11*(3), 237–252. doi:10.1002/1097-0355(199023)11:3<237::Aid-Imhj2280110306>3.0.Co;2-X

Burbach, J. P., Young, L. J., & Russell, J. (2006). Oxytocin: Synthesis, secretion, and reproductive functions. In J. D. Neill (Ed.), *Knobil and Neill's physiology of reproduction* (pp. 3055–3128). New York: Elsevier.

Chen, S., Boucher, H. C., & Tapias, M. P. (2006). The relational self revealed: integrative conceptualization and implications for interpersonal life. *Psychological Bulletin, 132*(2), 151–179.

Clark, M. S. (1986). Evidence for the effectiveness of manipulations of communal and exchange relationships. *Personality and Social Psychology Bulletin, 12*(4), 414–425. doi:10.1177/0146167286124004.

Collins, N. L., & Read, S. J. (1994). Cognitive Representations of Adult Attachment: The structure and function of working models. In K. Bartholomew & D. Perlman (eds.) *Advances in Personal Relationships, Vol. 5: Attachment Processes in Adulthood* (pp. 53–90). London: Jessica Kingsley.

Collins, N. L., & Allard, L. M. (1999) *Working models of attachment and social construal processes in romantic relationships.* Unpublished manuscript, Department of Psychology, University of California, Santa Barbara, CA.

Cook, W. L. (2000). Understanding attachment security in family context. *Journal of Personality and Social Psychology, 78*(2), 285–294.

Cozzarelli, C., Hoekstra, S. J., & Bylsma, W. H. (2000). General versus specific mental models of attachment: Are they associated with different outcomes? *Personality and Social Psychology Bulletin, 26*(5), 605–618. doi:10.1177/0146167200267008.

De Dreu, C. K. (2012). Oxytocin modulates the link between adult attachment and cooperation through reduced betrayal aversion. *Psychoneuroendocrinology, 37*(7), 871–880. doi:10.1016/j.psyneuen.2011.10.003.

De Dreu, C. K., Greer, L. L., Handgraaf, M. J., Shalvi, S., Van Kleef, G. A., Baas, M., & Feith, S. W. (2010). The neuropeptide oxytocin regulates parochial altruism in intergroup conflict among humans. *Science, 328*(5984), 1408–1411. doi:10.1126/science.1189047.

Declerck, C. H., Boone, C., & Kiyonari, T. (2010). Oxytocin and cooperation under conditions of uncertainty: The modulating role of incentives and social information. *Hormones and Behavior, 57*(3), 368–374. doi:10.1016/j.yhbeh.2010.01.006.

Dykas, M. J., & Cassidy, J. (2011). Attachment and the processing of social information across the life span: Theory and evidence. *Psychological Bulletin, 137*(1), 19–46. doi:10.1037/a0021367.

Gillath, O., Mikulincer, M., Fitzsimons, G. M., Shaver, P. R., Schachner, D. A., & Bargh, J. A. (2006). Automatic activation of attachment-related goals. *Personality and Social Psychology Bulletin, 32*(10), 1375–1388. doi:10.1177/0146167206290339.

Helgeson, V. S. (1994). Relation of agency and communion to well-being—evidence and potential explanations. *Psychological Bulletin, 116*(3), 412–428. doi:10.1037//0033-2909.116.3.412.

Hepper, E. G., & Carnelley, K. B. (2012). The self-esteem roller coaster: Adult attachment moderates the impact of daily feedback. *Personal Relationships, 19*(3), 504–520. doi:10.1111/j.1475-6811.2011.01375.x.

Kenny, D. A., & La Voie, L. (1984) The social relations model. In L. Berkowitz (Ed.) *Advances in experimental social psychology* (Vol. 18, pp. 141–182). Orlando: Academic Press.

Kosfeld, M., Heinrichs, M., Zak, P. J., Fischbacher, U., & Fehr, E. (2005). Oxytocin increases trust in humans. *Nature, 435*(7042), 673–676. doi:10.1038/nature03701.

La Guardia, J. G., Ryan, R. M., Couchman, C. E., & Deci, E. L. (2000). Within-person variation in security of attachment: A self-determination theory perspective on attachment, need fulfillment, and well-being. *Journal of Personality and Social Psychology, 79*(3), 367–384.

Lydon, J. E., Jamieson, D. W., & Holmes, J. G. (1997). The meaning of social interactions in the transition from acquaintanceship to friendship. *Journal of Personality and Social Psychology, 73*(3), 536–548. doi:10.1037/0022-3514.73.3.536.

Main, M. (1981). Avoidance in the service of proximity: A working paper. In Immelmann et al. (Eds.), *Behavioral development: The Bielefeld Interdisciplinary Project* (pp. 651–693). New York: Cambridge University Press.

Main, M., Kaplan, N., & Cassidy, J. (1985). Security in infancy, childhood and adulthood: A move to the level of representation. In I. Bretherton & E. Waters (Eds.), *Growing Points in Attachment, Monograph of the Society for Research in Child Development* (Vol. 50(1–2), pp. 66–104).

Man, K., & Hamid, P. N. (1998). The relationship between attachment prototypes, self-esteem, loneliness and causal attributions in Chinese trainee teachers. *Personality and Individual Differences, 24*(3), 357–371. doi: 10.1016/S0191-8869(97)00185-2.

McClure, M. J., & Lydon, J. E. (2014). Anxiety doesn't become you: How attachment anxiety compromises relational opportunities. *Journal of Personality and Social Psychology, 106*, 89–111.

McClure, M. J., Lydon, J. E., Baccus, J. R., & Baldwin, M. W. (2010). A signal detection analysis of chronic attachment anxiety at speed dating: being unpopular is only the first part of the problem. *Personality and Social Psychology Bulletin, 36*(8), 1024–1036. doi:10.1177/0146167210374238.

McClure, M. J., Bartz, J. A., & Lydon, J. E. (2013). Uncovering and overcoming ambivalence: The role of chronic and contextually activated attachment in two-person social dilemmas. *Journal of Personality, 81*(1), 103–117. doi:10.1111/j.1467-6494.2012.00788.x.

Meinlschmidt, G., & Heim, C. (2007). Sensitivity to intranasal oxytocin in adult men with early parental separation. *Biological Psychiatry, 61*(9), 1109–1111. doi:10.1016/j.biopsych.2006.09.007.

Mickelson, K. D., Kessler, R. C., & Shaver, P. R. (1997). Adult attachment in a nationally representative sample. *Journal of Personality and Social Psychology, 73*(5), 1092–1106. doi:10.1037//0022-3514.73.5.1092.

Mikulincer, M. (1998). Adult attachment style and affect regulation: Strategic variations in self-appraisals. *Journal of Personality and Social Psychology, 75*(2), 420–435.

Mikulincer, M., & Shaver, P. R. (2007). Boosting attachment security to promote mental health, prosocial values, and inter-group tolerance. *Psychological Inquiry, 18*, 139–156.

Mikulincer, M., Shaver, P. R., Sapir-Lavid, Y., & Avihou-Kanza, N. (2009). What's inside the minds of securely and insecurely attached people? The secure-base script and its associations with attachment-style dimensions. *Journal of Personality and Social Psychology, 97*(4), 615–633. doi:10.1037/A0015649.

Mikulincer, M., Shaver, P. R., & Avihou-Kanza, N. (2011). Individual differences in adult attachment are systematically related to dream narratives. *Attachment & Human Development, 13*(2), 105–123. doi:10.1080/14616734.2011.553918.

Milyavskaya, M., & Lydon, J. E. (2013). Strong but insecure: Examining the prevalence and correlates of insecure attachment bonds with attachment figures. *Journal of Social and Personal Relationships, 30*(5), 529–544.

Mischel, W. (1973). Toward a cognitive social learning reconceptualization of personality. *Psychological Review, 80*(4), 252–283. doi:10.1037/H0035002.

Mischel, W., & Shoda, Y. (1995). A cognitive-affective system theory of personality: Reconceptualizing situations, dispositions, dynamics, and invariance in personality structure. *Psychological Review, 102*(2), 246–268.

Norman, G. J., Cacioppo, J. T., Morris, J. S., Malarkey, W. B., Berntson, G. G., & Devries, A. C. (2011). Oxytocin increases autonomic cardiac control: Moderation by loneliness. *Biological Psychology, 86*(3), 174–180. doi:10.1016/j.biopsycho.2010.11.006.

Overall, N. C., Fletcher, G. J. O., & Friesen, M. D. (2003). Mapping the intimate relationship mind: Comparisons between three models of attachment representations. *Personality & Social Psychology Bulletin, 29*(12), 1479–1493.

Pierce, T., & Lydon, J. E. (2001). Global and specific relational models in the experience of social interactions. *Journal of Personality and Social Psychology, 80*(4), 613–631. doi:10.1037//0022-3514.80.4.613.

Rimmele, U., Hediger, K., Heinrichs, M., & Klaver, P. (2009). Oxytocin makes a face in memory familiar. *The Journal of Neuroscience, 29*(1), 38–42. doi:10.1523/JNEUROSCI.4260-08.2009.

Rockliff, H., Karl, A., McEwan, K., Gilbert, J., Matos, M., & Gilbert, P. (2011). Effects of intranasal oxytocin on 'compassion focused imagery'. *Emotion, 11*(6), 1388–1396. doi:10.1037/a0023861.

Ronen, S., & Baldwin, M. W. (2010). Hypersensitivity to social rejection and perceived stress as mediators between attachment anxiety and future burnout: A prospective analysis. *Applied Psychology—An International Review—Psychologie Appliquee-Revue Internationale, 59*(3), 380–403. doi:10.1111/j.1464-0597.2009.00404.x.

Ross, H. E., & Young, L. J. (2009). Oxytocin and the neural mechanisms regulating social cognition and affiliative behavior. *Frontiers in Neuroendocrinology, 30*(4), 534–547. doi:10.1016/j.yfrne.2009.05.004.

Rowe, A., & Carnelley, K. B. (2003). Attachment style differences in the processing of attachment-relevant information: Primed-style effects on recall, interpersonal expectations, and affect. *Personal Relationships, 10*(1), 59–75. doi:10.1111/1475-6811.00036.

Shaver, P. R., Collins, N. L., & Clark, C. L. (1996). Attachment styles and internal working models of self and relationship partners. In G. J. O. Fletcher & J. Fitness (Eds.), *Knowledge structures in close relationships: A social psychological approach* (pp. 25–61). Mahwah: Erlbaum.

Theodoridou, A., Rowe, A. C., Penton-Voak, I. S., & Rogers, P. J. (2009). Oxytocin and social perception: Oxytocin increases perceived facial trustworthiness and attractiveness. *Hormones and Behavior, 56*(1), 128–132. doi:10.1016/j.yhbeh.2009.03.019.

Trinke, S. J., & Bartholomew, K. (1997). Hierarchies of attachment relationships in young adulthood. *Journal of Social and Personal Relationships, 14*(5), 603–625. doi:10.1177/0265407597145002

Tversky, A., & Kahneman, D. (1974). Judgment under uncertainty—heuristics and biases. *Science, 185*(4157), 1124–1131. doi:10.1126/science.185.4157.1124.

Waters, H. S., & Waters, E. (2006). The attachment working models concept: Among other things, we build script-like representations of secure base experiences. *Attachment & Human Development, 8*(3), 185–197. doi:10.1080/14616730600856016.

Watson, J. S. (2001). Contingency perception and misperception in infancy: Some potential implications for attachment. *Bulletin of the Menninger Clinic, 65*(3), 296–320. doi:10.1521/bumc.65.3.296.19848.

Zayas, V., Shoda, Y., Mischel, W., Osterhout, L., & Takahashi, M. (2009). Neural responses to partner rejection cues. *Psychological Science, 20*(7), 813–821.

Part III
The Effect of Previous Experience on Adult Attachment Formation and Maintenance

Chapter 4
Attachment and Relationships Across Time: An Organizational-Developmental Perspective

Jeffry A. Simpson, W. Andrew Collins, Allison K. Farrell and K. Lee Raby

Two of the basic questions underlying attachment theory are how attachment bonds change across time and how relationship partners regulate (or fail to regulate) one another's emotional, cognitive, and behavioral responses in stressful situations. These questions are among the fundamental ones that inspired the current volume. They are central to Bowlby's fountainhead theory of attachment between infants and their parents or other caregivers, and they have helped to inspire other efforts to examine the normative development of relationships with partners other than parents across the life course (e.g., Ainsworth 1989; Mikulincer and Shaver 2007; Thompson 2008; Waters and Cummings 2000). Research findings from studies of infants and young children provide a case in point. These studies have revealed a reliable sequence in the development of attachments between infants and caregivers in early life (Schaffer 2002). Attachment behaviors are initially indiscriminant, as young infants are willing to receive care from nearly any capable adult. Gradually, infants' attachment behaviors become more specifically directed to the caregivers that infants most frequently encounter. It is with these partners that attachments are eventually formed.

Though not claiming that specific, functional connections with caregivers are identical with the elements of close relationships in adulthood, writers such as Ainsworth (1989), and Waters and Cummings (2000) have proposed that attachment-related events and experiences with parents and other caregivers early in social development influence how attachment-based relationships are formed, developed, and maintained in different relationships later in life. More specifically, romantic relationship partners are thought to serve as the primary attachment figure in adulthood (Hazan and Zeifman 1994). The normative sequence of attachment development between infants and caregivers may, therefore, also apply to attachments between romantic partners during adulthood.

However, several unique features of romantic partnerships complicate the extension of Bowlby's ideas to relationships between adults. For example, romantic

J. A. Simpson (✉) · W. A. Collins · A. K. Farrell · K. L. Raby
University of Minnesota, Minneapolis, USA
e-mail: simps108@umn.edu

V. Zayas, C. Hazan (eds.), *Bases of Adult Attachment*,
DOI 10.1007/978-1-4614-9622-9_4

relationships are voluntary, in contrast to parent-child relationships. One implication of voluntariness is that most romantic relationships are more easily terminated than parent–child relationships. In addition, although all relationships are bidirectional to some degree, parent–child relationships carry a stronger expectation of inequality between partners than romantic relationships do. As a result, comparing and contrasting early close relationships to later ones often confounds structural attributes with emotional and interpersonal ones. Despite these challenges, lessons and findings from studies of early attachment relationships provide useful guidance for how one might answer some of the provocative questions posed in the chapters of this volume.

For the past several years, our research group has been examining data collected as part of the Minnesota Longitudinal Study of Risk and Adaptation (MLSRA), a 35-year longitudinal study of individual development across the life-course. Our findings are yielding some provisional answers to several basic questions about the formation, maintenance, and dissolution of attachment relationships between young adults, potentially informing both our understanding of normative development in these relationships and the individual differences that are so pervasive in research on adult romantic attachment.

In this chapter, we first present the normative organizational-developmental perspective that has guided our thinking and research on how and why certain types of interpersonal experiences encountered earlier in life should be systematically related to individual-level and couple-level functioning in later relationships. We then overview the MLSRA project along with some of the core measures that have been collected on this novel longitudinal sample since our target participants were born in the mid-1970s. Next, we discuss the findings of several recently published studies examining how romantic relationships are maintained and sometimes dissolve during early adulthood (age 20–23) along with the ways in which these relationship processes are shaped by the quality of targets' early caregiving experiences. Following this, we describe how an organizational-developmental perspective can elucidate the normative processes through which adult romantic relationships develop, as well as the early interpersonal origins of adult romantic relationships. We conclude the chapter by pointing to some promising directions for future research.

An Organizational Perspective on Social Development

For many years, it was assumed that early interpersonal experiences can influence the developmental trajectory of individuals, including how they typically think, feel, and behave in their closest relationships across the entire life-course. This assumption is a cornerstone of several major theories, including those proposed by Freud (1940), Erikson (1963), and Bowlby (1969, 1973). Our research, which tests some of these cornerstone ideas, is grounded in an organizational perspective on normative social development. According to this framework, new relationships can be affected by prior experiences in earlier relationships. This organizational-developmental perspective contains four basic principles (see Salvatore et al. 2012; Sroufe et al. 2005), all of which provide insights into normative processes of relationship development and connections with earlier relationship experiences, both within and outside of the network of family members.

According to the first principle, mental representations (i.e., working models) of the self and significant others (i.e., attachment figures) formed early in life tend to guide interaction patterns in later relationships (Sroufe and Fleeson 1986). These internalized representations motivate most individuals to seek connections with others, including people outside the family. This is particularly true of relationships with long-term romantic partners, who often serve as the primary attachment figure in adulthood (Hazan and Zeifman 1994). Bowlby (1973), in fact, claimed that the quality of caregiving enacted by early caregivers acted as a "prototype" for what a person could expect in later relationships, which in turn should affect how he or she thinks, feels, and behaves with current and future partners (Fraley et al. 2013; Simpson and Rholes 2012).

However, these prototypes are not completely deterministic. The second principle is that experiences in early relationships (with parents) and later relationships (with close friends or romantic partners) should *jointly* affect what happens at later points in a person's development (Carlson et al. 2004; Collins et al. 1997; Collins and Sroufe 1999; Sroufe et al. 1990). For example, positive relationship experiences, such as becoming involved with a highly committed, caring, and emotionally well-adjusted partner later in life, may counteract or even change the insecure working models that developed in response to poorer quality relationship experiences earlier in life (such as experiencing rejection or inconsistent parenting during childhood; Ainsworth 1989; Sroufe et al. 2005). Alternatively, individuals who have a secure attachment history may become more insecurely attached if they get involved with partners who lead them to doubt their positive expectations and beliefs about romantic relationships (Rönkä et al. 2002; Tran and Simpson 2009).

Past relationship experiences not only affect working models; they also impact emotion regulation tendencies. The third principle suggests that the way in which people regulate their emotions in adult relationships should be associated with how they learn to regulate their emotions earlier in life, particularly in stressful or challenging situations (Sroufe and Fleeson 1986; Thompson 2008). Synchronous and supportive relationships with early caregivers (i.e., parents) are usually the initial social context in which functional and appropriate emotion-regulation skills are learned and honed (Sroufe et al. 2005). Consistent with this view, attachment security in infancy, which is a barometer of both synchrony between children and their primary caregivers and more effective emotion regulation during early childhood (Schore 2005), predicts more effective emotion-regulation skills in different types of relationships in later life (Thompson 2008). Similarly, attachment security later in life also predicts better emotion regulation in adult relationships (Mikucliner and Shaver 2007; Simpson and Rholes 2012).

Finally, the fourth principle claims that the meaning of a given behavior depends on how it fits with other actions in a specific social context. For example, although there are times when engaging in conflict has positive consequences for partners and their relationship, disengaging from conflict with a romantic partner when it is appropriate to do so should protect people from the corrosive effects of further conflict (Gottman 1994), whereas failure to disengage—especially when continued conflict is futile and the disagreement cannot be resolved—should harm relationship functioning in the future (Gottman and Levenson 1999). One implication of this principle, therefore, is that the behavior of partners in relationships cannot be fully understood unless one takes into account both partners' developmental histories and the broader social context in which they interact.

These four principles represent normative processes that are central to developmental and attachment models (Bowlby 1969, 1973, 1988; Sroufe et al. 2005). With these normative organizational-developmental principles in mind, we now describe the source of the data we have used to test how early social experiences are prospectively linked to later attachment and relationship outcomes.

The Minnesota Longitudinal Study of Risk and Adaptation

The MLSRA began in 1976–1977 when first-time mothers who were receiving free prenatal services at Minneapolis public health clinics were recruited for the study. (For a comprehensive overview of the entire project, including all of its measures and most of its findings, see Sroufe et al. 2005). The mothers' children, whom we call "target" participants, have been the primary focus of the study over the years. Since they were born, approximately 170 targets have been assessed at regular intervals at every major stage of development using numerous multi-method measures, which have included interviews, questionnaires, teacher-ratings, parent-ratings, and videotaped interactions with both their parents and their current romantic partners. Most of our research on adult romantic relationships has focused on approximately 75 targets (and their romantic partners) who were involved in an established relationship when targets were between 20 and 23 years old. These target participants are demographically representative of the full project sample.

Assessments were conducted at critical points of development when the targets were negotiating salient and important socioemotional developmental issues (cf. Erikson 1963), such as forming attachment bonds with their caregivers in infancy, navigating the peer environment in middle childhood, establishing close friendships in adolescence, and forming and maintaining romantic relationships in early adulthood. Each target's level of competence in each of these domains was assessed using different sets of age-appropriate methods and measures. We now describe some of the most important assessments of attachment security that have been conducted with our target participants across their lifetimes and have been used frequently in our research.

When targets were 12 and 18 months old, they were videotaped with their mothers in the Strange Situation (Ainsworth et al. 1978), a well-validated and widely used laboratory procedure that involves a series of separations and reunions between children (targets) and their caregivers (their mother). The Strange Situation procedure assesses a child's willingness and ability to use his or her caregiver to effectively reduce and manage distress, which results from (and is a proxy for) maternal presence and reassurance when a child is upset.

In the Strange Situation, children who are classified as securely attached typically use their caregivers (mothers) as a source of comfort to reduce their negative affect and regulate their negative emotions. This security allows the child to pursue other important tasks, such as exploring the environment and engaging in play. In contrast, children who are classified as insecurely attached do not use—and often act as if they cannot rely on—their caregivers to dissipate their negative affect and manage their negative emotions. Consequently, the attachment systems of insecurely attached children remain activated ("turned on"), and they often remain distressed throughout the entire Strange Situation procedure.

These attachment patterns are closely linked to the quality of caregiving that children receive from their primary caregivers in the home (Ainsworth et al. 1978; Egeland and Farber 1984). Securely attached children typically receive care that is sensitive, warm, and situationally appropriate, especially when they are upset. Insecure children, on the other hand, receive either emotionally distant, rejecting care (in the case of children classified as avoidant-resistant) or neglectful and inconsistent care (in the case of children classified as anxious-resistant). Trained observers then viewed the Strange Situation videotapes of each mother–child dyad and classified each target as having either a secure or an insecure (either anxious or avoidant) relationship with his/her caregiver (mother). Their scores, which could range from 0 (insecure at both 12 and 18 months) to 2 (secure at both times), reflected the number of times that the mother–child attachment relationship was classified as secure across the two Strange Situation assessments.

At several points during early childhood, targets and their parents also engaged in several age-appropriate tasks designed to assess the quality of parental care and the attention that each target received. Maternal supportive presence reflected each caregiver's degree of responsiveness and other behaviors designed to reassure his or her child while the child tried to perform new and somewhat stressful tasks. During home visits when targets were 30 months old, ratings were made of each mother's verbal and emotional responsiveness to her child on the HOME scale (Caldwell et al. 1966). Full descriptions, along with reliability and validity information for these measures, are reported in Sroufe et al. (2005). Standardized scores on each of these measures were calculated and then averaged to create a single indicator of the quality of early caregiving for targets who had at least two contributing measures.

In early and middle childhood, targets completed several measures that assessed their relationship representations and perceptions of different relationships (Carlson et al. 2004). For example, at ages 4–5, they completed the Preschool Interpersonal Problem-Solving Assessment (Shure and Spivack 1970), which assessed how each target resolved interpersonal dilemmas related to parent–child and peer relationships. Scores reflected theoretically derived ratings of the representational quality of the mother–child as well as peer relationships, including the degree of cognitive flexibility regarding these relationships.

When the targets were in elementary school (ages 6–8), several classroom teachers rated each child in terms of how closely she or he matched a standardized description of a socially competent child. Each child (target) was in a different classroom and school building, so corrections were made to account for different numbers of children in each classroom. Each target's score was his or her rank-order in the classroom (relative to his or her classmates) in the degree to which he or she matched the criterion description of a socially competent child.

At age 8, the organization of relationship representations was assessed again with family drawings (see Main et al. 1985), which were rated on theoretically-derived global scales (see Fury et al. 1997). The primary scores were ratings of the family relationship (e.g., each child's expectations of family interactions, his or her sense of pride in the family group) and ratings of each child's sense of self as being secure within the family group.

At age 12, targets completed several narrative tasks that involved parent–child and peer relationship themes. These included a sentence completion task, a story-telling task, an interpretation of a fable, and a friendship interview. Socioemotional expectations and attitudes across these tasks were assessed with theoretically derived rating scales.

At age 16, targets completed interviews that assessed the nature and quality of their relationship with their best friend, including how secure the relationship was and how conflicts were usually resolved. Ratings were made based on the extent to which targets said they could share all personal feelings with their best friend, regardless of the content, and the extent to which they trusted and felt they could count on their best friends in different situations.

At age 19, targets completed the Adult Attachment Interview (AAI; George et al. 1985), during which they reflected on memories of being raised by their parents between the ages of 5–12. The interview was audiotaped, transcribed, and then scored by trained raters for its degree of coherence. Individuals who are classified as secure on the AAI present a clear, well-supported description of their past relationship with both parents. Their episodic memories of childhood tend to be vivid and coherent, and secure individuals have little difficulty recalling important childhood experiences, even if their childhood upbringing was difficult. Individuals classified as insecure, on the other hand, have less coherent narratives. More specifically, those classified as dismissive (avoidant) typically describe their parents and their upbringing as normal or even "ideal," but fail to support these claims with clear, specific episodic memories of significant childhood events. Rather, they tend to disregard or dismiss the importance of attachment figures or attachment-related emotions and behavior. Individuals who are preoccupied on the AAI often discuss their childhood experiences with attachment figures very extensively during the interview. Their AAI interviews tend to reveal deep-seated, unresolved anger toward one or both parents, which taints their descriptions and interpretations of past experiences.

As targets entered early adulthood (age 20–21), those who were involved in a committed (6 months or longer) romantic relationship participated in an assessment of romantic relationship functioning. During this assessment, targets and their romantic partners engaged in a videotaped 10-min conflict resolution task during which they tried to resolve the most major point of conflict or disagreement in their relationship. This was immediately followed by a 5-min conflict recovery task, which is described later in the chapter. Both of these tasks were designed to assess how well each target regulated her or his emotions with his/her romantic partner. Both interactions were then rated by trained coders.

Targets and their romantic partners also independently completed the Current Relationship Interview (CRI; Crowell and Owens 1996). The CRI contains a series of questions similar to the AAI, but that focus on representations and memories of the relationship with one's current romantic partner. Targets' responses are scored for discourse properties (e.g., coherence) similar to the AAI. Individuals who are secure on the CRI tend to provide a clear, well-supported description of their current partner and relationship. Insecure individuals (dismissive or preoccupied), in contrast, provide less clear, more confusing, and/or more poorly supported descriptions of experiences with their current partner/relationship.

At age 23, we assessed whether targets were still dating the same romantic partner with whom they were videotaped in the conflict resolution and conflict recovery discussions 2 years earlier. Targets who were involved with a romantic partner of 4 months or longer at age 23 were also interviewed about their current romantic relationship, including their feelings of closeness, acceptance, approaches to conflict resolution, and commitment. These interviews were then coded for the overall quality of the relationship.

Finally, at ages 23, 26, and 32, targets completed measures assessing their anxious and depressive symptoms. Specifically, targets completed the Young Adult Self-Report measure (YASR; Achenbach 1997) as part of the 23-year and 26-year assessments, and they completed the Adult Self-Report measure (ASR; Achenbach 2003) at the 32-year assessment. Targets also rated themselves, their feelings, and their behavior during the past 6 months on self-report scales at ages 23 and 26 years.

Attachment Relationships Across the Lifespan: Recent MLSRA Findings

Findings from the MLSRA illustrate how social experiences earlier in life are systematically tied to attachment representations and relationship outcomes at multiple time-points of social development, culminating with romantic relationships in early adulthood. In this section, we describe five recent studies that each address at least one of the four normative principles of our organizational-development framework. Together, the studies exemplify the relevance of this perspective to questions about the normative maintenance and dissolution of adult attachments.

Direct Links Between Infant Attachment and Adult Romantic Attachment

The question of whether attachment security early in life is linked to romantic attachment security years later is fundamental and longstanding. Roisman et al. (2005) addressed this question with the MLSRA data when targets were 20–21 years old. As discussed previously, in addition to assessing the attachment security of targets when they were 12–18 months old in the Strange Situation, targets also completed the CRI to index their attachment status with their current romantic partners at age 20–21.

Individuals who were rated as secure on the CRI had higher quality conflict interactions with their romantic partners (rated by independent coders) and also reported greater closeness and more positive perceptions of their partner and relationship. More importantly, targets who were classified as secure as infants were significantly more likely to be classified as secure on the CRI nearly 20 years later. Thus, consistent with Principle 1, young adults' states of mind with regard to their current romantic partner/relationship appear to stem, at least in part, from their attachment experiences with primary caregivers in infancy nearly 20 years earlier.

Links Between Relationship Representations and Social Behavior over Time

Consistent with attachment theory (Bowlby 1973), the organizational-developmental perspective regards an infant's attachment security or insecurity as the launching point of a "transactional process" between relationship representations and social experiences and behavior that occurs repeatedly across the lifespan (Principle 2; Carlson et al. 2004). The process is termed "transactional" because relationship representations and social experiences/behavior often influence one another reciprocally over time, such that relationship representations affect social experiences/behavior, which then affect representations in return, and so on. To predict an individual's future relationship outcomes from his or her interpersonal past, one needs to identify the critical developmental experiences and issues that an individual has had to negotiate at each major transitional stage of her or his life. Each developmental stage entails addressing (and hopefully resolving) certain kinds of social and emotional challenges along with developing specific skills that must be mastered for social development to proceed in a normal fashion (Erikson 1963; Sroufe et al. 1999). During infancy, for example, children must become attached to a stronger/older/wiser caregiver who potentially can help them regulate their emotions and facilitate their survival in the world. The unique importance of infant-caregiver attachment bonds begin to wane during the preschool years as children meet new peers and start interacting with them. Although caregivers remain central components of their social environments and lives, children's attention usually shifts toward peers and the opportunities afforded by these new partners and relationships.

Peers continue to play a significant role in the lives of nearly all children during middle childhood and early adolescence, but children gradually must learn to balance their involvement in friendship groups with their involvement in romantic relationships (Sroufe et al. 2005).

Carlson et al. (2004) modeled the transactional nature of targets' relationship representations and social experiences/behavior across multiple developmental periods with the MLSRA dataset. According to their model, which is shown in Fig. 4.1, the connection between early care experiences and later adolescent social behavior depends on the transactions that occur between relationship representations and social behavior at different points of each target's life. As discussed earlier, relationship representations in early childhood, middle childhood, and early adolescence were assessed by interviews and projective drawings (Carlson et al. 2004). Targets' social behavior was also assessed at each developmental period by teachers' rankings of each target's peer competence and emotional health in classroom settings.

Structural equation modeling revealed that the transactional model shown in Fig. 4.1 fit the data best. In other words, representations of relationships at earlier points in development predicted meaningful changes in social behavior/experience at later points in development, and vice versa, across time. These findings support Bowlby's (1973) premise that early experiences with initial attachment figures (parents) initiate social functioning pathways, which are then propagated by later relationship representations and social experiences at each successive developmental period.

In line with Principle 2, this model also accounts for predictable, patterned changes in representations and behavior across development. Developmental change occurs in part because the pathways from mental representations to behavior are never perfect. An individual's representations of what partners and relationships should be like, for example, guides but does not determine how his or her relationships actually function. At each developmental stage, individuals have opportunities to form new relationships with different people, which are impacted by both the skills they have learned in prior relationships as well as their current relationship representations. However, when relationship experiences deviate sharply from expected patterns (whether good or bad), this can alter an individual's representations and future behavior (e.g., Simpson et al. 2003).

These developmental findings extend our understanding of the developmental origins of close relationships during adulthood. Adult attachment relationships are not the direct product of early parent–child relationship experiences; rather, they represent an outgrowth of a continuous, transactional process that occurs across development. As such, studying experiences with parents and close others beyond infancy helps us understand adult relationships more fully. In addition, these findings suggest that individuals' romantic relationship experiences have the capacity to produce changes in subsequent relationship representations. In other words, close interpersonal experiences in adulthood are both the product of prior developmental experiences *and* a contributor to future functioning.

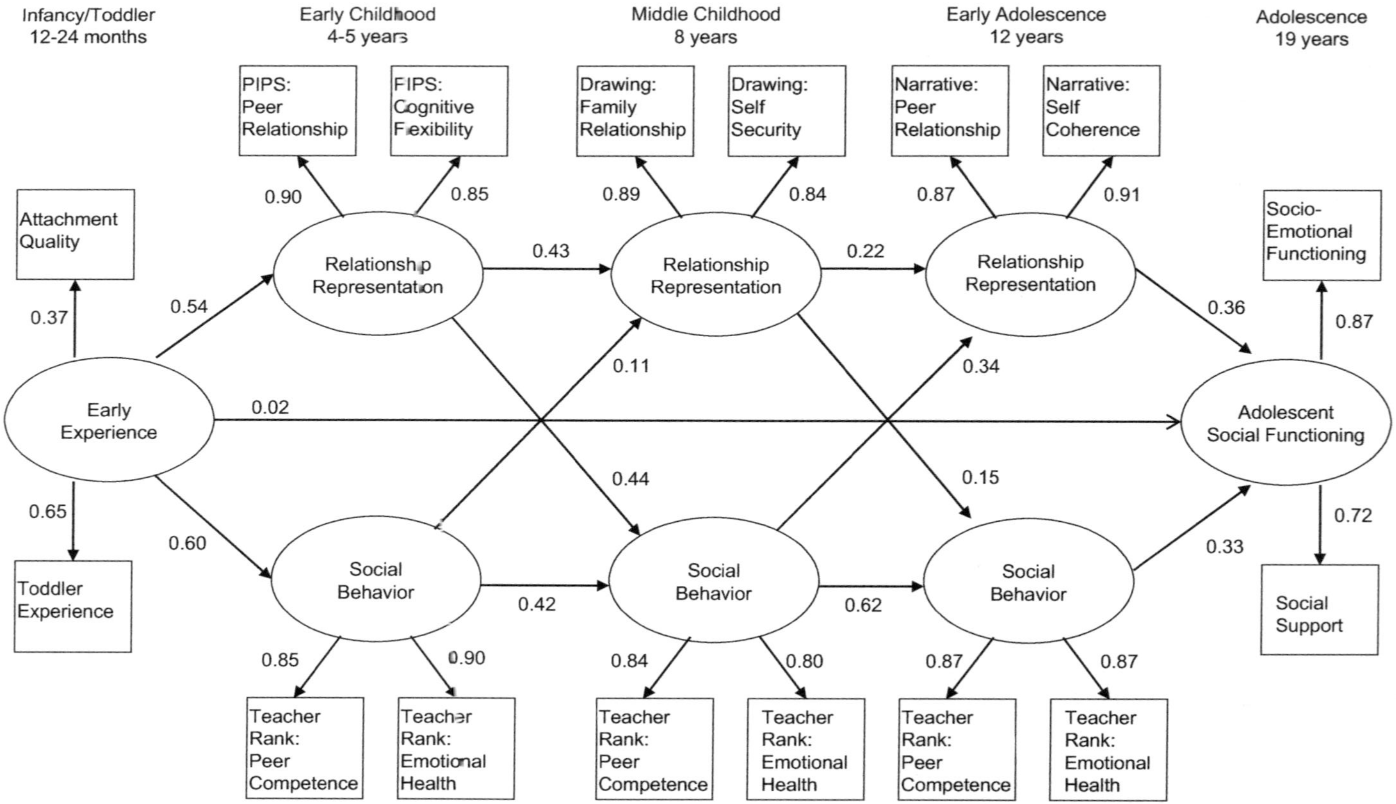

Fig. 4.1 A cross-lagged model linking representations and social behavior over time. The numbers in the figure are standardized path coefficients. Reprinted from Carlson et al. 2004. Copyright 2007 by Blackwell Publishing. Reprinted with permission

Links Between Early Relationship Representations, Romantic Relationship Quality, and Relationship Outcomes in Adulthood

As we have noted, our organizational-developmental perspective proposes that an individual's adaptation reflects the combination of his or her developmental history *in combination with* his/her current life circumstances (Principle 2; Sroufe et al. 1990). But why are some people able to form high quality, secure romantic relationships even though they received less-than-optimal parental care earlier in life? To address this question, Haydon et al. (2012) investigated the shared and distinct origins of targets' attachment representations of their early caregivers (i.e., parents) as well as their current romantic partners in early adulthood. Representations of caregiving experiences with parents and with current romantic partners were assessed by the AAI (when targets were 19 years old) and by the CRI (when targets were 20–23 years old).

The results revealed that targets' experience of early parenting quality (assessed when they were 24 months old) predicted their classifications on both the AAI and the CRI nearly 20 years later, with better early care resulting in a higher probability of being secure on both the AAI and the CRI. However, ego resiliency measured in preschool, which refers to the capacity to flexibly exert attentional and behavioral control and regulate negative affect, uniquely predicted later CRI security. These findings suggest that romantic relationship functioning might have somewhat different developmental origins than parent–child relationships functioning. Social functioning outside the family-of-origin may be another developmental pathway through which individuals who receive poorer care early in life can form and maintain more satisfying romantic relationships in adulthood and thus develop more secure representations of their adult romantic partners, all which should result in better romantic relationship functioning. It also is possible that ego resiliency helps people who have insecure attachment histories to override certain potentially maladaptive responses in adulthood (see, for example, Ayduk et al. 2008).

Links Between Infant Attachment and Emotion Regulation in Adult Romantic Relationships

Evidence shows that adult relationships are rooted in previous relationship experiences. However, which aspects of relationships are most likely to be linked over time? Given the fundamentally emotional nature of attachment bonds, Simpson et al. (2007) predicted that emotional experiences in relationships with adult romantic partners should show continuity with security in very early relationships with caregivers. Their results confirmed that targets' attachment status in the Strange Situation predicted how they regulated their emotions, both on a daily basis in their romantic relationships and when they engaged in major conflict discussions with their romantic partners at age 20–21. In particular, they found that if targets had an insecure attachment relationship with their mothers at 12 months (assessed in the

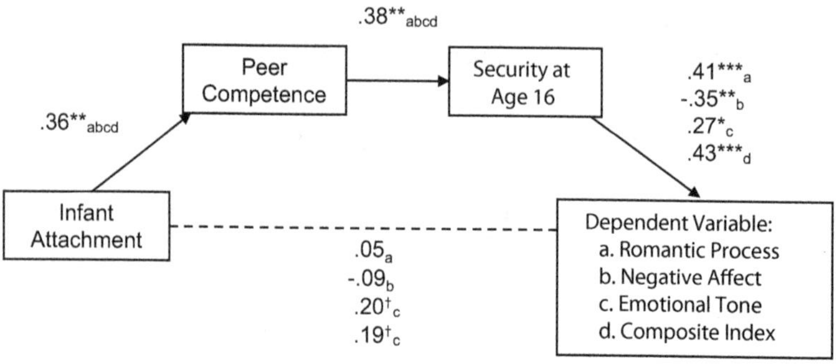

Fig. 4.2 A partial mediation model linking infant attachment security and early adulthood romantic relationship outcomes. The numbers in the figure are standardized path coefficients. Reprinted from Simpson et al. 2007. Copyright 2007 by the American Psychological Association. Reprinted with permission

Strange Situation), these targets reported and behaviorally expressed more negative than positive emotions when trying to resolve a major relationship conflict with their romantic partner in the lab approximately 20 years later. As shown in Fig. 4.2, this "early attachment effect" was partially mediated by targets' level of social competence in elementary school (rated by three of their grade-school teachers), along with the quality of their relationship with their best friend at age 16. This partial mediation pattern fit the data significantly better than did several other plausible models. These findings, which support Principle 3, illustrate one interpersonal pathway through which the degree of early attachment security is probabilistically linked to how targets regulate their emotions in the context of their adult romantic relationships.

Links Between Infant Attachment and Conflict Recovery in Adult Romantic Relationships

Salvatore et al. (2011) explored whether attachment security early in life predicts how well individuals *recover* from major romantic relationship conflicts. Conflict recovery refers to how quickly, how well, and how completely individuals are able to shift both emotionally and behaviorally from a negative state (such as discussing a major relationship problem) in order to achieve another, more positive goal (such as discussing topics on which both partners agree). Thus, conflict recovery is one type of emotion regulation skill or ability in the context of relationships. Gottman and Levenson (1999) contend that recovering from conflict entails a different set of skills, abilities, and behaviors than resolving conflicts in a fair and constructive fashion.

Salvatore and her colleagues found that targets who were securely attached in the Strange Situation as infants rebounded from major conflict discussions with their romantic partners significantly better than insecurely attached targets did at age 20–21, statistically controlling for how difficult each conflict discussion had been. Moreover, their romantic *partners* recovered better if targets had been securely attached as infants. In addition, having a romantic partner who displayed better conflict recovery was associated with greater relationship satisfaction and more positive daily emotions in the relationship. Finally, targets who had been insecurely attached early in life were more likely to still be involved with the same partner 2 years later (at age 23), but only if their partner had displayed better conflict recovery 2 years earlier.

Consistent with Principle 3, these findings reveal that attachment status in infancy predicts better emotion regulation (indexed by conflict recovery) with romantic partners in adulthood. In line with Principle 4, our results indicate that the way in which people behave in relationships cannot be completely understood unless one considers both the developmental histories that partners bring into their current relationships along with the social context in which they are currently interacting. Moreover, secure individuals appear to buffer their partners in conflict situations, as do partners who display better recovery following conflict. This ability is not only useful in conflict situations, but it also seems to have positive ramifications for relationship maintenance and stability over time.

Advantages of an Organizational-Developmental Perspective

Together, these studies showcase the relevance of our normative organizational-developmental perspective for addressing questions pertaining to the formation, maintenance, and dissolution of adult attachment relationships. Regarding relationship formation, our findings indicate that individuals carry forward expectations and beliefs about relationships from earlier interpersonal experiences into their current romantic relationships, which could affect processes associated with the selection of romantic partners. Once relationships are formed, individuals' cumulative histories of relationship experience continue to guide their interpersonal dynamics related to relationship maintenance, including their emotional experiences (Simpson et al. 2007), representations of their romantic partner (Haydon et al. 2012; Roisman et al. 2005), and emotion regulation abilities (Salvatore et al. 2011). In short, the likelihood of maintaining attachment-based relationships in adulthood is partly affected by the quality of earlier experiences with previous relationship partners. Relationship dissolution, which results from the breakdown of these maintenance processes, is also impacted by each partner's development history. As the study by Salvatore et al. (2011) illustrates, relationship dissolution is a dyadic phenomenon that is best understood by understanding contributions from both relationship partners (see also Attridge et al. 1995). In sum, the current set of findings showcase how the normative sequence of relationship development takes place within the context of each partner's unique developmental history, supporting the four principles of our organizational-developmental framework.

There are many advantages to adopting an organizational-developmental perspective. Perhaps the greatest advantage is that this perspective provides a basis for testing different predictions about an individual's future interpersonal functioning based on his or her current *and* past functioning with respect to salient developmental issues. As a result, individuals can arrive at the same personal or relational outcome, but from quite different beginning points. They can also arrive at very different outcomes from the same starting point. This explains why people who experience different developmental trajectories can show the same kind of adaptation at one time-point, but show different adaptations at later points in development (see Sroufe et al. 1990). According to an organizational-developmental viewpoint, these differences are predictable to the extent that an individual's current relationship functioning reflects his or her cumulative developmental history, rather than being completely governed by either his or her past or current life circumstances.

To make this important point clearer, consider two people—Tom and John—who have been happily married to their wives for many years. Each of them recently learned that their partners had extra-marital affairs in the recent past, which are now over. Tom and John both decide to try to repair their damaged relationships, and they both enter couples therapy. The powerful emotional strain and difficulties of the betrayals have led both men to experience and express a great deal of anger, negative affect, and hostility toward their wives in recent months. When their current "emotional profiles" are viewed cross-sectionally, Tom and John appear to be very similar. On the basis of this limited cross-sectional information, one might expect both men to have similar relationship trajectories and outcomes with respect to satisfaction, conflict, and stability in the not-too-distant future. However, different predictions are derived when Tom and John's current levels of emotional adaptation are viewed in relation to each man's distinctive developmental history. If Tom's therapy is successful and his issues of broken trust can eventually be resolved, Tom, with his secure attachment history, is likely to experience better relationship functioning and outcomes in the future, given the benevolent nature of his working models and his more constructive efforts to mend his damaged marriage. On the other hand, John, with his insecure attachment history, may not be able to rebound from the betrayal in his marriage nearly as well over time given his more negative working models and history of being "burned" in past relationships. According to an organizational perspective on social development, romantic relationship functioning and outcomes are a product of *both* an individual's relationship history as well as his or her current relationship circumstances.

New Research Directions and Conclusions

One particularly promising area for future research on the development of adult attachment relationships is the integration of biological perspectives and measures. The inclusion of molecular genetic measures is one approach that has become increasingly popular in recent investigations of adult attachment. For example, common genetic variants have been associated with several indicators of adult relationship functioning, ranging from empathy to attachment orientations to marital relationship quality (see Ebstein et al. 2010 for a review). Some of these findings have been interpreted as supporting the view that attachment security in infancy and adulthood is largely attributable to genetic factors, and that associations between early caregiving experiences and attachment-relevant adult outcomes may reflect genetic rather than environmental effects (see Harris 1998). In contrast to this position, we have argued that attachment security is largely a relationship phenomenon and, as such, it emerges from partners' histories of interaction (Collins et al. 2000).

We recently collected genetic information from our longitudinal participants (targets) to test these competing ideas about genetic contributions to attachment. In an initial investigation, we found that targets' genotypes were an important factor in predicting their emotional reactivity to a distressing event early in their lives (encountering the Strange Situation). However, target infants' attachment security assessed in the Strange Situation at 12 and 18 months was uniquely predicted by their *caregivers'* sensitivity during interactions with them (see Raby et al. 2012). These findings support theoretical predictions regarding the "relationship basis" of early attachment security, but they also indicate that genetic variation makes important contributions to early emotional development. We anticipate that attachment security during later developmental periods will be shaped by increasingly complex interactions between relationship and genetically based influences. Thus, the most fruitful future investigations are likely to be those that examine how genetic and relationship factors work together to support the development of adult attachment security and the functioning of adult attachment relationships, perhaps including close friendships.

A second area worthy of additional empirical attention is how early attachment experiences may "tune" certain biological systems within people. One straightforward hypothesis is that individuals who have a history of insecure attachments may show heightened activation of stress-regulatory systems, especially during emotionally salient interpersonal events. In line with this view, psychophysiological studies of adult attachment in both social and developmental psychology have demonstrated that insecurely attached individuals show elevated activation of the sympathetic nervous system and greater down regulation of the parasympathetic system during stressful situations (e.g., Diamond and Hicks 2005; Roisman 2007). Most of these investigations have used cross-sectional or short-term longitudinal designs, however. Long-term longitudinal studies investigating the developmental antecedents of these differences in psychophysiological regulation are needed. This is an important area for future research for many reasons, one of which is the potential implications for understanding the etiology of health problems. In the MLSRA study, for example, we have also found that adult targets' health problems are uniquely related to their histories of infant attachment security, with individuals who were insecurely attached as children reporting more physical health problems at age 32 (Puig et al. 2013). We suspect that differences in psychophysiological regulation may, at least in part, account for these developmental effects. However, complete tests of this question await future longitudinal research.

In conclusion, an organizational-developmental perspective focuses on the coherence of behavior in different types of relationships across the life-course. The manner in which relationship-relevant thoughts, feelings, and actions are patterned is what links individuals' early experiences with caregivers to their later experiences with peers and eventually romantic partners in adulthood. These experiences prior to adulthood shape and channel specific patterns of relating to others. Although competence in relationships may be expressed somewhat differently at each developmental stage, the latent meaning of competent and incompetent behavior remains the same across different developmental stages. As the findings of our research from the MLSRA demonstrate, relationship outcomes in adulthood *are* meaningfully tied to relationship experiences encountered much earlier in life. In fact, for many relationships, the past is an integral part of the present and the future.

References

Achenbach, T. M. (1997). *Manual for the young adult self-report and young adult behavior checklist*. Burlington: University of Vermont Department of Psychiatry.

Achenbach, T. M. (2003). *Manual for the adult self-report*. Burlington: University of Vermont Department of Psychiatry.

Ainsworth, M. (1989). Attachments beyond infancy. *American Psychologist, 44*(4), 709–716. doi:10.1037/0003-066X.44.4.709.

Ainsworth, M., Blehar, M., Waters, E., & Wall, S. (1978). *Patterns of attachment*. Hillsdale: Erlbaum.

Attridge, M., Berscheid, E., & Simpson, J. A. (1995). Predicting relationship stability from both partners versus one. *Journal of Personality and Social Psychology, 69,* 254–268.

Ayduk, O., Zayas, V., Downey, G., Cole, A. B., Shoda, Y., & Mischel, W. (2008). Rejection sensitivity and executive control: Joint predictors of borderline personality features. *Journal of Research in Personality, 42,* 151–168.

Bowlby, J. (1969). *Attachment and loss: Vol. 1. Attachment*. New York: Basic Books.

Bowlby, J. (1973). *Attachment and loss: Vol. 2. Separation: Anxiety and anger*. New York: Basic Books.

Bowlby, J. (1988). *A secure base: Parent–child attachment and healthy human development*. New York: Basic Books.

Caldwell, B., Heider, J., & Kaplan, B. (1966). *The inventory of home stimulation*. Paper presented at the American Psychological Association, New York.

Carlson, E. A., Sroufe, L. A., & Egeland, B. (2004). The construction of experience: A longitudinal study of representation and behavior. *Child Development, 75*(1), 66–83. doi:10.1111/j.1467-8624.2004.00654.x.

Collins, W. A., & Sroufe, L. A. (1999). Capacity for intimate relationships: A developmental construction. In W. Furman, B. B. Brown, & C. Feiring (Eds.), *The development of romantic relationships in adolescence* (pp. 125–147). New York: Cambridge University Press.

Collins, W. A., Hennighausen, K. H., Schmit, D. T., & Sroufe, L. A. (1997). Developmental precursors of romantic relationships: A longitudinal analysis. In S. Shulman & W. A. Collins (Eds.), *Romantic relationships in adolescence: Developmental perspectives*. San Francisco: Jossey-Bass.

Collins, W. A., Maccoby, E. E., Steinberg, L., Hetherington, E. M., & Bornstein, M. H. (2000). Contemporary research on parenting: The case for nature and nurture. *American Psychologist, 55,* 218–232.

Crowell, J. A., & Owens, G. (1996). *Current Relationship Interview and scoring system*. Unpublished manuscript, State University of New York at Stony Brook.

Diamond, L. M., & Hicks, A. M. (2005). Attachment style, current relationship security, and negative emotions: The mediation role of physiological regulation. *Journal of Social and Personal Relationships, 22,* 499–518.

Ebstein, R. P., Israel, S., Chew, S. H., Zhong, S., & Knafo, A. (2010). Genetics of human social behavior. *Neuron, 65,* 831–844.

Erikson, E. (1963). *Childhood and society*. New York: Norton.

Fraley, R. C., Roisman, G. I., Booth-LaForce, C., Owen, M. T., & Holland, A. S. (2013). Interpersonal and genetic origins of adult attachment styles: A longitudinal study from infancy to early adulthood. *Journal of Personality and Social Psychology, 104,* 817–838.

Freud, S. (1940). *An outline of psychoanalysis*. New York: Hogarth Press.

Fury, G., Carlson, E. A., & Sroufe, L. A. (1997). Children's representations of attachment relationships in family drawings. *Child Development, 68,* 1154–1164.

George, C., Kaplan, N., & Main, M. (1985). *The adult attachment interview*. Unpublished manuscript. University of California, Berkeley.

Gottman, J. M. (1994). *What predicts divorce? The relationship between marital processes and marital outcomes*. Hillsdale: Erlbaum.

Gottman, J. M., & Levenson, R. W. (1999). Rebound from marital conflict and divorce prediction. *Family Process, 38,* 287–292.

Harris, J. R. (1998). *The nurture assumption: Why children turn out the way they do*. New York: Free Press.

Haydon, K. C., Collins, W. A., Salvatore, J. E., Simpson, J. A., & Roisman, G. I. (2012). Shared and distinctive origins and effects of adult attachment representations: The developmental organization of romantic functioning. *Child Development*. doi:10.1111/j.1467-8624.2012.01801.x.

Hazan, C., & Zeifman, D. (1994). Sex and the psychological tether. In K. Bartholomew & D. Perlman (Eds.), *Advances in personal relationships: Vol. 5. Attachment processes in adulthood* (pp. 151–177). London: Jessica Kingsley.

Main, M., Kaplan, N., & Cassidy, J. (1985). Security in infancy, childhood, and adulthood: A move to the level of representation. In I. Bretherton & E. Waters (Eds.), *Growing points of attachment theory and research. Monographs of the Society for Research in Child Development, 50*(1–2), Serial No. 209, 66–104.

Mikulincer, M., & Shaver, P. R. (2007). *Attachment in adulthood: Structure, dynamics, and change*. New York: Guilford.

Puig, J., Englund, M. M.; Simpson, J. A., & Collins, W. A. (2013). Predicting adult physical illness from infant attachment: A prospective longitudinal study. *Health Psychology, 32,* 409–417.

Raby, K. L., Cicchetti, D., Carlson, E. A., Cutuli, J. J., Englund, M. M., & Egeland, B. (2012). Genetic and caregiving contributions to infant attachment: Unique associations with distress reactivity and attachment security. *Psychological Science, 23,* 1016–1023.

Roisman, G. I. (2007). The psychophysiology of adult attachment relationships: Autonomic reactivity in marital and premarital interactions. *Developmental Psychology, 43,* 39–53.

Roisman, G. I., Collins, W. A., Sroufe, L. A., & Egeland, B. (2005). Predictors of young adults' representations of and behavior in their current romantic relationship: Prospective tests of the prototype hypothesis. *Attachment and Human Development, 7,* 105–121. doi:10.1080/14616730500134928.

Rönkä, A., Oravala, S., & Pulkkinen, L. (2002). "I met this wife of mine and things got onto a better track": Turning points in risk development. *Journal of Adolescence, 25,* 47–63. doi:10.1006/jado.2001.0448.

Salvatore, J. E., Kuo, S. I., Steele, R. D., Simpson, J. A., & Collins, W. A. (2011). Recovering from conflict in romantic relationships: A developmental perspective. *Psychological Science, 22,* 376–383. doi:10.1177/0956797610397055.

Salvatore, J. E., Collins, W. A., & Simpson, J. A. (2012). An organizational-developmental perspective on functioning in adult romantic relationships. In L. Campbell & T. J. Loving (Eds.),

Interdisciplinary research on close relationships: The case for integration (pp. 155–177). Washington, DC: American Psychological Association. doi:10.1037/13486-007.

Schaffer, H. R. (2002). The early experience assumption: Past, present, and future. In W. W. Hartup & R. K. Silbereisen (Eds.), *Growing points in developmental science: An introduction* (pp. 24–46). Hove: Psychology Press.

Schore, A. N. (2005). Back to basics: Attachment, affect regulation, and the developing right brain: Linking developmental neuroscience to pediatrics. *Pediatrics in Review, 26,* 204–204.

Shure, M. B., & Spivack, G. (1970). *Preschool interpersonal problem-solving manual.* Philadelphia: Hahnemann Medical College and Hospitals.

Simpson, J. A., & Rholes, W. S. (2012). Adult attachment orientations, stress, and romantic relationships. In P. G. Devine, A. Plant, J. Olson, & M. Zanna (Eds.), *Advances in Experimental Social Psychology, 45,* 279–328. doi:10.1016/B978-0-12-394286-9.00006-8.

Simpson, J. A., Rholes, W. S., Campbell, L., & Wilson, C. L. (2003). Changes in attachment orientations across the transition to parenthood. *Journal of Experimental Social Psychology, 39,* 317–331. doi:10.1016/S0022-1031(03)00030-1.

Simpson, J. A., Collins, W. A., Tran, S., & Haydon, K. C. (2007). Attachment and the experience and expression of emotions in romantic relationships: A developmental perspective. *Journal of Personality and Social Psychology, 92*(2), 355–367. doi:10.1037/0022-3514.92.2.355.

Sroufe, L. A., & Fleeson, J. (1986). Attachment and the construction of relationships. In W. W. Hartup & Z. Rubin (Eds.), *Relationships in development.* Hillsdale: Erlbaum.

Sroufe, L. A., Egeland, B., & Kreutzer, T. (1990). The fate of early experience following developmental change: Longitudinal approaches to individual adaptation in childhood. *Child Development, 61*(5), 1363–1373. doi:10. 2307/1130748.

Sroufe, L. A., Egeland, B., & Carlson, E. A. (1999). One social world: The integrated development of parent–child and peer relationships. In W. A. Collins, B. P. Laursen, & W. W. Hartup (Eds.), *The 30th Minnesota symposium on child psychology: Relationships as developmental contexts* (pp. 241–261). Mahwah: Erlbaum.

Sroufe, L. A., Egeland, B., Carlson, E. A., & Collins, W. A. (2005). *The development of the person: The Minnesota study of risk and adaptation from birth to adulthood.* New York: Guilford.

Thompson, R. (2008). Early attachment and later development: Familiar questions, new answers. In J. Cassidy & P. R. Shaver (Eds.), *Handbook of attachment: Theory, research, and clinical applications* (2nd ed., pp. 348–365). New York: Guilford.

Tran, S., & Simpson, J. A. (2009). Prorelationship maintenance behaviors: The joint roles of attachment and commitment. *Journal of Personality and Social Psychology, 97,* 685–698. doi:10.1037/a0016418.

Waters, E., & Cummings, E. M. (2000). A secure base from which to explore close relationships. *Child Development, 71,* 164–172. doi:10.1111/1467-8624.00130.

Chapter 5
The Biobehavioral Legacy of Early Attachment Relationships for Adult Emotional and Interpersonal Functioning

Lisa M. Diamond

One of the chief contributions of attachment theory to relationship science is that it provides a coherent framework for understanding how individuals' earliest ties to their caregivers during infancy and childhood influence the quality of their adult romantic bonds. Historically, these linkages have been understood chiefly in terms of individuals' internalized, psychological models of relationships—the constellation of cognitions and expectations regarding attachment figures which provide the template for individuals' perceptions of, feelings about, and behaviors toward romantic partners. Yet an important development in attachment research over the past several decades is the increased attention to the *biological* implications of early attachment experiences. Specifically, we now know that early attachment experiences shape not only individuals' cognitions and emotions, but also a range of basic physiological systems involved in stress reactivity and regulation. The functioning of these systems, in turn, influences the development of multiple interpersonal processes which are critically implicated in the formation and maintenance of adult attachment bonds. The purpose of this chapter is to review this basic model. Specifically, (1) the quality of early caregiving, in interaction with genetically based temperament and overall stress exposure, calibrates the infant's basic stress-regulatory systems, most notably the autonomic nervous system (ANS) and the hypothalamic–pituitary–adrenocortical (HPA) axis; (2) the infant's resulting profile of ANS and HPA reactivity shapes his/her developing capacity for stress- and emotion-regulation and, as a result, his/her emerging interpersonal skills; (3) by adulthood, this variability in interpersonal and stress-regulatory skills affects the formation and maintenance of adult attachment bonds, by shaping individuals' abilities to seek and provide the safe haven and secure base components of attachment with their romantic partners during times of stress.

Yet importantly, this is not a biologically determinist model. One of the most exciting recent developments in research on the role of ANS and HPA functioning in child development is the emerging view that children's profiles of stress reactivity

---

L. M. Diamond (✉)
University of Utah, Salt Lake City, USA
e-mail: lisa.diamond@psych.utah.edu

V. Zayas, C. Hazan (eds.), *Bases of Adult Attachment*,
DOI 10.1007/978-1-4614-9622-9_5

do not represent global vulnerabilities, but rather *differential susceptibilities* to environmental input (Belsky et al. 2007; Belsky and Pluess 2009; Del Giudice et al. 2011; Ellis et al. 2011). Hence, when the environmental input changes from bad to good, individuals with highly reactive HPA and ANS systems might be disproportionately likely to benefit, in essence "absorbing" more developmental strengths and skills from highly nurturant attachments than their low-reactive counterparts. One intriguing possibility is that this differential susceptibility extends to early adulthood, potentially rendering highly reactive individuals more likely to develop enhanced interpersonal and self-regulatory skills if some of their earliest adult attachment bonds are particularly nurturant and supportive. Toward the end of this chapter, I outline promising directions for future research on such possibilities.

Attachment and the Biology of Stress and Emotion Regulation

Although attachment theory has historically been viewed as a theory of interpersonal functioning, Bowlby (1977) placed considerable emphasis on the role of the attachment system in governing *overall* responses to danger and threat. Confirming Bowby's view, researchers have demonstrated robust associations between attachment experiences and individuals' emotional responses to major and minor stressors (Ditzen et al. 2008; Maunder et al. 2006; Mikulincer and Florian 2004; Simpson et al. 2002), and studies have increasingly investigated the specific behavioral, cognitive, and physiological processes underlying the emotion-regulation functions of the attachment system. *Emotion regulation,* in this context, refers to the range of internal and transactional processes through which individuals consciously or unconsciously modulate the experience or expression of emotions elicited by environmental events (Gross 1999; Thompson 1994). Adaptive versus maladaptive patterns of emotion regulation shape the ways in which individuals perceive, appraise, and react to emotionally relevant experiences (reviewed in Diamond and Hicks 2004), and they are also fundamentally integrated with broader self-regulatory processes including executive functioning, response inhibition, and the regulation of attention (Koole 2009; Lewis et al. 2006; Ochsner and Gross 2007; Posner and Rothbart 2007). Hence, effective emotion regulation is critical for state regulation, social competence, and interpersonal behavior (Cicchetti et al. 1995; Frick and Morris 2004; Silk et al. 2003), and is considered a core developmental achievement for both children and adolescents (Collins et al. 1998; Denham 2006; Eisenberg et al. 2002).

Attachment figures foster the development and maintenance of the infants' emotion regulation abilities by continuously modulating the infant's affective and attentional state in response to changing situational demands. They achieve this on an ongoing basis by adjusting their own facial expressions, vocalizations, and physical touch during routine interactions with the infant, and by regulating the infant's direct engagement with the environment. This routine regulatory "scaffolding" supports the development of the infant's own self-regulatory capacities, as strong positive and negative emotions are repeatedly elicited, experienced, expressed, and modulated dyadically from situation to situation and moment to moment (Dickson et al. 1998; Fogel 2001; Fogel et al. 1999; Tronick 2007). Importantly, the attachment figure need not be perfectly attuned to the infant at each and every moment in order for these normative developmental processes to occur. Rather, even the periodic "mismatches" between the infant's and the caregiver's expressions, intensions, and affects are developmentally beneficial, as they provide opportunities for coordinated communicative "repair" that supports the infant's developing ability to cope with routine irritants and stressors (DiCorcia and Tronick 2011; Tronick and Beeghly 2011).

The cognitive and behavioral aspects of these normative dyadic processes have received extensive attention over the years, yet these processes also have physiological manifestations. Specifically, the processes by which attachment figures regulate their infants' ongoing emotional experiences is now understood to play a central role in "tuning" stress regulatory systems in the orbitofrontal cortex that provide the foundation for effective self- and emotion-regulation (Schore 1996; Siegel 2001). This emerging body of work is quite consistent with Bowlby's original formulation of the attachment system as fundamentally psychobiological. Specifically, he posited two different "rings" of homeostasis that assist the individual in responding to major and minor stressors so that emotional security could be maintained and environmental exploration fostered (Bowlby 1973). The inner ring comprises life-maintaining biological systems that govern ongoing physiological adaptation to external demands. The outer ring comprises behavioral (and particularly, interpersonal) strategies for coping and adaptation. From Bowlby's perspective, the integrated functioning of these two levels is critical for optimal self-regulation.

Extensive research confirms Bowlby's view. We now know that deficits in the quality of the infant–caregiver relationship disrupt not only children's social and behavioral development, but also their biological capacities for maintaining homeostasis in the face of threat (reviewed in Repetti et al. 2002). To understand these processes, developmentalists have increasingly adopted "biosocial" perspectives on the family (Booth et al. 2000), aimed at identifying the reciprocal influences among environmental, interpersonal, behavioral, psychological, and biological processes that unfold within family relations over time (Cairns et al. 1990; Gottlieb 1991). In this view, profiles of biological reactivity—established by interactions between genetic predispositions and early infant/caregiver interactions—set the stage for certain biological, cognitive, emotional, and behavioral responses to stress and challenge. These response patterns become regularized over time, especially as individuals self-select themselves into and out of environments that "fit" their patterns, and over time these patterns exert enduring influences on individuals' psychological functioning and the quality of their intimate relationships. Although such dynamics involve numerous biological processes, we focus below on two systems which have particular relevance for affect regulation: the autonomic system and the HPA axis of the endocrine system. We provide a brief review of these systems, followed by evidence for the critical role of early caregiving (including the quality of infant–caregiver attachment) in establishing enduring reactivity profiles. We then address the implications of these reactivity profiles for emotion regulation and, by extension, *adult* romantic attachment functioning. We conclude by highlighting recent research on the plasticity of these developmental processes, and identifying promising areas for future research on how individuals' earliest adult attachment bonds might prove differentially formative for individuals with different physiological reactivity profiles.

The HPA Axis

Our bodies regulate responses to psychological stress through two primary pathways: The hypothalamic–pituitary–adrenal (or HPA) axis, characterized by activation of the pituitary gland and release of adrenocorticotropic hormone (ACTH) and cortisol, and the sympathetic–adrenal medullary (SAM) axis, characterized by activation of the adrenal medulla (which is part of the autonomic nervous system, or ANS), release of catecholamines (such as norepinephrine and epinephrine) and immediate effects on cardiovascular functioning. Hence, both HPA and ANS activation provide markers of stress reactivity, but they represent distinct "channels" through which stress is regulated in the body, with different antecedents, different effects on other stress-induced biological processes (such as cellular immune function), and different long-term consequences for physical and mental health (Cacioppo 1994). Research has found that the manner in which individuals appraise the stressor at hand shapes the degree to which his/her physiological response is characterized by combined SAM/HPA activation versus SAM activation alone (Blascovich and Tomaka 1996; reviewed in Cacioppo 1994).

In cases where stressors are primarily appraised as challenges (i.e., in which one's resources are viewed as adequate for meeting the demand), the hypothalamus activates the adrenal medulla to release catecholamines, which activate the sympathetic nervous system (SNS) and inhibit the parasympathetic nervous system (PNS), producing increased heart rate, blood pressure, and respiration. In cases where stressors are primarily appraised as threats (i.e., in which one's resources are not viewed as adequate for meeting the demand), the hypothalamus activates the anterior pituitary in addition to the adrenal medulla. The pituitary is signaled to release ACTH, which in turn triggers the release of glucocorticoid hormones, primarily cortisol, into the bloodstream. The release of cortisol facilitates the body's response to stress by regulating glucose metabolism, inflammatory responses, localized blood flow, and the maturation of lymphocytes (Sapolsky et al. 2000). Hence, although most responses to stress involved combined patterns of HPA and SAM activation, the differences between the antecedents and consequences of these two different stress pathways (Blascovich and Tomaka 1996; Cacioppo 1994) makes it important to discus each system separately.

HPA Activation

Studies examining patterns of HPA reactivity to stress have generally followed two different approaches: The first involves measurement of increases in cortisol in response to a laboratory stress task, relative to a pre-task baseline (for a comprehensive review of published research using such paradigms, and a synthesis of the task characteristics most strongly associated with reactivity, see Dickerson and Kemeny 2004). Yet studies have also investigated how acute and chronic stressors influence sustained patterns of cortisol release over one or several days. Cortisol release follows a diurnal pattern, peaking in the first half hour after waking and then declining over the rest of the day.

Extensive research has found that exposure to major and minor stress can produce both transient and lasting alterations in this pattern of secretion (reviewed by Miller et al. 2007). Yet importantly, whereas laboratory studies of momentary HPA reactivity typically detect transient *increases* in cortisol in response to psychological stress, studies of longer-term patterns of cortisol release have found that sustained exposure to stress can elicit chronic increases *or* decreases in cortisol. Hence, stress-related dysregulation of the HPA axis appears to take two forms: Exaggerated cortisol release (paralleling the transient increases found in laboratory studies) and dampened or "blunted" cortisol release, in which the pattern of diurnal secretion is lowered or "flattened," lacking the pronounced morning rise or the evening fall that characterizes normal HPA functioning.

The processes through which chronic stress produces each pattern are thought to be somewhat different. Exaggerated HPA activity is thought to result from stress-related disruption of the normal feedback processes through which HPA activation is typically "shut down" once sufficient levels of cortisol are present in the bloodstream to meet environmental demands. Chronically low or "blunted" HPA activity, in contrast, has been interpreted as a potentially adaptive mechanism for protecting the brain from the detrimental effects of sustained stress-related exposure to cortisol. Awareness of both patterns of dysregulation is important, given that both patterns have been linked to early stress and caregiving experiences (Miller et al. 2011).

The Autonomic Nervous System

The classic "fight-or-flight" response to stress, with its well-known manifestations of increased heart rate, blood pressure, and sweat production, is part of a larger syndrome of physiological changes produced by the ANS, including increased cardiac output, widespread vasoconstriction, and changes in blood flow to the skeletal muscles, myocardium, brain, kidneys, gastrointestinal tract, and skin. All of these changes serve the purpose of redistributing metabolic energy throughout the body so that the organism can either "fight" or "flee" threats.

The ANS has two branches, the PNS and the SNS, which have antagonistic effects on autonomic functioning. Heightened activation of the SNS produces the physiological changes most commonly associated with fight-or-flight responses: acceleration in heart rate, increased blood pressure, increased sweating, etc. In contrast, the PNS is responsible for maintaining normal growth and restoration of internal organs, processes that are suspended in times of intense stress. Thus, stress-induced activation of the SNS is usually accompanied by some degree of "withdrawal" or "suppression" in the PNS, which functions to redistribute metabolic resources to cope with the external threat. Post-stress reengagement of the PNS channels metabolic energy back toward normal maintenance of internal organs and reestablishes homeostasis. Thus, PNS engagement produces the types of physiological changes associated with relaxation rather than arousal, such as decreased heart rate and blood pressure.

Correspondingly, each and every change in ANS activity must be understood as the product of parasympathetic and sympathetic influence, and thus stress responses such as heart rate acceleration can be brought about by activation of the SNS, withdrawal of the PNS, or some combination of the two. The specific balance of SNS and PNS control over cardiovascular functioning varies from situation to situation (Berntson et al. 1996) as well as from person to person (Berntson et al. 1994; Cacioppo et al. 1994).

ANS stress responses that involve a greater degree of PNS withdrawal than SNS activation appear to be more rapid, more flexible, and easier to disengage than SNS-dominated responses (Berger et al. 1989; Saul 1990; Spear et al. 1979), and thus individuals with more parasympathetically mediated patterns of cardiovascular reactivity are conceptualized as having nervous systems that more flexibly react to and recover from environmental stressors than those with sympathetically mediated patterns (Calkins 1997; DeGangi et al. 1991; Porges 1992; Porges et al. 1994).

Individual Differences in HPA and ANS reactivity: Links to Early Caregiving

Multiple studies of animals and humans have documented stable individual differences in both HPA and ANS stress reactivity that appear to have both genetic and environmental determinants (Kirschbaum et al. 1992; Piha et al. 1994; Propper et al. 2008; Snieder et al. 1997). Importantly, for both systems the major environmental determinants appear to be early adversity and early caregiving.

Specifically, research indicates that variations in stress and caregiving at sensitive periods of development can be particularly formative and can result in permanent alterations in the functioning of both the HPA-axis and the ANS (de Kloet et al. 2005; Gunnar and Quevedo 2007; Oitzl et al. 2010; Taylor et al. 2011). With respect to HPA functioning, inadequate parental care appears to have enduring detrimental effects on HPA regulation and broader neurodevelopment (Buss et al. 2007; Heim and Nemeroff 1999, 2001; Heim et al. 2008), particularly during the earliest years of life when brain systems such as the hippocampus and prefrontal cortex, which play key roles in the regulation of the HPA axis, undergo major development (Sanchez et al. 2001; Teicher et al. 2003). Notably, negative effects have been detected for *both* maternal and paternal care: Recent studies have found that paternal negativity is associated with heightened cortisol release to stress in infancy (Mills-Koonce et al. 2011) and heightened basal and reactive cortisol (in response to peer interactions) in adolescence (Byrd-Craven et al. 2012). In contrast to the detrimental effects of inadequate parental care, high levels of physical affection and warmth between a caregiver and his or her infant during stressful circumstances have been tied to normal HPA activation profiles in response to environmental demands (Chorpita and Barlow 1998; Gunnar 1998; Spangler et al. 1994), which is thought to promote overall biobehavioral regulation and well-being (Gunnar 2003; Gunnar and Donzella 2002).

Regarding ANS activity, studies have found that individual differences in PNS reactivity to stress among children are associated with the quality of parenting practices (Blandon et al. 2010; Calkins et al. 1998). In infants, PNS reactivity is associated with the degree of synchrony and symmetric responsiveness of mother–infant interaction (Moore and Calkins 2004; Porter 2003). Aspects of the home environment, such as marital conflict, are also significantly associated with PNS functioning (Porter et al. 2003). Links between early caregiving and ANS functioning appear to be preserved into adolescence and adulthood. For example, Luecken (1998) found elevated blood pressure reactivity among young adults who had undergone the loss of a parent as children, coupled with poor relationship quality in the family, and has documented interaction effects (between parental loss and parental caring) in predicting adult blood pressure reactivity and recovery (Luecken et al. 2009; Luecken et al. 2005).

Implications of HPA and ANS Activity for Emotion Regulation

Although the influence of early caregiving relationships on enduring profiles of HPA and ANS functioning is interesting and important in its own right, it is also important because dysregulated patterns of stress reactivity lead to deficits in social and interpersonal functioning that in turn have important implications for adult attachment relationships. In essence, individual differences in HPA and ANS functioning provides a potent biological mechanism through which deficits in childhood attachment bonds carry forward to reproduce deficits in *adult* attachment bonds, mediated by deficits in emotion regulation that make it difficult for adults to manage day-to-day interpersonal challenges that call for effective emotion regulation in the service of adaptive relationship functioning.

Accordingly, studies have found that individuals who show exaggerated HPA hyperreactivity to stress show deficient coping strategies and exaggerated experiences of negative affect (reviewed in Scarpa and Raine 1997; Stansbury and Gunnar

1994). Additionally, individuals whose HPA reactivity fails to habituate to *repeated* stressor administration are characterized by low self-esteem, low extraversion, high neuroticism, and multiple physical complaints (Kirschbaum et al. 1995). Similar findings were reported by Gerra et al. (2000), who found that adolescents with sustained HPA reactivity were more depressive and harm-avoidant. Other studies have found that youths with heightened HPA reactivity show greater inhibition (Kagan et al. 1987), and more rumination during stress anticipation (Roger and Najarian 1998). Links between HPA activity and emotion regulation have also been found for basal profiles: For example, elevated tonic cortisol levels have been found to be associated with general anxiety among adolescents girls (Schiefelbein and Susman 2006). Notably, research has found that dysregulation of cortisol can also manifest as chronically suppressed or "blunted" cortisol levels (reviewed extensively by Miller et al. 2007). For example, adult men with high levels of cynical hostility show flattened 24-hour cortisol profiles (Pope and Smith 1991) and tonically suppressed cortisol has been found to be associated with callous-unemotional traits in adolescent boys (Loney et al. 2006). Another study assessing diurnal profiles of cortisol release found that adolescents with higher levels of depressive symptoms had slightly lower basal cortisol levels, whereas adolescents with higher levels of trait anger had a significantly stronger cortisol response to awakening (Adam 2006).

Individual differences in ANS functioning are also associated with emotion regulation deficits. For example, excessive reactivity in the SNS system, typically indexed by skin conductance (SCL) reactivity to laboratory stressors, has been posited as a potential marker of children's hypersensitivity to environmental challenges (Boucsein 1991). Accordingly, heightened SCL reactivity predicts a variety of child and adolescent psychosocial outcomes, including reactive aggression (Hubbard et al. 2004, 2002), anxiety (Weems et al. 2005), shyness and inhibition (Kagan et al. 1987), emotional disorders (Garralda et al. 1991), and internalizing and externalizing problems (El-Sheikh 2005; El-Sheikh et al. 2007). In contrast to these reactivity effects, low SNS activity at baseline has been found to predict heightened risk for outcomes such as aggression and conduct problems (Beauchaine et al. 2007; Crowell et al. 2006; Lorber 2004; Raine et al. 1990).

The role of PNS functioning for emotion regulation is outlined in Thayer and Lane's (2000) neurovisceral integration model and Porges' polyvagal theory (Porges 2003), both of which suggest that PNS regulation of heart rate undergirds the constellation of self-regulatory and emotion-regulatory processes that are fundamental to adaptive socioemotional functioning. Generally, vagal activity provides a constant "brake" on cardiovascular functioning ("vagal" refers to the functioning of the 10th cranial nerve, which provides inhibitory input to the heart and plays a critical role in regulating metabolic output in response to environmental events). This tonic inhibitory control permits rapid and efficient modulation of cardiovascular activity in the service of changing environmental demands. Whereas SNS influences on heart rate are relatively slow-acting, typically taking several seconds, vagal inhibition can be suspended in a matter of milliseconds (Saul 1990). Hence, individuals with greater tonic PNS regulation of heart rate (often denoted *vagal tone,* and assessed via resting levels of respiratory sinus arrhythmia, or RSA) are conceptualized as having nervous systems that flexibly react to and recover from environmental stressors (Calkins 1997; DeGangi et al. 1991), which facilitates effective coordination of expressive and affective behavior in the service of social engagement (Porges 2003).

Numerous studies have provided empirical support for this model. For example, infants with low vagal tone (i.e., low baseline levels of RSA) show poor emotional control (Fox 1989; Porges 1991) and high behavioral inhibition (Snidman 1989). Children and adults with low vagal tone show ineffective behavioral coping in response to stress (Fabes and Eisenberg 1997; Fabes et al. 1993), as well as higher levels of anger, hostility, mental stress, and generalized anxiety (reviewed in Brosschot and Thayer 1998; Friedman and Thayer 1998; Horsten et al. 1999). Complementing these findings, recent research also suggests that vagal tone is associated with tonic positive affectivity (Oveis et al. 2009), which may provide a relational "building block" promoting approach-oriented behavior and fostering social resources (following Fredrickson 1998).

Although the majority of research on affect regulation and the PNS has focused on vagal tone (operationalized as resting levels of RSA), an increasing body of research assesses changes in PNS activity during stress and other environmental demands (operationalized as baseline-to-task changes in RSA). Polyvagal theory (Porges 2001) suggests a normative, adaptive pattern of reduced RSA during stress (often denoted vagal *suppression* or withdrawal, given that reductions in RSA represent reductions in PNS activity). Although most individuals typically think of stress as provoking heightened rather than reduced reactivity, reductions in PNS activity actually function to promote mobilization of energy and attention toward the task at hand because the PNS normally has an inhibitory influence on heart rate. Hence, suppressing this inhibitory influence produces a rapid and efficient increase in heart rate *without* requiring energy-costly SNS mobilization. Vagal suppression (indexed as baseline-to-task *reduction* in RSA) has been observed in numerous studies of children, adolescents, and adults engaged in stressful or affectively negative tasks (Beauchaine 2002; Beauchaine et al. 2001; Pieper et al. 2007), and studies suggest that individuals with greater reductions in RSA during stress have more adaptive patterns of emotional and interpersonal functioning (El-Sheikh and Buckhalt 2005; El-Sheikh and Whitson 2006; Hessler and Katz 2007; Huffman et al. 1998; Moore and Calkins 2004).

Yet it is not quite appropriate to characterize reduced RSA as "the" singular adaptive pattern of PNS activity during stress, given that an increasing body of research has found that PNS activity sometimes *increases* during stress (producing an increase in the inhibitory effect of the PNS on heart rate), especially in tasks that call for active *regulatory effort* (Beauchaine 2001; Kettunen et al. 2000; Segerstrom and Nes 2007; Thayer and Lane 2000). It has been theorized that this pattern (often denoted "vagal engagement" in contrast to "vagal suppression/withdrawal") may serve to facilitate attention and vigilance to environmental demands by slowing down cardiovascular activity. Hence, both vagal suppression and vagal engagement might be viewed as adaptive stress responses, albeit in different contexts, and researchers have not yet identified a stable set of criteria by which we might view one pattern or the other as "more appropriate." In addition to situational variation in PNS responses to stress, there also appear individual differences. Katz (2007) has argued that individuals exposed to *chronically* stressful environments may develop an *enduring* pattern of vagal engagement which may help them to monitor their environment and maintain control over their emotions and behavior. Yet although such a pattern might prove adaptive in the short term, it may prove taxing over the long term. Many researchers have begun to conceptualize regulatory capacity as relatively finite, analogous to a muscle that tires upon repeated use (Muraven and Baumeister 2000). Hence, individuals who show chronic patterns of increased RSA in response to stress might experience chronic regulatory "fatigue," leaving them vulnerable to frequent failures of self-control (Vohs et al. 2005). This may explain why individuals who show heightened RSA during stress show multiple indices of emotion dysregulation, such as depression, anxiety, and hostility (Hessler and Katz 2007; Neumann et al. 2004; Vella and Friedman 2007). It also bears noting that heightened RSA *during stress* is independent of—and appears to have quite different psychosocial correlates—than heightened RSA *during rest* (i.e., vagal tone). Hence, although the extant literature consistently suggests that high vagal *tone* is adaptive, the nature of stress-induced vagal engagement versus suppression remains a topic of ongoing debate and research.

Implications for Adult Attachment Functioning

How do these biologically based deficits in HPA and ANS functioning influence adult attachment functioning? Currently, there are no long-term longitudinal studies testing associations between childhood profiles of HPA and ANS reactivity and adults' feelings and behaviors in their romantic attachments. Yet as reviewed earlier, individuals with highly stress-sensitive ANS and HPA systems (due to early caregiving deficits, genetic factors, or their combination) are likely to manifest chronic difficulties regulating stress and negative emotions. These difficulties, in turn, may impede not only the quality of adults' attachment bonds, but their basic propensity to *form* such bonds. This is due to the fact that normative processes of attachment formation, at all stages of life, depend critically upon repeated experiences of comfort-seeking and security-provision via contact with the attachment figure. It is through repeatedly seeking contact with the attachment figure when distressed, and experiencing downregulation of distress as a result of this contact (and, in adulthood, through participation in specifically comforting and supportive behaviors) that individuals come to develop a conditioned, internalized representation of the attachment figure as a fundamental base of security.

Hence, individuals whose HPA and ANS systems show chronic difficulties with stress regulation, and who may consequently fail to experience rapid and reliable downregulation of stress as a result of contact with their romantic attachment partner, may be slower to internalize the partner as a fundamental base of security, and in some cases may never do so. Furthermore, their *partners* may have difficulties drawing emotional security from *them.* Previous research suggests that individuals with stress-regulatory deficits are often poor providers of support and security, since their own unregulated emotions can interfere with their capacity to accurately perceive and sensitively respond to the emotions of others, particularly during times of stress (reviewed in Diamond et al. 2012). Hence, because adult attachment formation and maintenance depends on repeated experiences of receiving *and* providing emotional security during major and minor stressors, individuals with biologically mediated deficits in emotion and stress regulation may show deficits in basic adult attachment dynamics.

The dual nature of these deficits (i.e., difficulties providing and benefiting from care and support) are particularly important, given that the bidirectional nature of adult attachment bonds is a fundamental characteristic of such ties which distinguishes them from infant/caregiver attachments. Specifically, whereas parents provide emotion regulation for their children but do not seek it in return, long-standing romantic partners have reciprocal influences on one another's emotional states, through a series of intentional and unintentional processes denoted as "co-regulation" (reviewed in Butler 2011; Sbarra and Hazan 2008). This is not to say that the ties between caregivers and infants are wholly unidirectional, and that they do not, as well, show reciprocal coregulaton. Yet the asymmetrical nature of infant/caregiver attachment, and the immature state of the infant's physiological, cognitive, and affective systems, suggests that the chains of influence from caregiver to infant—especially when informed by conscious intent, such as when the caregiver attempts to soothe the child—are more robust and developmentally salient than vice versa.

Coregulation in the context of adult attachment can be broadly defined as a state of mutual interconnectedness in which both partners in an adult attachment relationship provide subtle forms of regulatory scaffolding for one another. Research has provided consistent evidence for emotion coregulation in cohabiting couples, most typically in the form of one partner's emotions or physiological responses influencing the other's, either through specific disclosures or through simple time spent together in close proximity (Butner et al. 2007; Helm et al. 2012; Hicks and Diamond 2008; Reed et al. 2012; Saxbe and Repetti 2010; Schoebi 2008; Semin and Cacioppo 2008). Not only does effective coregulation provide a potential pathway through which well-functioning attachments influence individuals' physical and mental health (Diamond and Fagundes 2012), but Sbarra and Hazan (2008) have suggested, expanding on the seminal work of Hofer (1984), that the establishment of coregulation may in fact be a distinguishing characteristic of attachment bonds that distinguishes them from other affiliative ties. Accordingly, to the degree that individual differences in ANS and HPA reactivity to stress may interfere with the establishment of coregulation or bias its functioning (such that one partner has a greater influence on the other than vice versa, or such that emotional states co-ordinate in a manner that facilitates escalation rather than attenuation of negative affect), basic processes of attachment formation and functioning may be disrupted, potentially interfering with the ability of the bond to provide a reliable base of security for each partner.

The quality of the bond is also likely to suffer, due to the critical role of ongoing mutual emotion regulation in the course of effective relationship functioning. For example, effective maintenance of a well-functioning romantic relationship, in the face of day-to-day stress and conflict, requires inhibiting impulses to reciprocate negative affect or behavior, and sometimes even constraining one's own expressive behavior in order to avoid escalation; it requires active efforts at maintaining positive, relationship-enhancing interpretations of partner behavior; it requires periodically sacrificing one's immediate needs in the service of compromise and forgiving the partner's transgressions. Accordingly, researchers have increasingly acknowledged the importance of self-regulation and self-control in romantic relationship functioning (Finkel and Campbell 2001; Halford et al. 2007). Finkel and Campbell, for example, demonstrated that dispositional capacities for self-regulation are critical to couples' abilities to engage in *accommodation* (Rusbult et al. 1991), i.e., to respond constructively to one another's potentially destructive behavior and to resist reciprocating and escalating negative affect. As they noted, "all partners in romantic relationships behave badly at times…. should the nonoffending individual act on the self-interested, gut-level impulse to 'fight fire with fire,' or should he or she instead resist the temptation to retaliate, choosing to behave in a constructive, prorelationship manner?" (p. 263). Accommodation might take the form of apologizing to a partner, forgiving him/her for a transgression, introducing humor or affection into a potentially difficult interaction, or simply "letting go" of a complaint or a perceived slight. Accommodation is important because it can *interrupt* potentially negative chains of interaction, ensuring that periodic transgressions remain periodic (Arriaga and Rusbult 1998; Gottman 1993; Gottman and Levenson 1992; Rusbult et al. 1998). Yet it is not easy: Most individuals' immediate responses to negative interpersonal behavior tend to be self-centered, self-protective, and potentially destructive (Thibaut and Kelley 1978), and individuals must draw upon self-regulatory resources in order to consistently inhibit these impulses (Finkel and Campbell 2001; see also Robins et al. 2000). Not surprisingly, deficits in emotion regulation have been related to maladaptive aggression in intimate relationships (Marshall et al. 2011; McNulty and Hellmuth 2008; Shorey et al. 2011a; Shorey et al. 2011b).

Notably, heightened physiological reactivity may render self- and emotion-regulation in intimate relationships more difficult. Studies of HPA reactivity in particular have found that the excessive amounts of cortisol produced by HPA hyperreactivity to stress have detrimental effects on in situ cognitive processing, executive functioning, attention, and memory (Abercrombie et al. 2003; Cahill et al 2003; Lupien et al. 1994; McEwen et al. 1992) in a manner that may immediately interfere with the adoption of adaptive interpersonal strategies in the face of stress and threat. Hence, in the face of either generalized or relationship-specific stress (such as conflict), individuals with heightened HPA activity may prove less able to identify, select, and implement mature problem-solving approaches that call for heightened impulse control, self-awareness, and self-regulation, and might more quickly resort to more primitive, defensive, aggressive, and escapist approaches. Over time, the repeated adoption of such maladaptive coping strategies can introduce significant strains and burdens on one's romantic relationship, potentially leading to dissolution.

This scenario (in which deficits in biologically based capacities for emotion regulation have implications for adult romantic relationship functioning) applies to ANS functioning as well. Numerous researchers have highlighted the specific relevance of tonic PNS activity (vagal tone) for *social* functioning, given the critical role of affective and behavioral regulation in guiding children's reactivity and responsiveness to increasingly complex social situations as they mature (Beauchaine 2001). For example, researchers investigating links between vagal tone and tonic positive affect (Oveis et al. 2009) have argued that the positive and flexible disposition of individuals with high vagal tone may serve as a relational "building block" which promotes approach-oriented behavior and fosters social resources (following Fredrickson 1998). In contrast, the interpersonal hostility and defensiveness associated with low vagal tone (Brosschot and Thayer 1998; Demaree et al. 2004; Movius and Allen 2005; Sloan et al. 1994) directly hinders interpersonal functioning.

Supporting this view, one recent study (Diamond et al. 2011) found that individual differences in PNS regulation related to couples' day-to-day interpersonal behavior. Specifically, men with higher vagal tone (indexed by higher baseline RSA, and suggestive of more robust emotion regulation) were rated by their female partners as interacting more positively (i.e., expressing more connectedness and understanding) over 3 weeks of day-to-day assessment than were men with lower vagal tone. This study also found that on days when men with either low vagal tone (i.e., low baseline RSA) or high vagal reactivity (i.e., baseline-to-task increases in RSA in response to stress) reported high negative affect, their female partners described them as more critical and argumentative. Yet this was not the case for men with high vagal tone or low vagal reactivity. As for women, those with higher vagal tone interacted more positively with their partners (according to their partners' reports) on days when the women reported greater positive affect. This effect was not observed among women with lower vagal tone. These findings may suggest that women with higher vagal tone are better able to mobilize positive affect in the service of sensitive and responsive interactions with their romantic partners, or they might suggest that women with higher vagal tone experience stronger positive emotions *in response* to positive interactions with their romantic partners. Either interpretation is consistent with the notion that robust vagal regulation, potentially established by individuals' earliest interactions with caregivers, may allow adults to adaptively regulate negative emotions, foster positive emotions, and sustain adaptive interpersonal interactions with their romantic partners in the face of day-to-day stressors.

Directions for Future Research

Up until now, I have emphasized normative attachment processes such as the basic provision of safety, security, and mutual caregiving and coregulation. Yet there is, of course, an extensive body of research on individual differences in attachment security, commonly known as *attachment styles*. One promising direction for future research would involve bridging the conventional gap between research on normative attachment processes and research on individual differences in attachment styles by investigating how the (normative) activity of the HPA and ANS in response to stress contributes to the development and maintenance of adult attachment styles. Hence, although much adult attachment research has focused on the consequences of individual differences in attachment style for multiple aspects of couple functioning, an equally important question concerns the normative biobehavioral attachment processes that *give rise* to variation in adult attachment styles, and what these processes tell us about the total psychobiological complex of the attachment system.

Historically, attachment styles were conceived as trait-like expectations concerning the responsiveness of attachment figures, established through early infant/caregiver interactions, which function as mental prototypes for future relationship experiences (Ainsworth et al. 1978). Over the years, however studies have increasingly shown a key role for attachment styles in organizing the encoding, storage, retrieval, and manipulation of information related to affective states (Shaver and Mikulincer 2007), and attachment styles are now generally viewed as influencing not only interpersonal functioning, but psychosocial approaches to stress and to negative emotions more generally (reviewed in Mikulincer and Florian 2004; Nolte et al. 2012).

According to attachment theory, infants who did not receive adequate "external" emotion regulation from their attachment figures came to rely on secondary—and suboptimal—regulatory strategies. Specifically, individuals with high attachment *anxiety* have been found to maximize the experience and expression of negative affect, to be hypervigilant to threat cues, and to show patterns of spreading emotional reactivity such that one negative thought or memory triggers many others (Shaver and Mikulincer 2002). Individuals with high attachment *avoidance*, to the contrary, tend to minimize experiences of negative affect and to direct attention away from threat cues (Mikulincer et al. 2003). These "deactivating" strategies involve the denial or suppression of affective experience, the inhibition of affective expression, and distortion of encoding of affective experiences (Becker-Stoll et al. 2001; Kobak et al. 1993; Mikulincer et al. 2003). Importantly, both types of attachment insecurity are associated with the inability to derive emotion regulating benefits from contact with attachment figures. (Feeney 1999).

The cognitive, behavioral, affective, and interpersonal consequences of these two divergent strategies have received extensive attention over the years (reviewed in Mikulincer and Shaver 2008). Yet research has increasingly investigated their physiological manifestations. After all, if sensitive and responsive caregiving is responsible *both* for the development of attachment security *and* for the calibration of the stress regulation functions of the HPA axis and the ANS, one might expect to find that individual differences in attachment style relate directly to the functioning of these systems. Some research supports this view: Specifically, children with insecure patterns of attachment show heightened HPA responses to acute stress (Hertsgaard et al. 1995; Nachmias et al. 1996; Spangler and Grossman 1993; van

Bakel and Riksen-Walraven 2004), and a recent study found that attachment insecurity in adolescence is linked to heightened basal levels of cortisol (Oskis et al. 2011). As for adults, Quirin et al. (2008) found that adults' attachment anxiety was associated with heightened HPA reactivity to a standardized laboratory stressor, and both attachment anxiety and avoidance have been associated with lower vagal tone (Diamond and Hicks 2005; Maunder et al. 2006).

A shortcoming of this emerging body of research is that most studies investigate HPA or ANS functioning in response to relationship-specific rather than generalized stressors, and correspondingly interpret the physiological results as indicative of anxious or avoidant individuals' emotional responses to relationship events. Yet the model I have outlined in this chapter suggests that anxious and avoidant individuals may have *started out in childhood* with particularly reactive HPA or ANS systems, which may have developed due to deficits in early caregiving, genetic factors, or a combination of the two, and that this heightened reactivity may have contributed to the development of their attachment anxiety and avoidance. Yet research paradigms assessing associations between attachment style and physiological reactivity to relationship-specific stressors cannot reliably disentangle "pre-relationship" patterns of HPA/ANS reactivity from "relationship-triggered" HPA/ANS reactivity. For example, Powers et al. (2006) found that insecurely attached individuals showed greater HPA reactivity to (laboratory-induced) romantic conflict than did securely attached individuals. Specifically, attachment avoidance in female participants was related to increased HPA reactivity to couple conflict, whereas men showed elevated reactivity if they had high levels of anxiety combined with high avoidance. Individuals with high attachment anxiety also showed poorer recovery of HPA levels after the conflict (Laurent and Powers 2007). Dewitt and colleagues (Dewitte et al. 2010) led individuals to believe that they were going to have to watch a tape of their partner being interviewed about previous sexual and romantic relationships by an attractive opposite-sex experimenter. Participants with higher attachment anxiety showed heightened HPA reactivity while anticipating this stressful event, with the highest increases found among women with high anxiety *and* avoidance. Finally, during an *actual* 4–7-day physical separation from their romantic partner, individuals with high attachment anxiety showed tonically elevated levels of cortisol (Diamond et al. 2008).

All of these findings are consistent with the notion that anxiety is associated with a lower threshold for attachment-related threats (conflict, partner unavailability, jealousy, etc.), which manifests itself in a heightened physiological response. Yet it is also possible that, as outlined in this chapter, insecurely attached individuals possessed a *generalized* predisposition for heightened HPA or ANS stress reactivity, to relationship-specific as well as other stressors, and that this heightened reactivity contributed to the development of their attachment insecurity over the course of their development. This interpretation is consistent with the limited body of findings cited above on associations between attachment security and overall patterns of ANS and HPA functioning (Diamond and Hicks 2005; Maunder et al. 2006; Oskis et al. 2011; Quirin et al. 2008), but considerably more research is needed. In particular, future research should conduct comprehensive comparisons between anxious and avoidant individuals' physiological, cognitive, and emotional reactivity to relationship-related stressors *as well as* generalized stressors, at multiple points in time, in order to try and determine the degree to which patterns of reactivity reflect stable features of individuals (which "travel" from relationship to relationship and from situation to situation) versus the degree to which they reflect features of individuals' current relationship experiences (i.e., the degree of hostility or avoidance or support in this particular interaction). Such studies have enormous potential to contribute to our understanding of the complex links between early attachment experiences, biologically based patterns of emotion regulation, and adult attachment functioning.

Finally, one of the most intriguing areas for future research concerns the role of the HPA and the ANS systems in potentiating *plasticity* in attachment style and basic attachment-related interpersonal functioning over the lifespan. Historically, research on links between ANS and HPA functioning and socioemotional development adopted a diathesis-stress or "dual-risk" perspective, positing that children with heightened ANS and HPA responses to stress were disproportionately vulnerable to stressful rearing environments, due to their basic deficits in stress regulation (reviewed by Boyce and Ellis 2005). Yet recently an alternative perspective has emerged, denoted *differential susceptibility* (Belsky et al. 2007; Belsky and Pluess 2009; Del Giudice et al. 2011; Ellis et al. 2011) positing that the same factors that render children highly sensitive and reactive to negative environments also render them highly sensitive and reactive to positive environments. Hence, both dual-risk and differential susceptibility perspectives predict that children with certain patterns of ANS functioning will show disproportionately negative outcomes in negative environmental contexts (as shown by Boyce et al. 1995; Bubier et al. 2009; Cummings et al. 2007; El-Sheikh et al. 2007, 2009; Katz 2007). However, the differential susceptibility perspective additionally predicts that these children will show disproportionately positive outcomes in positive environments (reviewed in Belsky et al. 2007; Belsky and Pluess 2009), or might particularly show improvements in general socioemotional functioning when their environmental input changes from bad to good, due to the fact that they may be better able to "absorb" developmental strengths and skills from highly nurturant environments than their low-reactive counterparts.

Although most research testing the differential susceptibility model has focused on environmental inputs experienced during childhood (reviewed in Belsky and Pluess 2009), some researchers have argued that environmental inputs experienced at later ages also play a potentially important role. Specifically, Del Giudice et al. (2011) have argued that there may be additional "windows" of heightened susceptibility which open up during later developmental transitions, such as puberty (Del Giudice et al. 2011), which function to ensure that individuals adjust appropriately to the key environmental ingredients relevant to their changing developmental tasks. During adolescence, of course, mating and reproduction emerge as newly important life tasks, and one of the hallmarks of this transition involves the normative transfer of emotional attachment from parents to romantic partners (Diamond and Fagundes 2008; Hazan and Zeifman 1994; Trinke and Bartholomew 1997).

Most existing research on youths' first significant romantic attachments has focused on the degree to which the quality of these ties can be predicted from youths' preexisting interpersonal skills and deficits (see reviews in Crouter and Booth 2006), but little research has specifically investigated whether youths' first substantive romantic attachments have a particularly formative role with respect to adult attachment style. In light of the differential susceptibility model, one possibility is that youths' entry into mature adult attachments represents a normative window of heightened sensitivity to environmental input, *and* that highly reactive individuals will be disproportionately sensitive to these experiences, rendering their early romances particularly influential on their developing attachment cognitions and behaviors. For example, highly reactive youths whose first substantive romantic attachments are extremely positive and supportive might be particularly likely to develop robust interpersonal and self-regulatory skills as a result, even if they *began* these relationships with compromised skills. Moving forward, their improved social and regulatory capacities may improve the quality of their future adult attachment bonds, fostering an enduring sense of security and potentially attenuating the levels of anxiety and avoidance that they may have started with.

In contrast, highly reactive individuals whose first substantive ties are troubled, conflictual, and unsupportive might be particularly likely to become highly anxious or avoidant *as a result*, and to settle into maladaptive patterns of interpersonal behavior and emotion regulation that impede their abilities to form and sustain nurturant adult attachment bonds. Hence, although early appearing profiles of biological stress-regulation are likely to have important and enduring influences on attachment formation and functioning, these influences are not theorized as deterministic. Rather, the seeds for change in attachment-related skills and capacities may be a fundamental component of these profiles, and may be why they have been fundamentally preserved in our species as engines for lasting developmental adaptation.

Conclusion

The increasing body of psychobiological research on attachment and emotion regulation underscores the critical role of attachment relationships in fostering psychological, physical, and interpersonal functioning at all stages of the life course. Understanding the role of early attachment relationships in calibrating critical stress-regulatory systems, and the long-term implications of these systems for emotion regulation and interpersonal functioning, provides important new ways to understand the fundamental linkages between infant–child attachment and adult attachment, and potentially to bridge the long-standing bifurcation between these two separate research traditions. The development of integrative, lifespan, biobehavioral models of the attachment system should be a priority for future research, and greater emphasis on the emotion regulation functions of attachment, as they are manifested in different types of social and interpersonal challenges at different stages of life, can make an important contribution to this goal. After all, emotion regulation within attachment relationships is not a developmental task to be mastered at a certain age (after which attention turns to the psychological and behavioral implications of one's relative success or failure at this task), but rather a "moving target" that is continually sensitive to changing goals and contexts. The quality of individuals' parental attachments clearly has critical implications for both subjective and physiological aspects of emotion regulation and hence long-term interpersonal functioning, opening up a host of fascinating questions regarding the basic biopsychology of the attachment system, its multiple manifestations, and its potential developmental changes over the lifespan. Addressing these questions can help to integrate the increasingly sophisticated bodies of knowledge on social relationships and multiple domains of mental and physical functioning which have developed within the social-psychological, developmental, and behavioral medicine traditions—such an integration is critical for elucidating how and why attachment bonds play such a fundamental role in well-being over the life course.

References

Abercrombie, H. C., Kalin, N. H., Thurow, M. E., Rosenkranz, M. A., & Davidson, R. J. (2003). Cortisol variation in humans affects memory for emotionally laden and neutral information. *Behavioral Neuroscience, 117,* 505–516.

Adam, E. K. (2006). Transactions among adolescent trait and state emotion and diurnal and momentary cortisol activity in naturalistic settings. *Psychoneuroendocrinology, 31,* 664–679.

Ainsworth, M. D. S., Blehar, M. C., Waters, E., & Wall, S. (1978). *Patterns of attachment: A psychological study of the strange situation.* Hillsdale: Erlbaum.

Arriaga, X. B., & Rusbult, C. E. (1998). Standing in my partner's shoes: Partner perspective taking and reactions to accommodative dilemmas. *Personality and Social Psychology Bulletin, 24,* 927–948.

Beauchaine, T. P. (2001). Vagal tone, development, and Gray's motivational theory: Toward an integrated model of autonomic nervous system functioning in psychopathology. *Development and Psychopathology, 13,* 183–214.

Beauchaine, T. P. (2002). Autonomic substrates of heart rate reactivity in adolescent males with conduct disorder and/or attention-deficit/hyperreactivity disorder. In S. P. Shohov (Ed.), *Advances in psychology research* (Vol. 18, pp. 83–95). New York: Nova Science.

Beauchaine, T. P., Katkin, E. S., Strassberg, Z., & Snarr, J. (2001). Disinhibitory psychopathology in male adolescents: Discriminating conduct disorder from attention-deficit/hyperactivity disorder through concurrent assessment of multiple autonomic states. *Journal of Abnormal Psychology, 110,* 610–624.

Beauchaine, T. P., Gatzke-Kopp, L., & Mead, H. K. (2007). Polyvagal theory and developmental psychopathology: Emotion dysregulation and conduct problems from preschool to adolescence. *Biological Psychology, 74,* 174–184.

Becker-Stoll, F., Delius, A., & Scheitenberger, S. (2001). Adolescents' nonverbal emotional expressions during negotiation of a disagreement with their mothers: An attachment approach. *International Journal of Behavioral Development, 25,* 344–353.

Belsky, J., & Pluess, M. (2009). Beyond diathesis stress: Differential susceptibility to environmental influences. *Psychological Bulletin, 135,* 885–908. doi:10.1037/a0017376.

Belsky, J., Bakermans-Kranenburg, M. J., & van Ijzendoorn, M. H. (2007). For better and for worse: Differential susceptibility to environmental influences. *Current Directions in Psychological Science, 16,* 300–304.

Berger, R. D., Saul, J. P., & Cohen, R. J. (1989). Transfer function analysis of autonomic regulation: I. The canine atrial rate response. *American Journal of Physiology, 256,* H142–H152.

Berntson, G. G., Cacioppo, J. T., Binkley, P. F., Uchino, B. N., Quigley, K. S., & Fieldstone, A. (1994). Autonomic cardiac control. III. Psychological stress and cardiac response in autonomic space as revealed by pharmacological blockades. *Psychophysiology, 31,* 599–608.

Berntson, G. G., Cacioppo, J. T., & Fieldstone, A. (1996). Illusions, arithmetic, and the bidirectional modulation of vagal control of the heart. *Biological Psychology, 44,* 1–17.

Blandon, A. Y., Calkins, S. D., Keane, S. P., & O'Brien, M. (2010). Contributions of child's physiology and maternal behavior to children's trajectories of temperamental reactivity. *Developmental Psychology, 46,* 1089–1102.

Blascovich, J., & Tomaka, J. (1996). The biopsychosocial model of arousal regulation. In M. Zanna (Ed.), *Advances in experimental social psychology* (Vol. 28, pp. 1–51). New York: Academic.

Booth, A., Carver, K., & Granger, D. A. (2000). Biosocial perspectives on the family. *Journal of Marriage and the Family, 62,* 1018–1034.

Boucsein, W. (1991). *Electrodermal activity*. New York: Plenum.

Bowlby, J. (1973). *Attachment and loss: Vol. 2: Separation: Anxiety and anger*. New York: Basic.

Bowlby, J. (1977). The making and breaking of affectional bonds: I. Aetiology and psychopathology in the light of attachment theory. *The British Journal of Psychiatry, 130,* 201–210. doi: 10.1192/bjp.130.3.201.

Boyce, W. T., & Ellis, B. J. (2005). Biological sensitivity to context: I. An evolutionary-developmental theory of the origins and functions of stress reactivity. *Development and Psychopathology, 17,* 271–301.

Boyce, W. T., Chesney, M., Alkon, A., & Tschann, J. M. (1995). Psychobiologic reactivity to stress and childhood respiratory illnesses: Results of two prospective studies. *Psychosomatic Medicine, 57,* 411–422.

Brosschot, J. F., & Thayer, J. F. (1998). Anger inhibition, cardiovascular recovery, and vagal function: A model of the link between hostility and cardiovascular disease. *Annals of Behavioral Medicine, 20,* 326–332.

Bubier, J. L., Drabick, D. A. G., & Breiner, T. (2009). Autonomic functioning moderates the relations between contextual factors and externalizing behaviors among inner-city children. *Journal of Family Psychology, 23,* 500–510.

Buss, C., Lord, C., Wadiwalla, M., Hellhammer, D. H., Lupien, S. J., Meaney, M. J., & Pruessner, J. C. (2007). Maternal care modulates the relationship between prenatal risk and hippocampal volume in women but not in men. *The Journal Of Neuroscience, 27,* 2592–2595.

Butler, E. A. (2011). Temporal interpersonal emotion systems: The "TIES" that form relationships. *Personality and Social Psychology Review, 15,* 367–393. doi:10.1177/1088868311411164.

Butner, J., Diamond, L. M., & Hicks, A. M. (2007). Attachment style and two forms of affect coregulation between romantic partners. *Personal Relationships, 14,* 431–455.

Byrd-Craven, J., Auer, B. J., Granger, D. A., & Massey, A. R. (2012). The father-daughter dance: The relationship between father-daughter relationship quality and daughters' stress response. *Journal of Family Psychology, 26,* 87–94.

Cacioppo, J. T. (1994). Social neuroscience: Autonomic, neuroendocrine, and immune responses to stress. *Psychophysiology, 31,* 113–128.

Cacioppo, J. T., Uchino, B. N., & Berntson, G. G. (1994). Individual differences in the autonomic origins of heart rate reactivity: The psychometrics of respiratory sinus arrhythmia and preejection period. *Psychophysiology, 31,* 412–419.

Cahill, L., Gorski, L., & Le, K. (2003). Enhanced human memory consolidation with post-learning stress: Interaction with the degree of arousal at encoding. *Learning & Memory, 10,* 270–274.

Cairns, R. B., Gariepy, J. L., & Hood, K. E. (1990). Development, microevolution, and social behavior. *Psychological Review, 97,* 49–65.

Calkins, S. D. (1997). Cardiac vagal tone indices of temperamental reactivity and behavioral regulation in young children. *Developmental Psychobiology, 31,* 125–135.

Calkins, S. D., Smith, C. L., Gill, K. L., & Johnson, M. C. (1998). Maternal interactive style across contexts: Relations to emotional, behavioral, and physiological regulation during toddlerhood. *Social Development, 7,* 350–369.

Chorpita, B. F., & Barlow, D. H. (1998). The development of anxiety: The role of control in the early environment. *Psychological Bulletin, 124,* 3–21.

Cicchetti, D., Ackerman, B. P., & Izard, C. E. (1995). Emotions and emotion regulation in developmental psychopathology. *Development and Psychopathology, 7,* 1–10.

Collins, N. L., Shaver, P. R., & Collins, N. L. (1998). Attachment styles, emotion regulation, and adjustment in adolescence. *Journal of Personality and Social Psychology, 74,* 1380–1397.

Crouter, A. C., & Booth, A. (2006). *Romance and sex in adolescence and emerging adulthood: Risks and opportunities*. Mahwah: Erlbaum.

Crowell, S. E., Beauchaine, T. P., Gatzke-Kopp, L., Sylvers, P., Mead, H., & Chipman-Chacon, J. (2006). Autonomic correlates of attention-deficit/hyperactivity disorder and oppositional defiant disorder in preschool children. *Journal of Abnormal Psychology, 115,* 174–178.

Cummings, E. M., El-Sheikh, C. D., Kouros, C. D., & Keller, P. S. (2007). Children's skin conductance reactivity as a mechanism of risk in the context of parental depressive symptoms. *Journal of Child Psychology and Psychiatry, 48,* 436–445.

de Kloet, E. R., Sibug, R. M., Helmerhorst, F. M., & Schmidt, M. (2005). Stress, genes and the mechanism of programming the brain for later life. *Prenatal Programming Of Behavior, Physiology And Cognition, 29,* 271–281.

DeGangi, G. A., DiPietro, J. A., Greenspan, S. I., & Porges, S. W. (1991). Psychophysiological characteristics of the regulatory disordered infant. *Infant Behavior and Development, 14,* 37–50.

Del Giudice, M., Ellis, B. J., & Shirtcliff, E. A. (2011). The adaptive calibration model of stress responsivity. *Neuroscience and Biobehavioral Reviews, 35,* 1562–1592.

Demaree, H. A., Robinson, J. L., Everhart, D. E., & Schmeichel, B. J. (2004). Resting RSA is associated with natural and self-regulated responses to negative emotional stimuli. *Brain & Cognition, 56,* 14–23.

Denham, S. A. (2006). Emotional competence: Implications for social functioning. In J. L. Luby (Ed.), *Handbook of preschool mental health: Development, disorders, and treatment* (pp. 23–44). New York: Guilford.

Dewitte, M., De Houwer, J., Goubert, L., & Buysse, A. (2010). A multi-modal approach to the study of attachment-related distress. *Biological Psychology, 85,* 149–162.

Diamond, L. M., & Fagundes, C. P. (2008). Developmental perspectives on links between attachment and affect regulation over the lifespan. *Advances in Child Behavior and Development, 36,* 83–134.

Diamond, L. M., & Fagundes, C. P. (2012). Emotion regulation in close relationships: Implications for social threat and its effects on immunological functioning. In L. Cambell & T. J. Loving (Eds.), *Close relationships: An interdisciplinary perspective* (pp. 83–106). New York: Springer.

Diamond, L. M., & Hicks, A. M. (2004). Psychobiological perspectives on attachment: Implications for health over the lifespan. In J. A. Simpson & W. S. Rholes (Eds.), *Adult attachment: New directions and emerging issues* (pp. 240–263). New York: Guilford.

Diamond, L. M., & Hicks, A. M. (2005). Attachment style, current relationship security, and negative emotions: The mediating role of physiological regulation. *Journal of Social and Personal Relationships, 22,* 499–518.

Diamond, L. M., Hicks, A. M., & Otter-Henderson, K. A. (2008). Every time you go away: Changes in affect, behavior, and physiology associated with travel-related separations from romantic partners. *Journal of Personality and Social Psychology, 95,* 385–403.

Diamond, L. M., Hicks, A. M., & Otter-Henderson, K. A. (2011). Individual differences in vagal regulation moderate associations between daily affect and daily couples interactions. *Personality and Social Psychology Bulletin, 37,* 731–744.

Diamond, L. M., Fagundes, C. P., & Butterworth, M. R. (2012). Attachment style, vagal tone, and empathy during mother-adolescent interactions. *Journal of Research on Adolescence, 22,* 165–184.

Dickerson, S. S., & Kemeny, M. E. (2004). Acute stressors and cortisol responses: A theoretical integration and synthesis of laboratory research. *Psychological Bulletin, 130,* 355–391.

Dickson, K. L., Fogel, A., & Messinger, D. (1998). The development of emotion from a social process view. In M. F. Mascolo & S. Griffin (Eds.), *What develops in emotional development?* (pp. 253–271). New York: Plenum Press.

DiCorcia, J. A., & Tronick, E. (2011). Quotidian resilience: Exploring mechanisms that drive resilience from a perspective of everyday stress and coping. *Neuroscience and Biobehavioral Reviews, 35,* 1593–1602. doi:10.1016/j.neubiorev.2011.04.008.

Ditzen, B., Schmidt, S., Strauss, B., Nater, U. M., Ehlert, U., & Heinrichs, M. (2008). Adult attachment and social support interact to reduce psychological but not cortisol responses to stress. *Journal of Psychosomatic Research, 64,* 479–486.

Eisenberg, N., Spinrad, T. L., & Morris, A. S. (2002). Regulation, resiliency, and quality of social functioning. *Self and Identity, 1,* 121–128.

El-Sheikh, M. (2005). The role of emotional responses and physiological reactivity in the marital conflict-child functioning link. *Journal of Child Psychology and Psychiatry, 46,* 1191–1199.

El-Sheikh, M., & Buckhalt, J. A. (2005). Vagal regulation and emotional intensity predict children's sleep problems. *Developmental Psychobiology, 46,* 307–317.

El-Sheikh, M., & Whitson, S. A. (2006). Longitudinal relations between marital conflict and child adjustment: Vagal regulation as a protective factor. *Journal of Family Psychology, 20,* 30–39.

El-Sheikh, M., Keller, P. S., & Erath, S. A. (2007). Marital conflict and risk for child maladjustment over time: Skin conductance level reactivity as a vulnerability factor. *Journal of Abnormal Child Psychology, 35,* 715–727.

El-Sheikh, M., Kouros, C. D., Erath, S., Cummings, E. M., Keller, P., Staton, L., et al. (2009). Marital conflict and children's externalizing behavior: Interactions between parasympathetic and sympathetic nervous system activity. *Monographs of the Society for Research in Child Development, 74,* 1–79.

Ellis, B. J., Boyce, W. T., Belsky, J., Bakermans-Kranenburg, M. J., & Van Ijzendoorn, M. H. (2011). Differential susceptibility to the environment: An evolutionary-neurodevelopmental theory. *Development and Psychopathology, 23,* 7–28.

Fabes, R. A., & Eisenberg, N. (1997). Regulatory control in adults' stress-related responses to daily life events. *Journal of Personality and Social Psychology, 73,* 1107–1117.

Fabes, R. A., Eisenberg, N., & Eisenbud, L. (1993). Behavioral and physiological correlates of children's reactions to others in distress. *Developmental Psychology, 29,* 655–663.

Feeney, J. A. (1999). Adult romantic attachment and couple relationships. In J. Cassidy & P. R. Shaver (Eds.), *Handbook of attachment: Theory, research, and clinical applications* (pp. 355–377). New York: Guilford.

Finkel, E. J., & Campbell, W. K. (2001). Self-control and accommodation in close relationships: An interdependence analysis. *Journal of Personality and Social Psychology, 81,* 263–277.

Fogel, A. (2001). A relational perspective on the development of self and emotion. In H. A. Bosma & E. S. Kunnen (Eds.), *Identity and emotion: Development through self-organization* (pp. 93–119). New York: Cambridge University Press.

Fogel, A., Messinger, D. S., Dickson, K. L., & Hsu, H.-C. (1999). Posture and gaze in early mother-infant communication: Synchronization of developmental trajectories. *Developmental Science, 2,* 325–332. doi:10.1111/1467-7687.00078.

Fox, N. A. (1989). Psychophysiological correlates of emotional reactivity during the first year of life. *Developmental Psychology, 25,* 495–504.

Fredrickson, B. L. (1998). What good are positive emotions? *Review of General Psychology, 2,* 300–319.

Frick, P. J., & Morris, A. S. (2004). Temperament and developmental pathways to conduct problems. *Journal of Clinical Child and Adolescent Psychology, 33,* 54–68.

Friedman, B. H., & Thayer, J. F. (1998). Autonomic balance revisited: Panic anxiety and heart rate variability. *Journal of Psychosomatic Research, 44,* 133–151.

Garralda, M. E., Connell, J., & Taylor, D. C. (1991). Psychophysiological anomalies in children with emotional and conduct disorders. *Psychological Medicine: A. Journal of Research in Psychiatry and the Allied Sciences, 21,* 947–957.

Gerra, G., Zaimovic, A., Zambelli, U., Timpano, M., Reali, N., Bernasconi, S., & Brambilla, F. (2000). Neuroendocrine responses to psychological stress in adolescents with anxiety disorder. *Neuropsychobiology, 42,* 82–92.

Gottlieb, G. (1991). Experiential canalization of behavioral development: Theory. *Developmental Psychology, 27,* 4–13.

Gottman, J. M. (1993). The roles of conflict engagement, escalation, and avoidance in marital interaction: A longitudinal view of 5 types of couples. *Journal of Consulting and Clinical Psychology, 61,* 6–15.

Gottman, J. M., & Levenson, R. W. (1992). Marital processes predictive of later dissolution: Behavior, physiology, and health. *Journal of Personality and Social Psychology, 63,* 221–233.

Gross, J. J. (1999). Emotion regulation: Past, present, future. *Cognition and Emotion, 13,* 551–573.

Gunnar, M. R. (1998). Quality of early care and buffering of neuroendocrine stress reactions: Potential effects on the developing human brain. *Preventive Medicine, 27,* 208–211.

Gunnar, M. R. (2003). Integrating neuroscience and psychological approaches in the study of early experiences. In J. A. King, C. F. Ferris, & I. I. Lederhendler (Eds.), *Roots of mental illness in children* (pp. 238–247). New York: New York Academy of Sciences.

Gunnar, M. R., & Donzella, B. (2002). Social regulation of cortisol levels in early human development. *Psychoneuroendocrinology, 27,* 199–220.

Gunnar, M. R., & Quevedo, K. (2007). The neurobiology of stress and development. *Annual Review of Psychology, 58,* 145–173.

Halford, W. K., Lizzio, A., Wilson, K. L., & Occhipinti, S. (2007). Does working at your marriage help? Couple relationship self-regulation and satisfaction in the first 4 years of marriage. *Journal of Family Psychology, 21,* 185–194.

Hazan, C., & Zeifman, D. (1994). Sex and the psychological tether. In D. Perlman & K. Bartholomew (Eds.), *Advances in personal relationships: A research annual* (Vol. 5, pp. 151–177). London: Jessica Kingsley.

Heim, C., & Nemeroff, C. B. (1999). The impact of early adverse experiences on brain systems involved in the pathophysiology of anxiety and affective disorders. *Biological Psychiatry, 46,* 1509–1522.

Heim, C., & Nemeroff, C. B. (2001). The role of childhood trauma in the neurobiology of mood and anxiety disorders: Preclinical and clinical studies. *Biological Psychiatry, 49,* 1023–1039.

Heim, C., Newport, D. J., Mletzko, T., Miller, A. H., & Nemeroff, C. B. (2008). The link between childhood trauma and depression: Insights from HPA axis studies in humans. *Psychoneuroendocrinology, 33,* 693–710.

Helm, J. L., Sbarra, D., & Ferrer, E. (2012). Assessing cross-partner associations in physiological responses via coupled oscillator models. *Emotion, 12,* 748–762. doi:10.1037/a0025036.

Hertsgaard, L., Gunnar, M. R., Erickson, M. F., & Nachmias, M. (1995). Adrenocortical responses to the strange situation in infants with disorganized/disoriented attachment relationships. *Child Development, 66,* 1100–1106.

Hessler, D. M., & Katz, L. F. (2007). Children's emotion regulation: Self-report and physiological response to peer provocation. *Developmental Psychology, 43,* 27–38.

Hicks, A. M., & Diamond, L. M. (2008). How was your day? Couples' affect when telling and hearing daily events. *Personal Relationships, 15,* 205–228.

Hofer, M. A. (1984). Relationships as regulators: A psychobiologic perspective on bereavement. *Psychosomatic Medicine, 46,* 183–197.

Horsten, M., Ericson, M., Perski, A., Wamala, S. P., Schenck-Gustafsson, K., & Orth-Gomér, K. (1999). Psychosocial factors and heart rate variability in healthy women. *Psychosomatic Medicine, 61,* 49–57.

Hubbard, J. A., Smithmyer, C. M., Ramsden, S. R., Parker, E. H., Flanagan, K. D., Dearing, K. F., et al. (2002). Observational, physiological, and self-report measures of children's anger: Relations to reactive versus proactive aggression. *Child Development, 73,* 1101–1118.

Hubbard, J. A., Parker, E. H., Ramsden, S. R., Flanagan, K. D., Relyea, N., Dearing, K. F., et al. (2004). The relations among observational, physiological, and self-report measures of children's anger. *Social Development, 13,* 14–39.

Huffman, L. C., Bryan, Y. E., del Carmen, R., Pedersen, F. A., Doussard-Roosevelt, J. A., & Porges, S. W. (1998). Infant temperament and cardiac vagal tone: Assessments at twelve weeks of age. *Child Development, 69,* 624–635.

Kagan, J., Resnick, A., & Snidman, N. (1987). The physiology and psychology of behavioral inhibition in children. *Child Development, 58,* 1459–1473.

Katz, L. F. (2007). Domestic violence and vagal reactivity to peer provocation. *Biological Psychology, 74,* 154–164.

Kettunen, J., Ravaja, N., Naeaetaenen, P., & Keltikangas-Jaervinen, L. (2000). The relationship of respiratory sinus arrhythmia to the co activation of autonomic and facial responses during the Rorschach test. *Psychophysiology, 37,* 242–250.

Kirschbaum, C., Wust, S., Faig, H. G., & Hellhammer, D. H. (1992). Heritability of cortisol responses to human corticotropin-releasing hormone, ergometry, and psychological stress in humans. *Journal of Clinical Endocrinology and Metabolism, 75,* 1526–1530.

Kirschbaum, C., Prussner, J. C., Stone, A. A., Federenko, I., Gaab, J., Lintz, D., et al. (1995). Persistent high cortisol responses to repeated psychological stress in a subpopulation of healthy men. *Psychosomatic Medicine, 57,* 468–474.

Kobak, R. R., Cole, H. E., Ferenz-Gillies, R., Fleming, W. S., & Gamble, W. (1993). Attachment and emotion regulation during mother-teen problem solving: A control theory analysis. *Child Development, 64,* 231–245.

Koole, S. L. (2009). The psychology of emotion regulation: An integrative review. *Cognition & Emotion, 23,* 4–41.

Laurent, H., & Powers, S. (2007). Emotion regulation in emerging adult couples: Temperament, attachment, and HPA response to conflict. *Biological Psychology, 76,* 61–71.

Lewis, M. D., Lamm, C., Segalowitz, S. J., Stieben, J., & Zelazo, P. D. (2006). Neurophysiological correlates of emotion regulation in children and adolescents. *Journal of Cognitive Neuroscience, 18,* 430–443.

Loney, B. R., Butler, M. A., Lima, E. N., Counts, C. A., & Eckel, L. A. (2006). The relation between salivary cortisol, callous-unemotional traits, and conduct problems in an adolescent non-referred sample. *Journal of Child Psychology and Psychiatry, 47,* 30–36.

Lorber, M. F. (2004). Psychophysiology of aggression, psychopathy, and conduct problems: A meta-analysis. *Psychological Bulletin, 130,* 531–552.

Luecken, L. J. (1998). Childhood attachment and loss experiences affect adult cardiovascular and cortisol function. *Psychosomatic Medicine, 60,* 765–772.

Luecken, L. J., Rodriguez, A. P., & Appelhans, B. M. (2005). Cardiovascular stress responses in young adulthood associated with family-of origin relationship experiences. *Psychosomatic Medicine, 67,* 514–521.

Luecken, L. J., Kraft, A., Appelhans, B. M., & Enders, C. (2009). Emotional and cardiovascular sensitization to daily stress following childhood parental loss. *Developmental Psychology, 45,* 296–302.

Lupien, S., Lecours, A. R., Lussier, I., Schwartz, G., Nair, M. P., & Meaney, M. J. (1994). Basal cortisol levels and cognitive deficits in human aging. *Journal of Neuroscience, 14,* 2893–2903.

Marshall, A. D., Robinson, L. R., & Azar, S. T. (2011). Cognitive and emotional contributors to intimate partner violence perpetration following trauma. *Journal of Traumatic Stress, 24,* 586–590.

Maunder, R. G., Lancee, W. J., Nolan, R. P., Hunter, J. J., & Tannenbaum, D. W. (2006). The relationship of attachment insecurity to subjective stress and autonomic function during standardized acute stress in healthy adults. *Journal of Psychosomatic Research, 60,* 283–290.

McEwen, B. S., Angulo, J., Cameron, H., Chao, H. M., Daniels, D., Gannon, M. N., et al. (1992). Paradoxical effects of adrenal steroids on the brain: Protection versus degeneration. *Biological Psychiatry, 31,* 177–199.

McNulty, J. K., & Hellmuth, J. C. (2008). Emotion regulation and intimate partner violence in newlyweds. *Journal of Family Psychology, 22,* 794–797.

Mikulincer, M., & Florian, V. (2004). Attachment style and affect regulation: Implications for coping with stress and mental health. In M. B. Brewer & M. Hewstone (Eds.), *Applied social psychology* (pp. 28–49). Malden: Blackwell.

Mikulincer, M., & Shaver, P. R. (2008). Adult attachment and affect regulation. In J. Cassidy & P. R. Shaver (Eds.), *Handbook of attachment: Theory, research, and clinical applications* (2nd ed., pp. 503–531). New York: Guilford.

Mikulincer, M., Shaver, P. R., & Pereg, D. (2003). Attachment theory and affect regulation: The dynamics, development, and cognitive consequences of attachment-related strategies. *Motivation and Emotion, 27,* 77–102.

Miller, G. E., Chen, E., & Zhou, E. S. (2007). If it goes up, must it come down? Chronic stress and the hypothalamic-pituitary-adrenocortical axis in humans. *Psychological Bulletin, 133,* 25–45.

Miller, G. E., Chen, E., & Parker, K. J. (2011). Psychological stress in childhood and susceptibility to the chronic diseases of aging: Moving toward a model of behavioral and biological mechanisms. *Psychological Bulletin, 137,* 959–997.

Mills-Koonce, W. R., Garrett-Peters, P., Barnett, M., Granger, D. A., Blair, C., & Cox, M. J. (2011). Father contributions to cortisol responses in infancy and toddlerhood. *Developmental Psychology, 47,* 388–395.

Moore, G. A., & Calkins, S. D. (2004). Infants' vagal regulation in the still-face pradigm is related to dyadic coordination of mother-infant interaction. *Developmental Psychology, 40,* 1068–1080.

Movius, H. L., & Allen, J. J. B. (2005). Cardiac vagal tone, defensiveness, and motivational style. *Biological Psychology, 68,* 147–162.

Muraven, M., & Baumeister, R. F. (2000). Self-regulation and depletion of limited resources: Does self-control resemble a muscle? *Psychological Bulletin, 126,* 247–259.

Nachmias, M., Gunnar, M. R., Mangelsdorf, S., Parritz, R. H., & Buss, K. (1996). Behavioral inhibition and stress reactivity: The moderating role of attachment security. *Child Development, 67,* 508–522.

Neumann, S. A., Sollers, J. J., Thayer, J. F., & Waldstein, S. R. (2004). Alexithymia predicts attenuated autonomic reactivity, but prolonged recovery to anger recall in young women. *International Journal of Psychophysiology, 53,* 183–195.

Nolte, T., Guiney, J., Fonagy, P., Mayes, L. C., & Luyten, P. (2012). Interpersonal stress regulation and the development of anxiety disorders: An attachment-based developmental framework. *Frontiers in Behavioral Neuroscience, 5,* 1–21.

Ochsner, K. N., & Gross, J. J. (2007). The neural architecture of emotion regulation. In J. J. Gross (Ed.), *Handbook of emotion regulation* (pp. 87–109). New York: Guilford.

Oitzl, M. S., Champagne, D. L., van der Veen, R., & de Kloet, E. R. (2010). Brain development under stress: Hypotheses of glucocorticoid actions revisited. *Neuroscience and Biobehavioral Reviews, 34,* 853–866.

Oskis, A., Loveday, C., Hucklebridge, F., Thorn, L., & Clow, A. (2011). Anxious attachment style and salivary cortisol dysregulation in healthy female children and adolescents. *Journal of Child Psychology and Psychiatry, 52,* 111–118.

Oveis, C., Cohen, A. B., Gruber, J., Haidt, J., Keltner, D., & Shiota, M. N. (2009). Resting respiratory sinus arrhythmia is associated with tonic positive emotionality. *Emotion, 9,* 265–270.

Pieper, S., Brosschot, J. F., van der Leeden, R., & Thayer, J. F. (2007). Cardiac effects of momentary access to worry episodes and stressful events. *Psychosomatic Medicine, 69,* 901–909.

Piha, S. J., Ronnemaa, T., & Koskenvuo, M. (1994). Autonomic nervous system function in identical twins discordant for obesity. *International Journal of Obesity and Related Metabolic Disorders, 18,* 547–550.

Pope, M. K., & Smith, T. W. (1991). Cortisol excretion in high and low cynically hostile men. *Psychosomatic Medicine, 53,* 386–392.

Porges, S. W. (1991). Vagal tone: An autonomic mediator of affect. In J. Garber & K. A. Dodge (Eds.), *The development of emotion regulation and dysregulation* (pp. 111–128). New York: Cambridge University Press.

Porges, S. W. (1992). Autonomic regulation and attention. In B. A. Campbell, H. Hayne, & R. Richardson (Eds.), *Attention and information processing in infants and adults* (pp. 201–223). Hillsdale: Erlbaum. New York: Wiley.

Porges, S. W. (2001). The polyvagal theory: Phylogenetic substrates of a social nervous system. *International Journal of Psychophysiology, 42,* 123–146.

Porges, S. W. (2003). The polyvagal theory: Phylogenetic contributions to social behavior. *Physiology & Behavior, 79,* 503–513.

Porges, S. W., Doussard-Roosevelt, J. A., & Maiti, A. K. (1994). Vagal tone and the physiological regulation of emotion. In N. Fox (Ed.), The development of emotion regulation: Biological and behavioral considerations. *Monographs of the Society for Research in Child Development,* Vol. 59, (2–3, Serial no. 240), 167–186.

Porter, C. L. (2003). Coregulation in mother-infant dyads: Links to infants' cardiac vagal tone. *Psychological Reports, 92,* 307–319.

Porter, C. L., Wouden-Miller, M., Silva, S. S., & Porter, A. E. (2003). Marital harmony and conflict: Linked to infants' emotional regulation and cardiac vagal tone. *Infancy, 4,* 297–307.

Posner, M. I., & Rothbart, M. K. (2007). Research on attention networks as a model for the integration of psychological science. *Annual Review of Psychology, 58,* 1–23.

Powers, S. I., Pietromonaco, P. R., Gunlicks, M., & Sayer, A. (2006). Dating couples' attachment styles and patterns of cortisol reactivity and recovery in response to a relationship conflict. *Journal of Personality and Social Psychology, 90,* 613–628.

Propper, C., Moore, G. A., Mills-Koonce, W. R., Halpern, C. T., Hill-Soderlund, A. L., Calkins, S. D., et al. (2008). Gene-environment contributions to the development of infant vagal reactivity: The interaction of dopamine and maternal sensitivity. *Child Development, 79,* 1377–1394.

Quirin, M., Pruessner, J. C., & Kuhl, J. (2008). HPA system regulation and adult attachment anxiety: Individual differences in reactive and awakening cortisol. *Psychoneuroendocrinology, 33,* 581–590.

Raine, A., Venables, P. H., & Williams, M. (1990). Relationships between central and autonomic measures of arousal at age 15 years and criminality at age 24 years. *Archives of General Psychiatry, 47,* 1003–1007.

Reed, R. G., Randall, A. K., Post, J. H., & Butler, E. A. (2012). Partner influence and in-phase versus anti-phase physiological linkage in romantic couples. *International Journal of Psychophysiology*. doi:10.1016/j.ijpsycho.2012.08.009.

Repetti, R. L., Taylor, S. E., & Seeman, T. E. (2002). Risky families: Family social environments and the mental and physical health of offspring. *Psychological Bulletin, 128,* 330–366.

Robins, R. W., Caspi, A., & Moffitt, T. E. (2000). Two personalities, one relationship: Both partners' personality traits shape the quality of their relationship. *Journal of Personality and Social Psychology, 79,* 251–259.

Roger, D., & Najarian, B. (1998). The relationship between emotional rumination and cortisol secretion under stress. *Personality and Individual Differences, 24,* 531–538.

Rusbult, C. E., Verette, J., Whitney, G. A., Slovik, L. F., & Lipkus, I. (1991). Accommodation processes in close relationships: Theory and preliminary empirical evidence. *Journal of Personality and Social Psychology, 60,* 53–78.

Rusbult, C. E., Bissonnette, V. L., Arriaga, X. B., Cox, C. L., & Bradbury, T. N. (1998). Accommodation processes during the early years of marriage. In T. N. Bradbury (Ed.), *The developmental course of marital dysfunction* (pp. 74–113). New York: Cambridge University Press.

Sanchez, M. M., Ladd, C. O., & Plotsky, P. M. (2001). Early adverse experience as a developmental risk factor for later psychopathology: Evidence from rodent and primate models. *Development and Psychopathology, 13,* 419–449.

Sapolsky, R. M., Romero, L. M., & Munck, A. U. (2000). How do glucocorticoids influence stress responses? Integrating permissive, suppressive, stimulatory, and preparative actions. *Endocrine Reviews, 21,* 55–89.

Saul, J. P. (1990). Beat-to-beat variations of heart rate reflect modulation of cardiac autonomic outflow. *News in Psychological Science, 5,* 32–37.

Saxbe, D., & Repetti, R. L. (2010). For better or worse? Coregulation of couples' cortisol levels and mood states. *Journal of Personality and Social Psychology, 98,* 92–103.

Sbarra, D. A., & Hazan, C. (2008). Coregulation, dysregulation, self-regulation: An integrative analysis and empirical agenda for understanding adult attachment, separation, loss, and recovery. *Personality and Social Psychology Review, 12,* 141–167.

Scarpa, A., & Raine, A. (1997). Psychophysiology of anger and violent behavior. *Psychiatric Clinics of North America, 20,* 375–394.

Schiefelbein, V. L., & Susman, E. J. (2006). Cortisol levels and longitudinal cortisol change as predictors of anxiety in adolescents. *Journal of Early Adolescence, 26,* 397–413.

Schoebi, D. (2008). The coregulation of daily affect in marital relationships. *Journal of Family Psychology, 22,* 595–604.

Schore, A. N. (1996). Effects of a secure attachment relationship on right brain development, affect regulation, and infant mental health. *Infant Mental Health Journal, 22,* 269–276.

Segerstrom, S. C., & Nes, L. S. (2007). Heart rate variability reflects self-regulatory strength, effort, and fatigue. *Psychological Science, 18,* 275–281.

Semin, G. R., & Cacioppo, J. T. (2008). Grounding social cognition: Synchronization, coordination, and co-regulation. In G. R. Semin & E. R. Smith (Eds.), *Embodied grounding: Social, cognitive, affective, and neuroscientific approaches.* (pp. 119–147). New York: Cambridge University Press.

Shaver, P. R., & Mikulincer, M. (2002). Attachment-related psychodynamics. *Attachment & Human Development, 4,* 133–161.

Shaver, P. R., & Mikulincer, M. (2007). Adult attachment strategies and the regulation of emotion. In J. J. Gross (Ed.), *Handbook of emotion regulation* (pp. 446–465). New York: Guilford.

Shorey, R. C., Brasfield, H., Febres, J., & Stuart, G. L. (2011a). An examination of the association between difficulties with emotion regulation and dating violence perpetration. *Journal of Aggression, Maltreatment & Trauma, 20,* 870–885.

Shorey, R. C., Cornelius, T. L., & Idema, C. (2011b). Trait anger as a mediator of difficulties with emotion regulation and female-perpetrated psychological aggression. *Violence and Victims, 26,* 271–282.

Siegel, D. J. (2001). Toward an interpersonal neurobiology of the developing mind: Attachment relationships, "mindsight," and neural integration. *Infant Mental Health Journal, 22,* 67–94.

Silk, J. S., Steinberg, L., & Morris, A. S. (2003). Adolescents' emotion regulation in daily fife: Links to depressive symptoms and problem behavior. *Child Development, 74,* 1869–1880.

Simpson, J. A., Rholes, W. S., Minda, O. M., & Grich, J. (2002). Working models of attachment, support giving, and support seeking in a stressful situation. *Personality & Social Psychology Bulletin, 28,* 598–608.

Sloan, R. P., Shapiro, P. A., Bagiella, E., Boni, S. M., Paik, M., Bigger, J. T. Jr., et al. (1994). Effect of mental stress throughout the day on cardiac autonomic control. *Biological Psychology, 37,* 89–99.

Snidman, N. (1989). Behavioral inhibition and sympathetic influence on the cardiovascular system. In J. S. Reznick (Ed.), *Perspectives on behavioral inhibition* (pp. 51–70). Chicago: University of Chicago press.

Snieder, H., Boomsma, D. I., Van Doornen, L. J. P., & De Geus, E. J. C. (1997). Heritability of respiratory sinus arrhythmia: Dependency on task and respiration rate. *Psychophysiology, 34,* 317–328.

Spangler, G., & Grossman, K. E. (1993). Biobehavioral organization in securely and insecurely attached infants. *Child Development, 64,* 1439–1450.

Spangler, G., Schieche, M., Ilg, U., Maier, U., & Ackerman, C. (1994). Maternal sensitivity as an external organizer for biobehavioral regulation in infancy. *Developmental Psychobiology, 27,* 425–437.

Spear, J. F., Kronhaus, K. D., Moore, E. N., & Kline, R. P. (1979). The effect of brief vagal stimulation on the isolated rabbit sinus node. *Circulation Research, 44,* 75–88.

Stansbury, K., & Gunnar, M. R. (1994). Adrenocortical activity and emotion regulation. In N. Fox (Ed.), The development of emotion regulation: Biological and behavioral considerations. *Monographs of The Society for Research in Child Development*, Vol. 59, (2–3, Serial no. 240) 108–134.

Taylor, S. E., Karlamangla, A. S., Friedman, E. M., & Seeman, T. E. (2011). Early environment affects neuroendocrine regulation in adulthood. *Social Cognitive and Affective Neuroscience, 6,* 244–251.

Teicher, M. H., Andersen, S. L., Polcari, A., Anderson, C. M., Navalta, C. P., & Kim, D. M. (2003). The neurobiological consequences of early stress and childhood maltreatment. *Neuroscience and Biobehavioral Reviews, 27,* 33–44.

Thayer, J. F., & Lane, R. D. (2000). A model of neurovisceral integration in emotion regulation and dysregulation. *Journal of Affective Disorders, 61,* 201–216.

Thibaut, J. W., & Kelley, H. H. (1978). *Interpersonal relations: A theory of interdependence*. New York: Wiley.

Thompson, R. A. (1994). Emotion regulation: A theme in search of definition. In N. Fox (Ed.), The development of emotion regulation: Biological and behavioral considerations. *Monographs of the Society for Research in Child Development* Vol. 59, (2–3, Serial no. 240) pp. 225–252.

Trinke, S. J., & Bartholomew, K. (1997). Hierarchies of attachment relationships in young adulthood. *Journal of Social and Personal Relationships, 14,* 603–625.

Tronick, E. (2007). *The neurobehavioral and social-emotional development of infants and children*. New York: Norton.

Tronick, E., & Beeghly, M. (2011). Infants' meaning-making and the development of mental health problems. *American Psychologist, 66,* 107–119. doi:10.1037/a0021631.

van Bakel, H. J. A., & Riksen-Walraven, J. M. (2004). Stress reactivity in 15-month-old infants: Links with infant temperament, cognitive competence, and attachment security. *Developmental Psychobiology, 44,* 157–167.

Vella, E. J., & Friedman, B. H. (2007). Autonomic characteristics of defensive hostility: Reactivity and recovery to active and passive stressors. *International Journal of Psychophysiology, 66,* 95–101.

Vohs, K. D., Baumeister, R. F., & Ciarocco, N. J. (2005). Self-regulation and self-presentation: Regulatory resource depletion impairs impression management and effortful self-presentation depletes regulatory resources. *Journal of Personality and Social Psychology, 88,* 632–657.

Weems, C. F., Zakem, A. H., Costa, N. M., Cannon, M. F., & Watts, S. E. (2005). Physiological response and childhood anxiety: Association with symptoms of anxiety disorders and cognitive bias. *Journal of Clinical Child and Adolescent Psychology, 34,* 712–723.

Chapter 6
How Early Experiences Shape Attraction, Partner Preferences, and Attachment Dynamics

Marie E. Heffernan and R. Chris Fraley

How Early Experiences Shape Attraction, Partner Preferences, and Attachment Dynamics

One of the curious things about human relationships is that people sometimes fall in love with individuals who bear a striking resemblance to their parents—a phenomenon that has piqued the interest of psychoanalytic, evolutionary, and attachment scholars. Take Alison, for example (Perron 2009). Alison is married to a man who resembles her father in many ways. Both men are interested in politics and the stock market, and they both share the name *Mike*. They also physically resemble one another. Alison acknowledges the similarities between the two men, "I have a great relationship with my father, so I suppose I looked for a partner who shares some of his good qualities."

Why is it that people sometimes fall in love with others who resemble their caregivers?[1] In this chapter we review research from multiple disciplines that is designed to answer this question. Based on our review, we present a template-matching model that we believe can shed light on the formation and development of attachment bonds. Specifically, we discuss how early experiences can shape mate preferences. According to our model, individuals construct a mental representation of a prototypical person (a template) based on early caregiving experiences, and this mental representation is used as a standard against which potential mates are to be evaluated. We argue that, once initial attraction is established, the formation of an attachment bond is facilitated by the psychological match between early attachment figures and the new partner. We suggest that psychological transference may be a normative mechanism underlying this process. Thus, attraction and the

[1] In this chapter we will often claim that people are attracted to others who resemble their parents. Just to be clear: We mean that Person A is attracted to someone who resembles Person A's parents. We do not mean that Person A is attracted to someone (i.e., Person B) who resembles Person B's parents.

M. E. Heffernan (✉) · R. C. Fraley
University of Illinois at Urbana-Champaign, Champaign, USA
e-mail: heffern3@illinois.edu

V. Zayas, C. Hazan (eds.), *Bases of Adult Attachment*,
DOI 10.1007/978-1-4614-9622-9_6

development of an attachment bond are maximized when a potential mate matches an individual's physical and affective template.

We begin by reviewing theoretical perspectives that are designed to explain the way in which early experiences influence the traits that people find physically attractive. Next, we discuss how early experiences may impact the formation of an attachment bond in adulthood, beyond the effects of physical attraction per se. Finally, we present a template-matching model that integrates many of the theoretical ideas that have been discussed in the literature and that helps to explain how early experiences impact both mate preferences and attachment dynamics in adulthood.

We should note from the outset that although our theoretical interest is in understanding how early experiences might shape both what it is that people find attractive as adults and how those experiences might impact the development of an attachment bond, the majority of our discussion will highlight research and theory on the dynamics of physical attraction. There are two reasons for the emphasis on physical attraction. First, there is more empirical data on attraction than on attachment. Moreover, many of the interesting theoretical debates have emphasized feelings of attraction rather than attachment per se. Second, we consider physical attraction to be the first step in the development of romantic attachments. Although it is possible for people to become attached to one another in the absence of romantic interest (e.g., Diamond 2004), we assume that in many romantic relationships physical attraction often functions as a precursor to the development of attachment (e.g., Hazan and Zeifman 1994). Thus, investigating the dynamics of physical attraction may prove useful in advancing our understanding of the development of attachment relationships more generally.

Alternative Explanations for Associations Between Early Experiences and Partner Preferences

We opened with a colorful anecdote concerning Alison and Mike. Although Alison's situation is unusual, it is not necessarily outlandish. Indeed, there is a growing body of systematic, empirical research that suggests that people tend to fall in love with partners who resemble their caregivers.[2] For example, researchers have found that people who were born to older parents are more attracted to older faces than people who were born to younger parents (Heffernan and Fraley 2013; Perrett et al. 2002). In addition, researchers have demonstrated that individuals are more likely to marry and are more attracted to people of their parents' ethnicities (Heffernan and Fraley 2014; Jedlicka 1980) than to people of other ethnicities. In our own work, we found evidence that nonparental caregivers may also impact preferences.

[2] We should point out that in much of the research we review, the "caregivers" are parents, but we do not wish to restrict our discussion to parents. Other people such as nannies, grandparents, teachers, and siblings also play an important role in early social and emotional development and are potential candidates for the ideas we discuss in this chapter.

Participants who had a nanny when growing up showed a preference for faces of the nanny's ethnicity over other ethnicities, even after taking into account whether participants were the same ethnicity as their nannies (Heffernan and Fraley 2014).

Additionally, research on mate selection indicates that people are more likely to select partners who share the same hair and eye color as their parents. Little et al. (2003) assessed the hair and eye color of participants, participants' romantic partners, and participants' parents. They found that for women, paternal eye color was the best predictor of partner eye color and there were no significant predictors of partner hair color. For men, maternal eye color was the best predictor of partner eye color, and maternal hair color was the best predictor for partner hair color.

Finally, experiences with caregivers may also play a role in female preferences in partner body hair. In a study originally designed to test women's changing preferences across the menstrual cycle (Rantala et al. 2010), researchers first obtained images of men's torsos. Front-view and back-view photographs were taken of 20 shirtless men. Then, the men were given shaving cream and a razor (and a bottle of vodka, as compensation), and were asked to shave their entire torso. A second set of front-view and back-view photographs were taken. Next, 299 female participants engaged in a forced-choice task in which they were presented with two images of the same man's torso: one in which he had natural body hair, and one in which he was shaven. The women selected the image that they found most sexually attractive. Women also provided information about the hairiness of their romantic partner and father. Consistent with the hypothesis that caregivers may influence adult mate preferences, results indicated that women who had hairier fathers showed greater preference for the hairier torso photos, and were more likely to have a hairy romantic partner. Taken together, these results suggest that one's developmental experiences have the potential to influence the kinds of features that an individual considers attractive in adulthood.

Why is it the case that early experiences predict what it is that people find physically attractive as adults? There have been at least three explanations that have been discussed extensively in both the social psychological and the ethological literatures. First, there is evidence that a process similar to *sexual imprinting* occurs in humans by which adult sexual preferences are acquired during a sensitive period in childhood. During this time, an individual's social experiences subtly influence his or her expectations (or "search images") concerning desirable mates. Second, early caregiving experiences could influence later preferences through *mere exposure* or *familiarity* effects. For instance, caregiver-resembling others may seem more familiar, leading them to be evaluated more positively relative to others who do not resemble one's caregiver. Ultimately, this positivity bias lowers the threshold for what is judged as attractive or unattractive. Finally, the *optimal outbreeding* perspective combines both imprinting-like learning processes and habituation. According to this perspective, people acquire sexual preferences early in life through a learning process in which early caregiving experiences shape one's search image for a future mate. But a second process, habituation, weakens attraction to those specific individuals with whom one was raised. Next, we discuss each of these explanations in more depth.

Sexual Imprinting

Sexual imprinting is phase-sensitive learning that takes place in early life during which sexual preferences are shaped through social experience (Aronsson 2011). Konrad Lorenz (1937, 1970) pioneered research on this topic via the study of geese. He found that goslings raised by humans would imprint on humans. Moreover, once the goslings reached sexual maturity they would direct their sexual advances toward humans (rather than other geese). More recently, researchers have used cross-fostering experimental designs to study sexual imprinting in animals. In a typical cross-fostering experiment, young animals of one species are raised by adults of a different species. Using this method, researchers have found, for example, that zebra finches raised by Bengalese finches later preferred Bengalese finches as mates over zebra finches (Immelmann 1969). Similarly, sheep and goats that were cross-fostered preferred to mate with animals of their foster parents' species rather than their own species (Kendrick et al. 1998). Other researchers have shown that young animals will even imprint on artificial markings on their parents (ten Cate and Bateson 1989; Witte and Caspers 2006). For instance, ten Cate and Bateson (1989) exposed young Japanese quail to adult quail caregivers who had black dots painted on them with hair dye. When the young quail reached sexual maturity, they preferred to mate with adults who were also painted with dots rather than wild-type quail. Zookeepers' anecdotes provide additional evidence for sexual imprinting. Zoo animals often direct their sexual attention toward zookeepers (Wilson 1987) and human-raised chimpanzees direct sexual attention toward humans (Morris 1969).

In addition to the multitude of evidence for sexual imprinting in animals, a growing body of evidence has supported the possibility of an imprinting-like phenomenon in human attraction. Specifically, features that characterize people's caregivers are more likely to be considered sexually attractive in others in adulthood. Researchers have found evidence for imprinting-like effects with caregiver characteristics such as smoking habits (Aronsson et al. 2011), and maternal pregnancy and lactation (Enquist et al. 2011). Aronsson et al. (2011) assessed participants' sexual attraction to people who smoked, and also assessed the smoking habits of participants and their parents. Participants who had a parent who smoked when they were growing up were more likely to report being sexually attracted to people who smoked. Importantly, participants' own smoking habits were not associated with their sexual preference for smoking.

One of the assumptions of sexual imprinting is that a sensitive period exists in early life during which sexual imprinting occurs. There is evidence for a sensitive period for sexual imprinting in animal species, but the evidence in humans is limited. The only study to provide evidence of a sensitive period for sexual imprinting in humans of which we are aware examined the impact of maternal pregnancy and lactation on adult mate preferences (Enquist et al. 2011). Participants reported on their sexual attraction to pregnant and lactating women, and reported whether they were an older or younger sibling. Results indicated that older siblings were more likely to report sexual attraction to pregnancy and lactation than younger siblings.

The researchers reasoned that older siblings were more likely to have been exposed to maternal pregnancy and lactation in their childhood compared with younger siblings. Importantly, exposure to maternal pregnancy and lactation was only associated with adult preferences if the exposure occurred between 1.5 and 5 years of age, providing preliminary evidence that there may be a sensitive period during which caregiver characteristics and attachment experiences have the greatest impact on sexual preferences. The issue of sensitive periods remains an important one for future work on sexual imprinting.

Finally, research has suggested that the quality of the caregiver–child relationship (specifically, the father–daughter relationship) moderates the impact of early experiences on future mate preferences (Wiszewska et al. 2007). For instance, Wiszewska and colleagues recruited female participants and their fathers. The women rated target faces for attractiveness and their fathers' faces were photographed. The researchers took facial measurements of the target faces and the father faces, and used factor analytic techniques to derive factor scores for different facial regions. These factor scores were then used to correlate each woman's highest rated target face with her father's facial features. The women also reported on their relationships with their fathers during early childhood. Women who rated their relationship with their father as more positive showed a correlation between their father's central facial characteristics and the facial characteristics of their most highly rated target face. Women who reported less positivity in their relationships with their father did not show a correlation between father face and most highly rated target face. The authors reasoned that the central region of the face may be particularly important either because women paid most attention to this area or because these areas of the face are the least prone to change over time, due to weight gain or loss, for example. Although the quality of the father–daughter relationship was assessed retrospectively, these results suggest the possibility that the quality of the caregiver relationship may moderate the effects of sexual imprinting, such that a positive relationship with a caregiver increases one's attraction to caregiver-resembling others, whereas a negative relationship with a caregiver decreases one's attraction to caregiver-resembling others. However, the results of Wiszewska et al. cannot rule out two possible alternative explanations: first, that women who had good relationships with their fathers inherited the same preferences as their mother to a greater degree; and second, that women who had good relationships with their fathers were more physically similar to their fathers and rated the target photographs based on self-similarity. We will discuss these two alternative explanations shortly.

In summary, the sexual imprinting hypothesis suggests that people acquire sexual preferences during a sensitive period in early life when they learn the characteristics of their caregivers. A number of research studies support this hypothesis. However, the issue of sensitive periods, a critical component of this hypothesis, remains largely untested. Only one study has examined this issue in humans (Enquist et al. 2011). More research is needed to determine if the acquisition of sexual preferences occurs during a sensitive period, and if so, to determine the onsets and offsets of these periods across people. Next, we briefly present two alternative explanations that have been offered for the imprinting-like effects mentioned above, namely inherited preferences and phenotypic matching.

Inherited Preferences Inherited preferences is the idea that one may inherit mate preferences from one's parents, resulting in attraction to people who resemble one's parents. For instance if a young man's father had a preference for and married a green-eyed woman (the young man's mother), the young man may inherit this preference from his father and end up partnering with a green-eyed woman who resembles his mother in eye color, not because his mother helped set his search image for a future mate, but because his preferences were passed down genetically from his father.

This particular explanation is difficult to test because people tend to share genes with the people with whom they were raised. However, by studying natural variation in biological relatedness, it is possible to partly tease apart the role of potential learning processes (e.g., sexual imprinting) from inherited preferences. Studies of twins and their spouses have offered conflicting support of inherited preferences. Lykken and Tellegen (1993) examined 901 twin pairs and 1052 of their spouses and assessed the degree to which spouses of twins were similar to one another in personality, attitudes, and interests. If mate preferences were inherited, the spouses of monozygotic (MZ) twins (who share 100 % of their DNA) would be expected to be more similar than spouses of dizygotic (DZ) twins (who share only 50 % of their DNA). However, the authors found that the spouses of MZ twins were no more similar than the spouses of DZ twins, and only slightly more similar than randomly paired same-sex strangers. This suggests that whatever criteria people use when selecting a spouse, it was not more similar for MZ twins than DZ twins. Additionally, the authors surveyed 547 twin pairs about their cotwin's choices in areas such as clothing and vacation activities, and importantly, about their cotwin's choice of spouse. They found that MZ twins reported more positivity about their cotwin's choice of clothing and vacation than DZ twins. However, MZ twins did not approve of their cotwin's choice of spouse more than DZ twins. Finally, Lykken and Tellegen surveyed the spouses of twins about their feelings regarding their twin-in-law. The wives of MZ twins reported no special attraction to their husband's cotwin. The husbands of MZ twins were more likely to report that they found their wives' cotwin attractive than unattractive, but 25 % reported that they disliked their wives' cotwin. For spouses of DZ twins, both sexes reported more negative than positive attitudes toward their spouse's cotwin. If spouses' preferences were determined genetically, their attitudes toward their twin-in-law would be expected to be positively biased, rather than overwhelmingly negative.

However, in another twin study, researchers found greater similarity between the spouses of MZ twins than between the spouses of DZ twins. Rushton and Bons (2005) surveyed approximately 300 twin pairs, their spouses, and the twins' same-sex best friends on personality variables, social attitudes, and physical characteristics. Across these various attributes, they found that spouses of MZ twins were more similar to each other than spouses of DZ twins ($r=0.23$ vs. $r=0.14$), and friends of MZ twins were more similar to each other than friends of DZ twins ($r=0.22$ vs.

$r=0.18$). Correlational and model-fitting techniques suggested that 10–30 % of the variance in partner choice was due to genetic factors. It is worth noting that Rushton and Bons (2005) used a smaller sample size and item pool that Lykken and Tellegen (Study 1, 1993), which could, in part, explain the differences in their results.

The evidence for inherited preferences is mixed, but even the evidence in support of this alternative hypothesis suggests that other factors account for the majority of the variance in partner choice.

Self-Referential Phenotype Matching Another alternative explanation that has been offered for the imprinting-like effects mentioned in this section is self-referential phenotype matching. This is the idea that people are attracted to others who resemble the self. According to the self-referential phenotype matching explanation, people are attracted to and select mates based on how similar potential mates are to the self, rather than on similarity to a caregiver. For example, a redhead may prefer to date other redheads on the basis of phenotypic similarity. Indeed, a recently launched internet dating site, findyourfacemate.com, is premised on the idea that people are particularly attracted to others who resemble themselves.

A great deal of work in the animal literature has attempted to distinguish between self-referential phenotype matching and sexual imprinting. Research on a variety of species (e.g., finches: Immelmann 1969; sheep and goats: Kendrick et al. 1998) has suggested that when the young animals reach sexual maturity, they prefer to mate with animals of their foster parents' species rather than their own species, supporting a sexual imprinting hypothesis rather than a self-referential phenotypic matching hypothesis. Cross-fostering designs not only rule out the phenotypic matching explanation, but also help to rule out the inherited preferences explanation because the young animals are raised by adults with whom they share no genetic material, so their preference for the foster parents' species cannot be inherited. As one might expect, distinguishing between these alternative explanations in human studies is more difficult.

One way to address these alternative explanations in humans is to use adoptive samples. In adoptive samples, children do not share any genetic variance with their adoptive parents, so the inherited preferences account is not a potential explanation. Furthermore, adoptive studies are able to tease apart the effects of self-referential phenotype matching and imprinting-like effects because researchers can determine if a participant's romantic partner more closely resembles (1) the participant, supporting a self-referential phenotype matching hypothesis; or (2) the participant's adoptive parent, supporting an imprinting-like explanation.

Bereczkei et al. (2004) used this logic in a study of facial similarity among adopted women, their husbands, and the women's adoptive parents. First, the researchers collected photographs of adopted women, their husbands, and the women's adoptive parents when the parents were young (e.g., when their adopted children were growing up). Then the researchers had three separate samples of undergraduates provide facial similarity ratings. In the first study, participants were presented with tables of five photos. Each table contained one photo of a woman's adoptive father, her husband, and three other similar aged men. Participants ranked the photos of the woman's husband and the three other men on the basis of similarity to the adoptive father (participants did not know which of these photos was the woman's true husband). In a second study, participants were shown a picture of a woman's adoptive mother, the adopted woman's husband, and three similar aged men. Participants ranked the photos of the woman's husband and the three other men on the basis of similarity to the adoptive mother. And in a third study, participants were shown a photo of an adopted woman, her husband, and three other similar aged men. Again, participants ranked the woman's husband and three other men based on similarity to the adopted woman. The results of all three studies suggested that participants were more accurate in matching husbands with their wives' adoptive fathers than with the wives themselves, or with the adoptive mothers. This suggests that women's husbands more closely resembled the women's adoptive fathers than the women themselves, supporting an imprinting explanation rather than a self-referential phenotype matching explanation. Additionally, there was greater similarity between women's adoptive fathers and the women's husbands for women who reported receiving more emotional support from their adoptive fathers, echoing Wiszewska et al.'s (2007) finding that the quality of the father–daughter relationship moderates the impact of early attachment experiences on later preferences.

Lykken and Tellegen (1993) noted that although spouses tend to be similar on many variables, the model of selecting a partner based on self-similarity has not been shown to account for actual partner choice from a pool of candidates. They suggest that the observed correlations between spouses could be observed if people simply avoided partnering with 50 % of the population who are least similar to the self.

In our own research (Heffernan and Fraley 2014), we found that participants who had a nanny when growing up rated faces of the nanny's ethnicity as more attractive than faces of other ethnicities, even if the participant was not the same ethnicity as the nanny. Self-referential phenotype matching cannot account for this finding because people were more attracted to the nanny's ethnicity than other races, including their own ethnicity.

Nonetheless, there is some support for self-referential phenotype matching. DeBruine (2002) showed participants photographs of strangers with whom they would be playing a trust game. Using digital morphing techniques, strangers' faces were morphed with participant's own face, or with the face of an unknown person. Participants trusted strangers whose faces had been morphed with the participant's face more than strangers whose faces had been morphed with an unknown person's face. This finding appears compatible with self-referential phenotype matching: people trusted faces that looked more like the self. In summary, there is mixed evidence regarding self-referential phenotype matching. Bereczkei and colleagues' son-in-law study (Bereczkei et al. 2004) provides preliminary evidence against the self-referential phenotype matching hypothesis and instead supports the hypothesis of a sexual imprinting-like process in the acquisition of mate preferences. However, other research has shown that people trust self-resembling others more than non-self-resembling others.

Mere Exposure or Familiarity

In addition to sexual imprinting, another mechanism that may explain the association between early attachment experiences and adult mate preferences is mere exposure or familiarity effects (Zajonc 1968). Social psychological research has established that people prefer familiar objects over less familiar objects (Kunst-Williams and Zajonc 1980). Thus, it is possible that people are attracted to individuals who resemble their caregivers because individuals who share features with one's caregiver may seem familiar and safe.

Indeed, the mere exposure effect has been demonstrated in the realm of interpersonal attraction. Moreland and Beach (1992) manipulated students' exposure to some of their classmates and found that greater exposure resulted in greater attraction. Specifically, students were more likely to be attracted to confederate "students" who had attended their class 15 times than confederates who had only attended their class 5 times.

One reason that familiarity might lead to greater liking and attraction is that familiar stimuli are easier to process, and ease of processing may be misattributed to liking. This phenomenon is called perceptual fluency (Bornstein and D'Agostino 1994). In a series of three studies, Reber et al. (1998) found that increased fluency resulted in greater liking. For instance, participants preferred drawings that were preceded by a processing-facilitating prime over those that were preceded by processing-inhibiting prime. Also, participants preferred images of shapes that had greater contrast with the background. These shapes were more perceptually fluent than those with less contrast. Finally, participants rated shapes more positively if they had been exposed to the shapes for longer because longer exposure increased perceptual fluency.

It stands to reason that perceptual fluency might contribute to observed similarities between individual's romantic partners and the people with whom the individuals were raised. Caregiver-resembling others may be easier to process and this enhanced perceptual fluency might be attributed to liking or attraction. Thus, the attraction generated by a more fluent individual may pave the way to relationship initiation and perhaps eventually the development of an attachment bond with the individual.

Although the mere exposure effect has amassed a considerable amount of support in psychological research, this explanation has not yet been tested specifically in the realm of early experiences and their influence on adult attraction and mate preferences. Additionally, this explanation leads to several other predictions that warrant examination. First, if exposure to caregivers influences mate preferences, it might be expected that the primary caregiver, the caregiver to whom one has the greatest exposure, might have a greater influence on adult mate preferences. Second, it is also possible that other figures such as teachers and nannies would influence mate preferences through mere exposure. Indeed, we have found that people are more attracted to faces of their nanny's race than other races (Heffernan and

Fraley 2014). Ultimately, the mere exposure explanation requires further testing in the realm of early experiences and adult mate preferences.

Optimal Outbreeding

Bateson's optimal outbreeding model (1983) provides a third explanation for why people may be attracted to the characteristics of individuals with whom they were raised, but not the specific individuals themselves. This model suggests that a learning process leads people to find attractive the features of the individuals with whom they were surrounded in early life. A second process, habituation, weakens the desire to mate with those specific individuals (sometimes referred to as "incest avoidance"; e.g., Lieberman and Symons 1998). In support of this model, Bateson (1980) has demonstrated that quail are more likely to mate with first cousins than siblings or unrelated individuals. Similarly, humans may be attracted to their parents' hair and eye coloring in others, but regard the parent as an inappropriate mate (Little et al. 2003). This dual process model suggests that, upon encountering a potential mate, if the mate is too similar to one's caregivers, habituation will dominate and the potential mate will not be sexually appealing. On the other hand, if the potential mate is drastically different from one's caregivers, he or she will not map onto one's search image, and again may not be sexually appealing. Sexual attraction would be greatest, therefore, when a newly encountered individual embodies an optimal level of similarity to one's caregivers and novelty.

Fraley and Marks (2010) have found support for the optimal outbreeding perspective in studies in which they subtly activate mental representations of people's caregivers and kin. In one study, the researchers used photographs of participants' opposite sex parent to subliminally prime mental representations of the parent. Participants exhibited increased sexual attraction to others after nonconscious activation of their opposite-sex parent mental representations compared with participants who had been primed with images of someone else's parent (yoked control). In another experiment, the researchers used computerized facial morphing techniques to subtly infuse an image of the participant with unfamiliar faces. Participants rated faces as more sexually attractive if they were morphed with an image of the self (a digital proxy for kin), and found the faces more attractive as the degree of morphing increased. In a third study, when participants were told that the images they were rating had been morphed with their own faces, participants found the faces less sexually attractive. From an optimal outbreeding perspective, these findings suggest that people find others more sexually attractive if they resemble or activate mental representations of kin, but if this resemblance is too obvious or is known, sexual attraction decreases dramatically. Attraction appears to be maximized when a potential partner is partly familiar and partly novel.

The optimal outbreeding model accounts for how people may develop mate preferences based on caregiver characteristics, and how these mate preferences function to increase people's attraction caregiver-similar (but not too similar) others. It allows for other mechanisms such as sexual imprinting and mere exposure to play a role in the development of mate preferences. It also adds the idea of habituation to explain why people are not attracted to the individuals with whom they were raised. It would be useful for future research to examine habituation more closely. For instance, how much caregiver resemblance is too much? How similar to one's caregivers can an unknown target look, before they become unappealing?

Summary

Sexual imprinting, mere exposure, and optimal outbreeding provide potential mechanisms for the associations between early caregiving experiences and adult mate preferences that have been observed in numerous empirical studies. Next, we move beyond attraction and discuss how early experiences may play a more direct role in the formation of an attachment in adulthood.

Early Experiences and Attachment Formation

As we have discussed, early experiences are associated with attraction and mate preferences, which may potentiate the development of a relationship and an attachment bond. Early experiences may also be more directly associated with attachment formation. In this section we first review briefly some of the work that suggests that people prefer others who match their preexisting working models of attachment. Then we discuss how psychological transference may be a mechanism through which early experiences influence attachment formation. For instance, when people encounter strangers who resemble a significant other (e.g., caregivers), mental representations of caregivers may become activated and lead individuals to interact with and relate to strangers in ways that resemble preexisting relationships. In this way, it is possible that individuals transfer mental representations concerning their caregivers to potential romantic partners. Moreover, forming an attachment with a new romantic partner may be facilitated if that partner activates mental representations of already established attachment figures.

A great deal of research has suggested that people prefer partners with an attachment style similar to their own (see Holmes and Johnson 2009 for a review). Because one's own attachment models are based, in part, on early experiences with caregivers, this suggests that one may prefer others whose attachment models correspond with one's models of early caregivers. In a series of correlational and experimental studies, Frazier et al. (1996) found that individuals tended to be in relationships with partners who matched their attachment style (e.g., anxious individuals tended to be paired with anxious partners) and people were more attracted to hypothetical partners who had similar attachment styles to their own. Importantly, these researchers also found that participants' ratings of their mothers' caregiving styles were associated with attachment preferences. Specifically, people who rated their mother as cold or ambivalent were less attracted to secure potential partners. Similarly, Collins and Read (1990) found that men who rated their mothers as cold and inconsistent were more likely to be dating women who were high in attachment-related anxiety. Taken together, these findings suggest that people are more romantically interested in others who have working models of attachment that are similar to one's own, and moreover, that this romantic interest leads people to be more likely to enter into relationships with others who share similar working models of attachment.

How might one's own attachment models come into play in the context attraction and attachment formation? The availability and accessibility of attachment models is a possible mechanism. For instance, Baldwin et al. (1996) asked participants to nominate individuals with whom they had a secure, avoidant, or anxious-ambivalent attachment relationship. Several days later, participants were primed with one of these relationships and subsequently asked to rate their interest in a potential dating partner. Participants generally reported greater interest in dating secure potential partners, but they also reported greater romantic interest in potential partners who possessed the attachment style with which they had just been primed. The authors suggested that the similarity of the targets to accessible working models facilitated romantic interest.

More broadly, we suggest that *psychological transference* may be one mechanism through which one's own attachment models, which are shaped, in part, by early caregivers, influence attraction to potential partners and attachment formation with a new partner. Transference is a process by which a person's mental representations concerning a significant other are activated and applied to another person (typically a stranger in experimental research; Andersen and Glassman 1996; Chen and Andersen 1999). Kraus and Chen (2010) have found that people transfer evaluations and inferences about a significant other to a stranger if the stranger physically resembles the significant other. Participants were shown a facial photograph of a stranger with whom they expected to have an interaction. In an earlier study session, participants rated 200 faces based on similarity to the participant's significant other (e.g., a person the participant selected whom they knew well, liked, and considered to be important). In the experimental condition, the stranger in the photograph resembled the participant's significant other. In a yoked control condition, the stranger resembled someone else's significant other. Participants rated the stranger more positively if the face resembled their own significant other compared with yoked participants. Additionally, participants presented with the significant-other resembling face inferred that the stranger was more likely to possess attributes consistent with the significant other. The authors suggested that transference was responsible for this pattern of results.

Günaydin et al. (2012) objectively manipulated facial resemblance using digital techniques to morph photographs of strangers with a photograph of a participant's romantic partner, and with a yoked participant's partner. People rated partner-resembling races more favorably than faces that did not resemble their partner. However, this effect was qualified by participant sex. Women, but not men, judged partner-resembling faces more favorably. Additionally, for both men and women, greater relationship satisfaction was associated with more positive evaluations of the partner-resembling faces. The authors reasoned that evaluative transference triggered by partner-resembling faces was due to activation of partner-specific representations, rather than due to familiarity.

Brumbaugh and Fraley (2007) examined transference of both romantic partner representations and parental representations to novel targets. Participants rated how they thought they would feel in a friendship with an unknown target who had been idiographically described as similar to participants' romantic partners, parents, or controls. Their results suggested that participants applied their representations of partners only when they encountered the partner-similar target, whereas representations of parents were applied more generally (e.g., to both partner-similar and parent-similar targets). The authors suggested that the more general application of parental representations might be due to their developmental origins. If parental representations serve as the foundation upon which representations of new people are built (Bowlby 1969), then parental representations may be applied more broadly in a variety of contexts, rather than in a selective fashion. These researchers also found that people were more interested in dating unknown targets who descriptively resembled their former romantic partner than targets who did not resemble their former romantic partner (Brumbaugh and Fraley 2006). Participants provided a list of traits describing their former partners and the researchers used these lists to create descriptions of unknown targets (potential dating partners). Later, participants returned and rated unknown targets who idiographically resembled their former partner or another participant's former partner (yoked control). Participants transferred attachment representations of their former partners to the descriptively similar targets, and they expressed greater interest in dating these targets relative to control targets. Even participants who were relatively insecure in their past relationships were more interested in dating the target that was descriptively similar to their former partner, despite feeling more insecure with this target.

Up to this point we have highlighted research on people's attachment preferences suggesting that people may feel more romantically interested in partners who match their preexisting attachment representations, and we have explained how a social-cognitive process such as transference may account for these findings. However, there is also an emerging body of prospective research that indicates that early caregiving experiences can shape attachment-related dynamics in established romantic relationships. For example, Roisman et al. (2005) found that people who were securely attached to their mother in infancy were more likely to have a secure relationship with their romantic partner, as assessed with the Current Relationship Interview (CRI: Crowell and Owens 1996) at age 20. In addition, Dinero et al. (2008) found that adolescents who had more positive interactions with their parents at ages 15 and 16 were more likely to have positive interactions with their romantic partners at age 25, and were more likely to exhibit secure attachment, as assessed with self-report instruments, with their romantic partners at age 25. Finally, Zayas et al. (2011) found similar results using observers' coding of mothers' behavior toward their toddler-aged children in a semi-structured free play situation and self-reports of attachment when the children reached adulthood. Specifically, self-reports of secure attachment to romantic partners at age 22 were associated with having a mother who provided supportive care when the individual was 18 months old.

In summary, there is some support for the idea that individuals are more romantically interested in others who share the same working models of attachment. Additionally, research suggests that people are more attracted to and more frequently date partners who share psychological (e.g., attachment) similarities to their parents. It stands to reason, then, that if a potential partner is psychologically similar to one's caregiver, this will facilitate attachment to that partner. We suggest that these effects may come about through a transference process. Fraley and Brumbaugh (2007) found that romantic partner representations were transferred to partner-similar unknown targets, but parental representations might be applied more broadly. Thus, parental representations appear to have a persistent influence on person perception. Finally, longitudinal research supports the idea that attachment experiences with early caregivers influence not only attachment preferences, but also people's attachment within established romantic relationships.

Closing Thoughts and Future Directions for Research

It is well established that individuals often end up attracted to and bonded with others who are physically and behaviorally similar to their caregivers. We have reviewed several explanations for this phenomenon. First, the sexual imprinting hypothesis suggests that people acquire sexual preferences through social experiences during a sensitive period in early life. Second, a mere exposure or familiarity explanation suggests that people may develop a preference for individuals who resemble their caregivers because the characteristics of those individuals are familiar and may be processed more fluently. Third, the optimal outbreeding explanation suggests that a learning process results in sexual attraction to the characteristics of those people with whom one was raised and a second process, habituation, reduces attraction to the specific individuals with whom one was raised. These mechanisms may result in increased attraction to caregiver-similar others, thus setting the stage for a romantic relationship and potentially an attachment bond to develop.

Furthermore, research suggests that early experiences may also play a role in attachment formation beyond the effects of physical attraction per se. Psychological transference may result in a preference for others who are similar to one's preexisting working models of attachment, which are, in part, based on caregiver representations developed in early life. Thus, it may be easier to develop an attachment bond with an individual who is more similar than dissimilar to one's caregivers. Finally, longitudinal research suggests that attachment security with early caregivers predicts attachment security with partners in established romantic relationships in adulthood.

Template Matching Hypothesis

One of the arguments we have been developing in recent years is that a template-matching process underlies the way in which people evaluate potential mates—an idea that brings together themes from both the sexual imprinting and attachment literatures. Specifically, on the basis of early caregiving experiences, individuals construct a mental representation of a prototypical person and this representation functions in part as a standard or template against which potential mates are evaluated. When a potential mate physically resembles the template, attraction is maximized. To the extent to which the target deviates from the template, attraction is diminished.

These dynamics can be represented with a rudimentary equation:

$$\text{Attraction} = C + B_1 \times U + B_2 \times (T - A)^2 + E$$

In this example we are considering attraction to targets that vary in a specific attribute—age. The basic dynamics of the equation, however, generalize to a variety of traits. The first term, *C*, is simply a constant that can potentially vary from one person to the next. *U* represents the normative effects of variation in the age of the targets in question, weighted by a coefficient, B_1. In this example, $B_1$is likely to be negative because, on average, men tend to find younger women more appealing than older women (Kenrick and Keefe 1992). Paired with this normative effect is an idiosyncratic one represented by $(T-A)^2$ and weighted by B_2. This component suggests that attraction will be maximized when a target's age (A) resembles the person's template (T) for the attribute in question (e.g., age). *E* is an error term.

Figure 6.1 illustrates some of the dynamics of this model with respect to the attribute of age. The person represented in the upper panel has a *T* value of 20 (i.e., his template represents a person who is approximately 20 years of age). Notice that for the person described in the upper panel, he is generally attracted to targets who are younger instead of targets who are older (i.e., $B_1 \times U$ represents a negative linear slope for target age and attraction). But, despite this tendency, his attraction to targets is maximized when the targets are 20 years old. As targets exceed this age, his attraction to them begins to diminish.

In contrast, the person depicted in the lower panel has a *T* value of 30. Again, although this person is generally more attracted to younger targets than older ones due to the $B_1 \times U$ term, his attraction to targets is maximized when the targets are 30 years old.

Although this model is relatively simple, we believe that it can account for many of the empirical findings we have reviewed. For example, it is capable of explaining why it is that people born to older parents may be more attracted to older individuals than people born to younger parents (e.g., Perrett et al. 2002; Heffernan and Fraley 2013). The model is compatible with the sexual imprinting hypothesis, the mere exposure effect, and the learning process proposed in the optimal outbreeding perspective because each of these mechanisms could contribute to the formation of one's template. Moreover, the model is relatively robust to the kinds of alternative explanations that have been offered for imprinting-like effects. If the template is

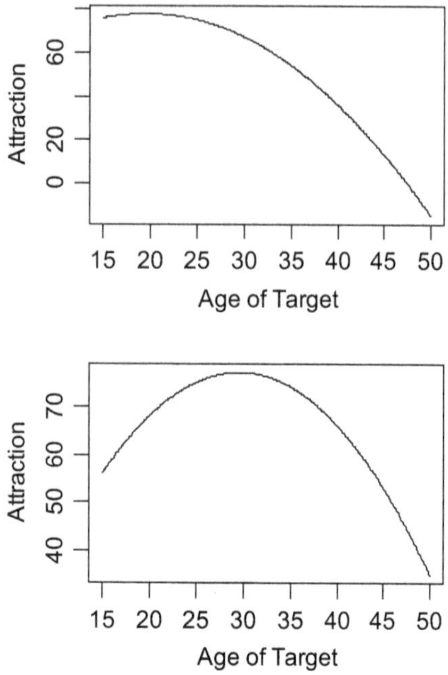

Fig. 6.1 A model for early experiences, attraction, and attachment. The first panel illustrates predicted attraction values for a person with a template value of 20. The model (Attraction $=80-0.1\times$(Age of Target)$-0.1\times$(20$-$[Age of Target])^2) implies that the person would find younger people more attractive than older individuals, but attraction is maximized for targets who are 20 years of age. The second panel illustrates the predicted attraction values for a person with template value of 30. The model (Attraction $=80-0.1\times$(Age of Target)$-0.1\times$(30$-$[Age of Target])^2) implies that attraction will be maximized for targets who are 30 years of age. The model also implies that, on average, younger targets will be rated more favorably than older targets

based, in part, on the physical characteristics of other individuals in the caregiving environment, that suggests that mate preferences are not necessarily inherited, nor are they necessarily the result of self-similarity.

The template-matching model can also explain incest avoidance. Recall that the optimal outbreeding perspective suggests that one reason why individuals may not mate with others who are too similar to their relatives is that a habituation process has the effect of making "too similar" others less appealing than they would be otherwise. We do not wish to suggest that habituation is not operative. But we think the template-matching approach can explain some of the incest avoidance data without necessarily requiring habituation. In this respect, it may offer a more parsimonious account of certain findings.

To elaborate, we find it helpful to consider the way templates or prototypes are constructed in the context of connectionist models (see Fraley 2007, for a discussion of connectionist models in the context of attachment dynamics). In connectionist models, networks are exposed to repeated exemplars over a period of trials. When those networks are then tested for their "memory" of the exemplars, they typically perform well. However, when they are tested with a prototype—a statistical average of all the exemplars that had been previously presented—neural networks produce a stronger response than normal. Importantly, this is the case even when the network was never exposed to the prototype per se.

As an analogy, consider exam performance in the classroom. If students were to take 10 exams or quizzes over the course of a semester, psychometric theory and instructor intuition would suggest that the best predictor of a student's 11th exam grade would be the average of all his or her previous exam scores. We would not necessarily bet that his or her grade on exam 1 or exam 10 would be a better predictor than the *average* of his or her performance to date. Similarly, in a template-matching model, we would not necessarily expect attraction to be maximized when a target matches perfectly someone from an individual's early caregiving environment. (In other words, the model *does not* predict that individuals will find their parents or siblings the most attractive targets.) What the model predicts is that some kind of composite of all the features represented in the early caregiving environment will produce the maximum response. Therefore, the model predicts that an individual's sibling, for example, who is just one of the exemplars from the individual's early caregiving experiences, would be less attractive than someone who better represents the composite of people from the individual's developmental history. This also suggests that a target who somewhat resembles an individual's early caregivers should be evaluated as more attractive than they would be evaluated by other people, but they will not necessarily be evaluated as more attractive than every other possible target.

Thus far, we have explained how the template-matching model accounts for how early caregiving experience may shape adult mate preferences. Furthermore, we believe the template-matching model can also provide a way of understanding the dynamics of attachment. Indeed, attachment theorists commonly use the language of template-matching to describe attachment dynamics. For example, it is often assumed that people will be more likely to form an emotional attachment to someone in adulthood if that individual resembles the psychological qualities of their primary caregivers. In fact, John Bowlby (1973) noted that people often form attachment bonds with others who maximize the similarity between current attachment experiences and preexisting models of attachment.

The template-matching model produces potentially counterintuitive predictions in this context. For example, if someone were raised in an environment in which his or her caregivers were cold, distant, or rejecting, the individual should develop insecure working models of attachment. However, because the individual has also developed the expectation that close others are likely to be unsupportive and rejecting, he or she should be most likely to feel comfortable with a partner who is also unsupportive and rejecting because that partner confirms the working models that the individual already has (Swann et al. 1992).

To date, most research on attachment has focused on what might be best described as "main effects" of parental models on relationship functioning rather than the match or mismatch between working models and partner behavior. This work suggests that, in general, people are more likely to feel comfortable opening up to and depending on others who are warm, responsive, and supportive. Indeed, in the realm of attraction research, Latty-Mann and Davis (1996) have referred to this as the "attachment-security hypothesis." The implication of this kind of work is that people should not find rejecting or cold partners as desirable or likely to facilitate emotional bonding. Instead, people prioritize feeling security in their relationships, and thus secure partners are more desired over insecure partners, regardless of one's own attachment models and expectations.

One interesting finding that is difficult to explain in the absence of the template-matching hypothesis comes from the transference study by Brumbaugh and Fraley (2006). Although people who were relatively insecure in their past relationship were also more likely to feel insecure with a potential partner who had some attributes of their former partner relative to potential partners who had attributes of another participant's former partner (i.e., a transference effect), they also reported a greater interest in dating that particular individual relative to the yoked control. In other words, despite the fact that the familiar other made them feel more insecure, they were more interested in pursuing an intimate relationship with that person.

In short, potential dating partners who resembled people's preexisting templates were the ones who roused the most romantic interest. The template-matching model predicts that the development of an attachment relationship will be maximized when the partner in question matches the individual's template for an ideal partner—one that we think is shaped over the course of a person's development. When a person's prototype suggests that others are warm, responsive, and caring, the person will be most likely to develop an attachment to others who exhibit those qualities. When a person's prototype suggests that others are cold, unresponsive, and unsupportive, the person will be most likely to develop an attachment to others who exhibit those qualities. However, in this particular case, that tendency exists in opposition to a "main effect" that leads supportive partners to be more desirable than unsupportive ones (e.g., Latty-Mann and Davis 1996), so the effect may only be observable in carefully controlled conditions.

Future Directions, Open Questions, and Conclusions

Sensitive Periods The sexual imprinting hypothesis suggests that mate preferences are acquired during a sensitive period. However, only one research study of which we are aware has examined this issue carefully in humans (Aronsson et al. 2011). Determining whether humans do indeed have a sensitive period for the acquisition of mate preferences, and if so, when the sensitive period occurs, is critical for the sexual imprinting hypothesis. For instance, it is possible that humans are more sensitive to caregiver characteristics in early childhood, and are less sensitive to caregiver characteristics that appear only in later adolescence and adulthood. This leads to the expectation that if one's mother was a brunette for most of one's early life, but began to dye her hair blonde in one's adult life, the person's mate preferences would be more closely associated with the mother's brunette, rather than blonde hair. Alternatively, it is possible that people are sensitive to caregiver characteristics throughout childhood and early adulthood.

Aronsson and colleagues' (Aronsson et al. 2011) study provided preliminary evidence for a sensitive period for acquiring sexual preferences. Maternal pregnancy and lactation was associated with preferences only if people had been exposed to maternal pregnancy between the ages of 1.5–5 years. Exposure after that developmental window was not associated with mate preferences. Determining whether there is a sensitive period for acquiring mate preferences is an important direction for future research and will help to understand whether something similar to sexual imprinting occurs in humans.

Quality of Caregiver–Child Relationship as a Moderator Some research has suggested a potential moderator of the association between people's caregivers and their mate preferences. Specifically, the quality of the caregiver–child relationship may function as a moderator such that people with positive relationships with their caregivers would be more likely to end up paired with and attracted to a person who resembles their caregiver. Several studies have supported this prediction (Bereczkei et al. 2004; Wiszewska et al. 2007). For example, adopted women who had a more positive relationship with their adoptive fathers chose spouses who resembled their adoptive fathers more than adopted women who had less positive relationships with their adoptive fathers (Bereczkei et al. 2004). Additionally, women who had more positive relationships with their fathers were attracted to faces that more closely resembled their fathers' face than women who had less positive relationships with their fathers (Wiszewska et al. 2007). If people have a more positive relationship with their caregivers, then encountering a stranger who resembles a caregiver may lead to increased liking and attraction. On the other hand, if people's relationship with their caregivers is more negative, encountering someone who resembles a caregiver may lead to decreased liking for and attraction to the stranger. In this case, people might be more likely to pair with others who are dissimilar to the caregiver.

We should note that this particular hypothesis, although theoretically compelling, is inconsistent with the predictions entailed by a template-matching hypothesis. Namely, a template-matching hypothesis leads to the prediction that attraction will be maximized when evaluating someone who resembles a caregiver regardless of whether one's relationship with that caregiver was positive or negative. Indeed, one of the potential benefits of the template-matching model is that it provides an explanation for why people might be attracted to individuals who possess attributes that most people would find unappealing (e.g., individuals who behave in cold or unresponsive ways). The "relationship quality moderator" hypothesis, in contrast, would suggest that the general dynamics we have reviewed in this chapter would be less relevant to explaining attraction and attachment among people with insecure relationships to their caregivers. We hope that future research will be able to clarify exactly where these two models converge and diverge in their predictions so they can be systematically evaluated.

Conclusion In closing, there are several potential explanations for why Alison is attracted to Mike, a man who is strikingly similar to Alison's father (who, perhaps incidentally, is also named Mike). Alison's mate preferences may have developed through a specialized learning process akin to sexual imprinting and through mere exposure to her caregivers. In other words, Alison may have developed a template for a future mate that was based, in part, on her father. In adulthood, her mate preferences may have been expressed through a number of mechanisms that would have made it more likely that she end up paired with Mike. For instance, because Mike resembles Alison's father, he may have been more familiar and perceptually fluent, which would increase Alison's attraction to Mike. Additionally, she may have transferred her representation of her father to Mike, making Mike a more desirable dating partner and facilitating the formation of an attachment with him. In sum, the explanatory mechanisms that we have reviewed may be partially responsible for the associations between people's early caregiving experiences and adult mate preferences, and account for why people like Alison end up falling in love with partners who resemble their parents.

References

Andersen, S. M., & Glassman, N. S. (1996). Responding to significant others when they are not there: Effects on interpersonal inference, motivation, and affect. In R. M. Sorrentino & E. T. Higgins (Eds.), *Handbook of motivation and cognition: Vol. 3. The interpersonal context* (pp. 262–321). New York: Guilford.

Aronsson, H. (2011). Sexual imprinting and fetishism: An evolutionary hypothesis. In P. R. Adriaens & A. De Block (Eds.), *Maladapting minds* (pp. 65–90). New York: Oxford University Press.

Aronsson, H., Lind, J., Ghirlanda, S., & Enquist, M. (2011). Parental influences on sexual preferences: The case of attraction to smoking. *Journal of Evolutionary Psychology, 9,* 21–41.

Baldwin, M. W., Keelan, J. P. R., Fehr, B., Enns, V., & Koh-Rangarajoo, E. (1996). Social-cognitive conceptualization of attachment working models: Availability and accessibility effects. *Journal of Personality and Social Psychology, 71*(1), 94–109. doi: http://dx.doi.org/10.1037/0022-3514.71.1.94.

Bateson, P. (1980). Optimal outbreeding and the development of sexual preferences in Japanese quail. *Zeitschrift für Tierpsychologie, 53,* 231–244.

Bateson, P. (1983). Optimal outbreeding. In P. Bateson (Ed.), *Mate choice* (pp. 257–277). Cambridge: Cambridge University Press.

Bereczkei, T., Gyuris, P., & Weisfeld, G. E. (2004). Sexual imprinting in human mate choice. *Proceedings of the Royal Society B, 271,* 1129–1134.

Bornstein, R. F., & D'Agostino, P. R. (1994). The attribution and discounting of perceptual fluency: Preliminary tests of perceptual fluency/attributional model of the mere exposure effect. *Social Cognition, 12,* 103–128.

Bowlby, J. (1969). *Attachment and loss: Vol. 1. Attachment*. New York: Basic Books.

Bowlby, J. (1973). *Attachment and loss: Vol. 2. Separation*. New York: Basic Books.

Brumbaugh, C. C., & Fraley, R. C. (2006). Transference and attachment: How do attachment patterns get carried forward from one relationship to the next? *Personality and Social Psychology Bulletin, 32,* 552–560.

Brumbaugh, C. C., & Fraley, R. C. (2007). Transference of attachment patterns: How important relationships influence feelings toward novel people. *Personal Relationships, 14,* 513–530.

Chen, S., & Andersen, S. M. (1999). Relationships from the past in the present: Significant-other representations and transference in interpersonal life. In M. P. Zanna (Ed.), *Advances in experimental social psychology* (Vol. 31, pp. 123–190). San Diego: Academic.

Collins, N. L., & Read, S. J. (1990). Adult attachment, working models, and relationship quality in dating couples. *Journal of Personality and Social Psychology, 58*(4), 644–663. doi: http://dx.doi.org/10.1037/0022-3514.58.4.644.

Crowell, J., & Owens, G. (1996). *Current relationship interview*. Unpublished manuscript, State University of New York at Stony Brook.

DeBruine, L. M. (2002). Facial resemblance enhances trust. *Proceedings of the Royal Society London B, 269,* 1307–1312.

Diamond, L. M. (2004). Emerging perspectives on distinctions between romantic love and sexual desire. *Current Directions in Psychological Science, 13,* 116–119.

Dinero, R. E., Conger, R. D., Shaver, P. R., Widaman, K. F., & Larsen-Rife, D. (2008). Influence of family of origin and adult romantic partners on romantic attachment security. *Journal of Family Psychology, 22,* 622–632.

Enquist, M., Aronsson, H., Ghirlanda, S., Jansson, L., & Jannini, E. A. (2011). Exposure to mother's pregnancy and lactation in infancy is associated with sexual attraction to pregnancy and lactation in adulthood. *Journal of Sexual Medicine, 8,* 140–147.

Fraley, R. C. (2007). A connectionist approach to the organization and continuity of working models of attachment. *Journal of Personality, 75,* 1157–1180.

Fraley, R. C., & Marks, M. J. (2010). Westermarck, Freud, and the incest taboo: Does familial resemblance activate sexual attraction? *Personality and Social Psychology Bulletin, 36,* 1202–1212.

Frazier, P. A., Byer, A. L., Fischer, A. R., Wright, D. M., & DeBord, K. A. (1996). Adult attachment style and partner choice: Correlational and experimental findings. *Personal Relationships, 3*(2), 117–136. doi: http://dx.doi.org/10.1111/j.1475-6811.1996.tb00107.x.

Günaydin, G., Zayas, V., Selcuk, E., & Hazan, C. (2012). I like you but I don't know why: Objective facial resemblance to significant others influences snap judgments. *Journal of Experimental Social Psychology, 48,* 350–353.

Hazan, C., & Zeifman, D. (1994). Sex and the psychological tether. In D. Perlman & K. Bartholomew (Eds.), *Advances in personal relationships* (pp. 151–180). London: Sage.

Heffernan, M. E., & Fraley, R. C. (2013). Do early caregiving experiences shape what people find attractive in adulthood? Evidence from a study on maternal age. *Journal of Research in Personality, 47,* 364–368.

Heffernan, M. E., & Fraley, R. C. (2014). An examination of attraction in adulthood and early life experiences with race and culture. Unpublished manuscript.

Holmes, B. M., & Johnson, K. R. (2009). Adult attachment and romantic partner preference: A review. *Journal of Social and Personal Relationships, 26,* 833–852. doi:10.1177/0265407509345653.

Immelmann, K. (1969). Über den Einfluss frühkindlicher Erfahrungen auf die geschlechtliche Objektfixierung bei Estrildiden. *Zeitschrift für Tierpsychologie, 26,* 677–691.

Jedlicka, D. (1980). A test of the psychoanalytic theory of mate selection. *The Journal of Social Psychology, 112,* 295–299.

Kendrick, K. M., Hinton, R. M., Atkins, K., Haupt, M. A., & Skinner, J. D. (1998). Mothers determine sexual preferences. *Nature, 395,* 229–230.

Kenrick, D. T., & Keefe, R. C. (1992). Age preferences in mates reflect sex-differences in reproductive strategies. *Behavioral Brain Science, 15,* 75–133.

Kraus, M. W., & Chen, S. (2010). Facial-feature resemblance elicits the transference effect. *Psychological Science, 21,* 518–522.

Kunst-Wilson, W. R., & Zajonc, R. B. (1980). Affective discrimination of stimuli that cannot be recognized. *Science, 207,* 557–558.

Latty-Mann, H., & Davis, K. E. (1996). Attachment theory and partner choice: Preference and actuality. *Journal of Social and Personal Relationships, 13,* 5–23.

Lieberman, D., & Symons, D. (1998). Sibling incest avoidance: From Westermarck to Wolf. *Quarterly Review of Biology, 73,* 463–466.

Little, A. C., Penton-Voak, I. S., Burt, D. M., & Perrett, D. I. (2003). Investigating an imprinting-like phenomenon in humans: Partners and opposite-sex parents have similar hair and eye colour. *Evolution and Human Behavior, 24,* 43–51.

Lorenz, K. Z. (1937). The companion in the bird's world. *The Auk, 54,* 245–273.

Lorenz, K. Z. (1970). *Studies in animal and human behavior* (Vol. 1). Cambridge: Harvard University Press.

Lykken, D. T., & Tellegen, A. (1993). Is human mating adventitious or the result of lawful choice? A twin study of mate selection. *Journal of Personality and Social Psychology, 65,* 56–68.

Moreland, R. L., & Beach, S. R. (1992). Exposure effects in the classroom: The development of affinity among students. *Journal of Experimental Psychology, 28,* 255–276.

Morris, D. (1969). *The human zoo*. London: Jonathan Cape.

Perrett, D. I., Penton-Voak, I. S., Little, A. C., Tiddeman, B. P., Burt, D. M., Schmidt, N., Oxley, R., & Barrett, L. (2002). Facial attractiveness judgements reflect learning of parental age characteristics. *Proceedings of the Royal Society B, 269,* 873–880.

Perron, C. (2 Feb 2009). Why you're likely to marry your parent. CNN. http://articles.cnn.com/2009-02-11/living/lw.programmed.to.marry.parents_1_share-mom-parent?_s=PM:LIVING. Accessed 28 June 2012.

Rantala, M. J., Polkki, M., & Rantala, L. M. (2010). Preference for human male body hair changes across the menstrual cycle and menopause. *Behavioral Ecology, 21,* 419–423.

Reber, R., Winkielman, W., & Schwarz, N. (1998). Effects of perceptual fluency on affective judgments. *Psychological Science, 9,* 45–48.

Roisman, G. I., Collins, W. A., Sroufe, L. A., & Egeland, B. (2005). Predictors of young adults' representations of and behavior in their current romantic relationship: Prospective tests of the prototype hypothesis. *Attachment and Human Development, 7,* 105–121. doi:10.1080/14616730500134928.

Rushton, J. P., & Bons, T. A. (2005). Mate choice and friendship in twins. *Psychological Science, 16,* 555–559.

Swann, W. B., Hixon, J. G., & de la Ronde, C. (1992). Embracing the bitter "truth": Negative self-concepts and marital commitment. *Psychological Science, 3*(2), 118–121. doi: http://dx.doi.org/10.1111/j.1467-9280.1992.tb00010.x.

ten Cate, C., & Bateson, P. (1989). Sexual imprinting and a preference for 'supernormal' partners in Japanese quail. *Animal Behavior, 38,* 356–358.

Wilson, G. D. (1987). An ethological approach to sexual deviation. In G. D. Wilson (Ed.), *Variant sexuality: Research and theory* (pp. 84–115). Baltimore: Johns Hopkins University Press.

Wiszewska, A., Pawlowski, B., & Boothroyd, L. G. (2007). Father–daughter relationship as a moderator or sexual imprinting: A facial-metric study. *Evolution and Human Behavior, 28,* 248–252.

Witte, K., & Caspers, B. (2006). Sexual imprinting on a novel blue ornament in zebra finches. *Behavior, 143,* 969–991.

Zajonc, R. B. (1968). Attitudinal effects of mere exposure. *Journal of Personality and Social Psychology, 9,* 1–27.

Zayas, V., Mischel, W., Shoda, Y., & Aber, J. L. (2011). Roots of adult attachment: Maternal caregiving at 18 months predicts adult peer and partner attachment. *Social Psychological and Personality Science, 2,* 289–297. doi:10.1177/1948550610389822.

Part IV
Development and Change in Adult Attachment Bonds

Chapter 7
Insights into the Formation of Attachment Bonds from a Social Network Perspective

Omri Gillath and Gery Karantzas

Attachment bonds—the social ties one has with people who fulfill attachment needs for love, comfort, and security—play a central role in people's well-being and functioning (Bowlby 1982). In the early stages of life, attachment bonds are formed between a child and her or his primary caregivers. However, as people navigate through life, they develop multiple attachment relationships with various other people within their social network, such as kin, peers, and mentors (e.g., Hazan and Zeifman 1994; Roberts and Dunbar 2011; Trinke and Bartholomew 1997). Thus, one's social network can be conceptualized as the candidates' pool of affiliations from which attachment bonds are formed.

The process of forming an attachment bond is likely to be gradual and selective in nature. Initial strangers become acquaintances; some of these acquaintances become close personal relationships, and of those, some eventually develop into attachment bonds. Thus, over time, acquaintances can evolve to function as *attachment figures*—people that provide a safe haven and secure base to individuals in times of need for help and protection (Bowlby 1982). How this normative process of attachment bond formation takes place is still unclear (e.g., Hazan et al. 2004; see also Chap. 1 in this volume). That is, "how does a person unknown to an individual transform from a complete stranger, to a member of one's social network, to then become an attachment figure?" In the current chapter, we provide insights into the formation of attachment bonds by integrating social network theory and research with Bowlby's behavioral systems perspective. We specifically focus on the associations between the attachment and affiliation behavioral systems, and situate the interplay between these systems within the context of social networks (e.g., Kadushin 2012).

O. Gillath (✉)
Department of Psychology, University of Kansas,
1415 Jayhawk Blvd. Rm 518, Lawrence, KS 66045-7556, USA
e-mail: ogillath@ku.edu

G. Karantzas
Deakin University, 221 Burwood, Hwy. Burwood, Victoria 3125, Australia

V. Zayas, C. Hazan (eds.), *Bases of Adult Attachment*,
DOI 10.1007/978-1-4614-9622-9_7

In an attempt to better understand the process of attachment formation, scholars have investigated various questions; with one of the most common being "what does it mean to be attached?" (Hazan et al. 2004). Here we are guided by two slightly different yet related questions: (1) exactly who becomes an attachment figure and (2) what is the social context in which attachment bonds are developed and formed? To answer these questions, one needs to look beyond the attachment system, to a complimentary behavioral system—the affiliation system (e.g., Mikulincer and Selinger 2001; Schwartz et al. 2007). The affiliation system relates to the formation of social relationships more broadly, and one's network of affiliation serves as the basis or pool for—among other things—the development of new attachment bonds (e.g., Kobak et al. 2007). Studying the normative functioning of the affiliation system, the interplay between the affiliation and attachment systems, and contextualizing this interplay within a social networks framework provides a promising avenue to improve the understanding of the formation of attachment bonds.

Chapter Overview

We commence the chapter with a review of the attachment and affiliation behavioral systems, followed by a discussion of the interplay between these systems. Then after giving a short introduction to the topic of social networks, we propose how the dynamic between the two systems is likely to influence the formation of attachment bonds within one's social network. As part of this chapter, we also review our research program which has focused on: (1) the associations between attachment and social network characteristics—namely density and multiplexity, (2) attachment and the management of social networks, and, (3) outcomes of the associations between attachment and social network configuration and management. In doing so, we interpret our research in terms of what it means for the formation, maintenance, and dissolution of attachment bonds. We conclude the chapter by highlighting the theoretical and practical implications of our work as well as outline future research in the area.

The Attachment Behavioral System

According to Bowlby and Ainsworth (e.g., Ainsworth et al. 1978; Bowlby 1982) an infant's tendency to seek close proximity to a primary caregiver when threatened or distress is driven by the attachment system. The main goal of the attachment system is felt security—a state of psychological and physical safety necessary for optimal human functioning. Thus, the attachment system serves a survival function by mobilizing an infant to seek refuge in the presence of a stronger wiser other. Repeated experiences with significant others who are able to provide love, comfort, and security (termed attachment figures) result in the development of a person's *attachment style*—their most chronically accessible way of thinking, feeling, and acting in close relationships.

Attachment style is conceptualized as two orthogonal dimensions, termed attachment avoidance and attachment anxiety (Brennan et al. 1998; Simpson et al. 1992). Attachment avoidance is characterized by a discomfort with closeness, a lack of confidence in others to attend to attachment needs, and an excessive self-reliance (Brennan et al. 1998). Attachment anxiety is characterized by an excessive need for approval, a preoccupation with relationship-related issues, and a fear of abandonment (Brennan et al. 1998). Individuals who are low on both attachment avoidance and anxiety are thought to be securely attached and are characterized by a comfort with emotional closeness, trust in close others, and a tendency to have longer more satisfying relationships as compared with their insecure counterparts (Bartholomew and Horowitz 1991; Simpson 1990). Attachment style has been found in numerous studies to predict various relationship-related outcomes (e.g., satisfaction, stability; for reviews see Cassidy and Shaver 2008; Mikulincer and Shaver 2007a) and the way people perceive and manage their social relationships with close others (e.g., Bippus and Rollin 2003; Jang et al. 2002; Kirkpatrick and Davis 1994). This suggests that attachment style is also a likely predictor of social network management and characteristics (e.g., density—how close network members are to each other, and multiplexity—the number of functions fulfilled by each network member).

Normative Processes in Attachment Although Bowlby (1982) conceptualized the formation of attachment bonds in terms of a normative process, much of the work in the field of attachment has focused on individual differences with regards to attachment (for a review see Mikulincer and Shaver 2007a). As a result of this emphasis, much less research has been dedicated to studying the normative developmental aspects of attachment formation (Hazan et al. 2004). That said, a few things are already known about normative attachment processes. First, as Bowlby theorized, evidence suggests that everyone, even those with abusive or neglectful caregivers, become attached to attachment figures (Crittenden 1995). Second, people tend to attach to their primary caregivers at first (often mom; e.g., Campa et al. 2008), and later develop attachment bonds with significant others such as siblings and peers (i.e., friends and romantic partners). Research also suggests that for some, attachment bonds may develop with nonhumans or inanimate objects (e.g., developing an attachment to god or a pet, Kirkpatrick and Shaver 1992).

Irrespective of whom one chooses as an attachment figure, the process of attachment formation takes time, and it unfolds through an identifiable set of phases—preattachment, attachment-in-the-making, clear-cut attachment, and goal-corrected partnership (Bowlby 1982). Once permanently separated from an attachment figure, attachment bonds are thought to dissolve through another set of stages: the first of which involves feelings of protest, the second—feelings of despair, and the third and final stage—detachment. Here we suggest that as people navigate through life they inevitably experience attachment and detachment. We propose that the relinquishment of attachment bonds can motivate an individual to form new attachment bonds—bonds that they form with members of their broader social networks.

Scholars have relied on specific markers in determining when someone is attached or when an attachment bond has formed (e.g., Hazan et al. 2004). These markers are often based on Bowlby's (1982) four distinct interrelated classes of behaviors or attachment functions: safe haven, secure base, separation distress, and proximity seeking/maintenance. Supporting Bowlby's conceptualization, these behaviors have been observed in both children and adults' attachment relations (e.g., Campa et al. 2008; Mikulincer et al. 2002). An attachment bond is thought to have formed when the attachment figure fulfills these attachment functions, or when these attachment-related behaviors (e.g., separation distress, proximity seeking) are directed toward a given person.

Although existing knowledge does not provide a clear depiction of the manner by which attachment bonds form (especially in adults), here, we suggest that development of attachment bonds shares much in common with other relationship formation processes. Whether it be falling in love (Bowlby 1979), developing a sexual attraction towards someone (Gillath et al. 2008; Zeifman and Hazan 1997), or becoming best friends; the process of forming close and intimate relationships consists of similar phases. We further suggest that the formation of new attachment bonds can be initiated by the affiliation behavioral system and as time goes by and the tie strengthens, the attachment system takes over, and a bond of affiliation evolves into an attachment bond (for a fuller example regarding the formation of an attachment bond with a romantic partner see Hazan et al. 2004; Fagundes and Schindler 2012). To understand this process we first review the affiliation system and its related processes and constructs.

The Affiliation Behavioral System

Bowlby (1982) articulated that the attachment system is one of various inherent behavioral systems that govern human functioning. Of interest to this chapter, Bowlby noted that social behavior of a nonattachment nature was associated with an alternate behavioral system—the affiliation system. According to Cassidy (2008) the affiliation system, like the attachment system, functions to promote survival through the phylogenic need to be sociable with others. From an evolutionary standpoint, this need for sociability is thought to protect humans and nonhuman primates from predators, increases the likelihood of mating, and enhances the abilities to collect food, build shelter, and explore the environment (Cassidy 2008; Mikulincer and Selinger 2001).

Unlike the set goal of the attachment system which pertains to enhancing a person's tendency to seek proximity to attachment figures when facing threats, the set goal of the affiliation system is to develop social ties to fulfill social functions that are distinct, but related, to attachment functions. According to Weiss (1998) these social functions include turning to others for: (1) companionship and friendship, (2) the development of knowledge and skills, (3) intellectual and social stimulation, and (4) diverse social activities such as play and the development of alliances to defend against protagonists or outgroup members.

While both the attachment and affiliation behavioral systems are associated with enhancing the survival through seeking proximity with others, Bowlby (1982) suggested that the contextual triggers that activate proximity seeking differ across the systems. In the case of attachment, proximity seeking behaviors are associated with seeking closeness to a stronger and wiser person to meet one's needs for love, comfort, and security especially in times of distress or ill-health. In the case of affiliation, proximity seeking behaviors are associated with seeking out friends and acquaintances when one is of good psychological and physical health and is clear of the whereabouts of their attachment figure. As Mikulincer and Selinger (2001) aptly put it: "attachment behaviors tend to be elicited by distress arousal, whereas affiliation behaviors tend to occur whenever a person is in a good mood and there is no immediate source of stress." (p. 84). Once activated, the affiliation system ensures that individuals can associate with others in order to exchange instrumental resources such as knowledge and information, as well as socioemotional resources such as experiencing positive mood and social connection in the presence of others.

The two systems—attachment and affiliation—while related, are underpinned by different goals, triggers, and responses. Thus, their activation, even in reaction to the same cue or stimulus (e.g., a stranger), can generate contrasting behaviors (Baron 1993; Cicchetti and Serafica 1981). As a case in point, when in the presence of a stranger, the attachment behavioral system is likely to result in avoidance of the stranger and the seeking of proximity to an attachment figure. However, when in the presence of a stranger, the affiliation system may actually encourage approach behavior towards the stranger. Another distinction between the systems has to do with the target of the behavior. The attachment system motivates an individual to seek proximity to an attachment-security-providing figure, whereas the affiliation system focuses an individual to direct behavior towards a potential or existing friend (Sheldon and West 1989).

Associations Between the Attachment and Affiliation Behavioral Systems

In describing the interplay between the attachment and the affiliation behavioral systems, Bowlby (1982) developed the concept of "attachment–affiliation balance." Affiliation behavior is enacted during periods when an individual is in a state of felt security vis-à-vis—the attachment system is in a state of deactivation. However, when an individual experiences distress or threat and the attachment system is activated, affiliation behaviors (in a similar fashion to behaviors guided by other behavioral systems; e.g., Gillath et al. 2005) are inhibited. This allows an individual to focus on proximity seeking strategies meant to re-establish security with an attachment figure. Once security is restored, the individual can re-engage their attention and behaviors towards affiliation activities. According to Bowlby (1982), this interplay between the two systems reflects the normative functioning of these complementary behavioral systems.

Despite the theoretical and functional associations between the attachment (Bowlby 1982) and affiliation (Bemporad 1984) behavioral systems (e.g., both are thought to involve hormones such as oxytocin [Kosfeld et al. 2005] and vasopressin (Pitkow et al. 2001), and behaviors such as self-disclosure [Bowlby 1982]), relatively little work has directly examined the interplay between the systems. Furthermore, of the few studies conducted, the focus was on individual differences, rather than on the normative processes of these systems (e.g., Florian et al. 1995; Mikulincer and Selinger 2001; Schwartz et al. 2007).

In one of the few studies examining the interplay between the two systems, Mikulincer and Selinger (2001) investigated attachment–affiliation balance in the context of adolescents' same-sex best friends relationships. Mikulincer and Selinger suggested that secure adolescents positive working models, and perceptions of attachment figures as a secure base from which to explore the social world, fosters their engagement in affiliation behaviors with peers. Moreover, peers are not only perceived by secure adolescents as a source of security, but are perceived as meeting nonattachment needs such as companionship and other social or instrumental needs. Thus secure individuals can selectively attend to peers to have both their attachment and affiliation needs met. In contrast, insecure adolescents remain preoccupied with their attachment needs, which interfere, and even inhibit affiliation activities. Specifically, the self-focused concerns and intense distress experienced by anxious adolescents, and the excessive self-reliance and lack of trust characteristic of avoidant adolescents, can disrupt affiliation behaviors with peers.

Behavioral System Functioning Within the Four-Phase Model of Attachment Formation: The Interplay Between Attachment and Affiliation The interplay between the attachment and affiliation behavioral system outlined above affords us the opportunity to further extend on the theoretical and empirical work conducted by Hazan and colleagues (e.g., Zeifman and Hazan 1997) on Bowlby's (1982) four-phase model. Our extension is meant to capture the process of forming an attachment bond via an affiliative route. In this way we can examine the interplay between the attachment and affiliation behavioral systems through a different lens. Further, we outline how the development of an attachment bond through the initial activation of the affiliation system can subsequently result in the formation of an attachment relationship.

Initially, in what can be perceived as the preattachment phase, people become interested in a social interaction with someone else. This interest can be due to various reasons such as the need to affiliate (e.g., Murray 1953; Schultheiss 2008), the need to belong (Baumeister and Leary 1995), loneliness (e.g., Cacioppo and Patrick 2008), or the fear of social exclusion (Mead et al. 2011). The target can be a potential friend/colleague/spiritual or professional mentor or anyone that is a part of a person's social network. It is in the preattachment phase that people begin to develop mental representations of others (Zeifman and Hazan 1997).

Within the preattachment phase, it is the affiliation system that primarily guides one's behavior. As a result, the first interactions between a person and a member of their social network are likely to consist of playful, explorative, positive activities. People exchange information, find common interests, and start to enjoy each other's company (for an extensive review and model of friendship formation see [Gottman and Graziano 1983]). With the passing of time, people become a little closer, spend more time together, and start to self-disclose, potentially treating each other as more than a mere acquaintance. It is at this point in the relationship that processes such as exclusivity and reciprocation may come into play (Parker et al. 2005).

The activation of these relationship processes may be indicative of the second phase: attachment-in-the-making. In this stage, the relationship partner may become a secondary or tertiary attachment figure (i.e., not as influential and important as the primary attachment figure, but important nonetheless; see Bretherton 1985; Trinke and Bartholomew 1997). People may start developing expectations about these relationship partners meeting attachment needs (see more about this below) but are unlikely to turn to these relationship partners in the first instance to fulfill their attachment functions (Hazan et al. 2004). The third phase—clear-cut attachment—involves the selective enactment of the four attachment behaviors (secure base, safe haven, proximity maintenance, and separation-distress) toward the new relationship partner. As suggested by Hazan and colleagues, and by Fagundes and Schindler (2012), the four behaviors are directed at a new partner at a different rate (e.g., partners may start by fulfilling the function of proximity and safe haven roughly 4 months after commitment, but secure base may transfer after 2 years). Within this stage, partner representations are likely to be activated when people are threatened and the attachment system is activated (Mikulincer et al. 2002). As a result, relationship partners are likely to play an increasingly important role in one's emotion-regulation processes. The fourth and final stage—goal-corrected partnership—as suggested by Zeifman and Hazan (1997), is characterized by a reduction in the overt display of attachment-related behaviors, and reliance on mental representations. It is at this stage that the close other becomes a primary attachment figure, and a main target for one's attachment needs and behaviors.

As mentioned previously, the target person of the new bond is being selected out of the accessible pool in ones' social network. Next we provide a short introduction to social networks research and then further discuss the interplay between the attachment and affiliation system within the framework of social networks.

Social Networks

Close relationships do not occur in a social vacuum, rather they are formed, developed, maintained, and dissolved in the context of a complex *social network* of family members, friends, and acquaintances (e.g., Antonucci et al. 2004; Milardo and Allan 1997; Sprecher 2011). A social network is defined as a relational system characterized by a set of people and their social relationships to one another (van

Duijn and Vermunt 2006). For example, a person can have a network of people that go to school together, a network of work colleagues, a friendship network, or a network of attachment figures. These different groups tend to fulfill different needs and provide different benefits to a given individual (McPherson et al. 2001). In the current work, we focus on a network that is less studied with regard to attachment relationships—the friendship social network.

An individual's social network has specific characteristics that make it unique and distinct from the social networks of other individuals (e.g., Antonucci et al. 2004). Two widely studied network characteristics, which we argue are central to the study of nonattachment as well as attachment relationships, are network density and network multiplexity (Kadushin 2012; McPherson et al. 2001). *Network density* refers to the extent to which network members are closely knit and known to one another (e.g., Allan 2006; Granovetter 1973). *Network multiplexity* refers to the number of social functions a network member fulfills for another, such as providing emotional or instrumental support (e.g., Campbell et al. 1986). The more functions each member fulfills the higher the multiplexity. The greater the density and the mulitplexity, the more positively the network is perceived, and the more benefits it is thought to provide to the individual (e.g., Lewin 1935; Kruglanski et al. 2002; Snyder et al. 1983).

Network density has been found to have important functional outcomes for individuals, such as general wellbeing and buffer against loneliness (e.g., Mesch and Talmud 2006; Wellman and Wellman 1992). For instance, a number of studies have found that people reporting highly dense social networks do not experience as much loneliness as those with less dense networks (e.g., Bell 1991; Cacioppo et al. 2009). Similarly, while studying older adults, Dykstra et al. (2005) found that a reduction in network density (and size) was associated with an increase in loneliness. Other researchers have found similar results such that having a dense network was positively associated with outcomes like happiness, subjective wellbeing, and greater life expectancy (e.g., see reviews by Berkman 1995; Watt and Badger 2009). These outcomes are thought to occur due to the increased sense of safety and social support inherent in denser networks (Kadushin 2012).

Multiplexity is also associated with various beneficial outcomes, such as the experience of relationship closeness (Boissevain 1974; Knoke and Kuklinski 1982; Lang and Carstensen 1994; Stoller et al. 2001), relationship strength, and duration (Mesch and Talmud 2006). Multiplexity was also found to enhance trust and relationship functioning between network members (Baker and Faulkner 1993). Finally, Berg and McQuin (1989) found that the more social functions network members fulfilled for people (i.e., higher multiplexity) the less loneliness those people experienced.

Despite the role of network density and multiplexity in predicting various psychological outcomes, research on density and multiplexity suffers from the same gaps as the general research on social networks—the extent that individual difference variables influence these networks characteristics is still unclear (e.g., Mischel 2011). Furthermore, as Antonucci and her colleagues suggest (e.g., Antonucci and Akiyama 1994; Antonucci et al. 2004), to fully understand the way network characteristics shape psychological outcomes, researchers need to embed the study of social network in a theory of relationships. Specifically, Antonucci et al. (2004) argue that attachment theory (Bowlby 1982), which encompasses central tenants about the formation, maintenance, and dissolution of social bonds, as well as the role of these bonds in fulfilling various social functions, would serve as a useful framework for studying social networks (see also Henderson 1977).

Attachment and Affiliation System Functioning in Social Networks: A Window into the Formation of Attachment Relationships

The fact that the social ties of young people seem to meet affiliation as well as attachment needs highlights the potential for network members to start out as meeting social and instrumental functions, and then evolve to meeting attachment functions. However, understanding how this process takes place has been mitigated by attachment researchers' primary focus on the study of attachment networks. We contend that expanding the study of social ties beyond attachment networks (i.e., to the broader social network) can facilitate the investigation of how social network members go from being mere acquaintances and social allies, to becoming attachment figures and thereby occupying a position in a person's attachment hierarchy.

Given that the affiliation system is driven by the goal of seeking out others to meet social and instrumental social functions, it stands to reason that people's structuring of social ties, and the management of social networks, reflect affiliation system functioning. Specifically, we suggest that people's capacities to initiate, maintain and relinquish social ties, and the properties of social networks such as their size, density, and multiplexity, represent manifestations of the affiliation system functioning.

From a normative standpoint, the development of social relationships outside the family home is not only seen as meeting the primary goal of the affiliation system, but is regarded as a key developmental task in young adulthood (Havighurst 1972). Therefore, managing one's network, that is initiating, maintaining, and dissolving social relationships beyond one's existing set of attachment figures is regarded as critical for the healthy socioemotional development of young adults. From a social network perspective, this normative functioning of the affiliation system during young adulthood is likely to be associated with an increase in social network size, such that individuals develop more acquaintances from whom one can acquire social resources and develop social skills. We suggest that such an increase in network size has also important normative benefits from an attachment perspective, insomuch as the development of acquaintances increases the pool of individuals who could serve as future attachment figures.

Normative functioning of the affiliation system is also likely to be associated with an increase in network density and multiplexity. As noted earlier in the chapter, network density refers to the extent to which network members are closely knit and known to one another. The more frequently people fulfill or act upon their affiliative needs and interact with other network members, the more likely they are to feel closer to these members (e.g., mere exposure effects; Zajonc 1968), and perceive the network in general as denser. Similarly, normative functioning of the affiliation system is likely to influence network multiplexity, such that individuals are motivated to establish social relations with other that meet more than one social function or need. In this manner, the affiliation system may drive affiliation behavior towards individuals that can provide diverse social resources, all of which can enhance a person's capacities and skills to navigate and explore the social world. Furthermore, turning to a variety of network members to fulfill various social functions—be they nonattachment or attachment in nature—offers opportunities for experiential learning. By interacting with social network members on a variety of levels, individuals begin to develop beliefs and expectations regarding the ability of social ties to reliably and competently meet their needs. While these social needs may initially relate to affiliation, social network members deemed particularly reliable and trustworthy may be experienced as meeting attachment needs, and over the course of time, become consistently relied upon as attachment figures. In such instances, these members of one's social network may be called upon when either the affiliation or attachment systems are activated.

Our theoretical hypotheses pertaining to the links between attachment, affiliation, and social networks shares commonalities with the work of Mary Levitt and colleagues (1980, 1991, 1994, 2005), which focused on understanding the role of social networks in the development of attachment bonds. In articulating a case for how social network members may become attachment figures, Levitt et al. outline a normative model of attachment formation that draws on the work of John Watson's (1972) social contingency game hypothesis. As such, Levitt viewed attachment bond formation as underpinned by the expectancies that a person develops regarding a social network member's behavior towards him or her over time. In brief, Levitt and colleagues (Levitt 2005; Levitt et al. 1994) propose that the familiarity and responsiveness of an acquaintance are important in the initiation of an affiliation bond. In addition to repeated interactions fostering familiarity, interactions over time build expectations about another's behaviour. Specifically, interactions that enhance an individual's self-efficacy (or "broaden and build" the capacities of the individual, in Fredrickson's [2001] terms) yield positive emotions regarding the sensitivity and responsiveness of the acquaintance and their potential to act as a secure base. Levitt (2005) suggests that "a long period of familiarity, coupled with efficacy enhancing interactions with potential attachment figures, should promote the development of attachment bonds" (p. 35).

Across various studies, Levitt found that while familiarity did play a role in the development of affiliation, changes in a relationship to either promote or attenuate attachment-like behaviors was more strongly associated with network members behaving in ways consistent with established social contingencies (Levitt 1980, 1991; Levitt et al. 1994). According to Levitt (2005), length of familiarity and efficacy enhancing interactions with an acquaintance can promote the transition of an affiliation bond to an attachment bond. Furthermore, Levitt contended that: (a) relationships are enhanced when the behavior of a social network member exceeds one's expectations; (b) relationships are maintained when a social network member's behavior meets one's expectations, and (c) relationships may be threatened when a social network member's behavior violates one's expectations. Thus, the meeting or exceeding of expectations can be viewed as either fostering the maintenance of an affiliative or attachment relationship, or drive an affiliative relationship to become an attachment relationship. If however the behavior of social network members' falls short of a person's expectations, then this is likely to result in some attenuation of the attachment relationship such that it may only fulfill affiliation functions, or result in relationship dissolution.

The notion that social network ties first develop on the basis of affiliation, and then evolve to encompass social bonds not dissimilar to those of attachment relationships has been present across various theories and studies relating to friendship and romantic relationship development. For instance, Knapp (1984) identified five stages of relationship development, namely: (1) initiating—the making of acquaintances and forming of first impressions; (2) experimentation—developing shared activities, common acquaintances and issues and determining the extent to which the relationship meets social functions; (3) intensifying—expressions of intimacy through reciprocal disclosure and responsiveness, an increase in time spent together and declarations of affection; (4) integrating—disclosure becomes more personal and lives become integrated through such milestones as becoming flat mates; and (5) bonding—the development of a highly committed relationship characterized by deep attachment and affection.

Importantly, in drawing on the work of Levitt and colleagues and Knapp, it appears that familiarity is an important factor that facilitates the transition from an affiliation bond to an attachment bond. Moreover, it appears that friendships that deepen over time are likely to experience a shift in intimacy. Intimacy is defined within Reis and Shaver's (1988) intimacy model as a dyadic process involving disclosure on behalf of one individual and a sensitive response to the disclosure by another. From this perspective, one can argue that having friends in one's social network that respond to disclosure in this way elevates the significance of the friendship such that the peer is deemed as a significant close other—similar to an attachment figure.

Using a network analysis, Milardo (1982) found that college students' networks of mutual friends changed as a function of the degree of intimacy across stages of friendship development. Specifically, he found that intimacy fostered the deepening of friendships among social network members. Similarly, Hays (1985) examining the longitudinal development of same-sex friendships amongst college students found peers that became close friends over time differed behaviorally and attitudinally from peers that did not develop a close friendships. Again, intimacy was regarded as an important factor in the qualitative changes that occurred in friendships over time. In reviewing some of the early friendship development literature, Tesch (1983) suggested that friendship develops from a basis of mutual liking and shared activities to loyalty and mutual aid, and later, intimate self-disclosure.

In reviewing the above literature, it appears that development of attachment relationships from young people's social networks is a gradual process that requires the interplay of both the affiliation and the attachment system. In the first instance, the affiliation behavioral system motivates people to initiate new ties, thus broadening the social network. As acquaintances become more familiar to one another, the affiliation system assists in motivating people to turn to social network members to fulfill various social functions and develop friendships. The history of the interactions one develops with various social network members yield beliefs and expectations about social network members' capacities to reliably meet the socioemotional needs of the individual. The greater the confidence one has in turning to a social network member to meet social functions, the more trust the individual puts in a given network member, which likely results in the increase of intimacy and disclosure. Overall positive experiences based on these interactions are likely to elevate some network members from friendship status to best friend status. As such, individuals may start directing attachment behaviors toward these close friends, until at some point friends become fully attached to one another—fulfilling the various attachment functions for one another. To this end, these friends are likely to fulfill both affiliation and attachment needs for a given individual. Moreover, individuals that can seamlessly turn to close friends for affiliation and attachment needs are likely to be secure and encompass a state of attachment-affiliation balance.

Research on Attachment and Social Networks

Almost 40 years had passed since Henderson (1977) suggested using attachment theory as a way to understand the psychological function of social networks. Despite this, relatively little empirical work has followed-up Henderson's initial idea (e.g., Wallace and Vaux 1993). Recently, researchers have applied attachment theory to study various aspects of social networks such as people's perceptions of their closeness to network members (e.g., Antonucci et al. 2004; Doherty and Feeney 2004; Rowe and Carnelley 2005). Most of these studies, however, have focused on a very specific type of social network—a network comprised of the people who fulfill one's attachment needs for love, comfort, and security—termed an attachment network (e.g., Doherty and Feeney 2004; Rowe and Carnelley 2005; Uchino 2009).

For example, Rowe and Carnelley (2005) examined how young adults' attachment style was associated with the configuration of their attachment networks. They found that people differed with regard to the number of attachment figures that were included in their attachment network. Specifically, securely attached individuals included a greater number of people in their attachment network compared to insecure individuals. Especially important for the current work, secure individuals also mapped close others as closer to the self as compared with insecure individuals, suggesting security to be positively associated with density. This association between attachment style and network characteristics seems to support the idea that attachment style is also related to the density of friendship social networks—the focus of the present chapter.

Whereas attachment has been applied to the understanding of attachment networks and to what might be considered as network density, little work has linked attachment style directly to multiplexity. A few studies, however, have examined attachment and the functions network members fulfill, using measures like the WHO-TO (Fraley and Davis 1997; Hazan and Zeifman 1994). For example, Fraley and Davis found that attributing more attachment functions (proximity maintenance, secure base, and safe haven) to a network member was associated with greater trust, care, and intimacy in the relationship with that member. Furthermore, the more functions fulfilled by a network member the more likely they were to serve as an attachment figure. To date, however, no study—to our knowledge—has examined the direct associations between attachment style and multiplexity, especially within friendship networks.

In the second half of the chapter, we review our program of research which has set to examine numerous aspects of the association between attachment and social networks. Specifically, our research has focused on the associations between: (1) attachment and social network characteristics—namely density and multiplexity, and (2) attachment and the management of social networks. Based on the above mentioned literature we hypothesized that: (1) Attachment style would be associated with network density. Specifically insecurely attached people would perceive their friendship networks as less dense as compared with their secure counterparts. (2) Attachment style would be also associated with multiplexity, such that insecurely attached people would report experiencing lower mutiplexity as compared with their secure counterparts. To test these predictions we used ego-centered networks (Burt 1984; van Duijn and Vermunt 2006) in our studies, where all the reports about the network characteristics are generated by the participant (i.e., ego).

A Review of our Research Program

Attachment Style, Network Density, and Multiplexity Our first series of three studies focused on the friendship network characteristics (density and multiplexity) of college students and their association with attachment anxiety and avoidance. We collected data from two samples—one focusing specifically on online friends and the other focusing on face-to-face friends. Density was operationalized as perceived closeness between participants to each network member, and perceived closeness amongst network members themselves. Multiplexity was operationalized as the perceived amount of functions each network member fulfilled. Included within these functions were attachment functions, social support functions, affiliation functions, and academic functions. We asked people to report only on the ten most important people in their networks, in line with other studies on social networks (Antonucci and Akiyama 1987). Across the three studies we found attachment anxiety to be associated with perceived network density, such that the higher one's anxiety the lower the perceived density. With regard to attachment avoidance, it was not associated with network density in any consistent way; however, it was associated with multiplexity. The higher one's attachment avoidance the lower the multiplexity.

To validate these findings in another context, culture, and age group, we examined the associations between the attachment dimensions and network density and multiplexity in a large online community sample of Australian people experiencing arthritis (Karantzas et al. 2012). Density and multiplexity were operationalized in the same manner as in our college samples. Similar to the findings of Gillath et al. (2012), we again found attachment anxiety to be negatively associated with network density, while attachment avoidance was negatively associated with multiplexity.

We have also investigated the associations between attachment and multiplexity in organizational contexts. In a study by Kavadas and Karantzas (2012) attachment avoidance was found to be negatively associated with three functions of organizational networks—the perceptions of coworker trust, perceptions of support during workplace difficulties, and perceptions of validation from coworkers during workplace achievements. Thus, people high on avoidance sought less support from co-workers during times of strain or accomplishment, and were less trusting of co-workers. The findings from the workplace study again suggest attachment avoidance is negatively associated with multiplexity.

There are at least two potential explanations for the findings between attachment anxiety and network density. First, anxiously attached people may constantly try to get closer to people in their social network, leading these people to pull away as they feel smothered (Feeney 2008), thus, anxious people's perception may reflect the reality. An alternative explanation has to do with anxiously attached people's tendencies to have a high need for reassurance and love, and to perceive others as not as close as they would like them to be (Brennan et al. 1998; Shaver et al. 2005). As a part of this general perception, anxiously attached people would also underestimate closeness in their network—that is—in their eyes their network members are not as close as they would like. Anxiously attached people may have the same biased perceptions when making inferences about the closeness amongst network members, possibly assuming that the relationships between other members of their network are also not as close, resulting with an overall perception of lower network density.

The findings pertaining to the negative association between attachment avoidance and multiplexity fits with avoidant people's tendency to distance themselves from others, as well as their lack of confidence in depending on others to meet their needs (Collins and Feeney 2004; Mikulincer 1998; Rowe and Carnelley 2005). By allowing each friend to fulfill only a few functions or just one, avoidant individuals reduce their dependence on each specific friend, making friends more replaceable. This approach to friendship is in line with Lewin's (1935) conceptualization and Kruglanski et al.'s (2002) empirical work on differences in friendship. According to these scholars, low multiplexity (or unifinality as termed by Kruglanski) is associated with friendships that are less deep, less committed, and easier to replace.

Attachment Style and Network Management In our research into attachment and social networks we also investigated the associations between attachment style and network management. To assess network management in our studies we developed the Network Management Inventory (Gillath et al. 2011). This self-report measure consists of three reliable factors assessing the extent to which individuals *initiate* (e.g., "I like meeting new people"), *maintain* (e.g., "I keep my contact with my old social network members") and *dissolve* (e.g., "It is easy for me to let go of old friends") social ties. Each factor assesses the tendency to engage in relevant behaviors and the ease or perceived ability to do so. The factors we identified are in line with conceptualizations by Kadushin (2012) and others (e.g., Milardo 1988) on the motivations driving the management of networks.

In one set of studies examining network management, Gillath et al. (2011) found that attachment avoidance was significantly negatively associated with the maintenance of social ties and significantly positively associated with the dissolution of social ties. The association between attachment avoidance and the initiation of social ties was not significant; however it was in the expected negative direction. Attachment anxiety was not associated with any of the social network management strategies. However, a significant two-way interaction was found (attachment avoidance × attachment anxiety) such that individuals scoring low on both dimensions (i.e., securely attached individuals) reported greater maintenance of social ties. In a different set of studies on transition into college, Karantzas and Gillath (2012), using an Australian sample, also found attachment avoidance to be negatively associated with the initiation and maintenance of ties and positively associated with the dissolution of ties.

Overall our findings suggest that attachment avoidance is a key factor affecting the management of social networks. In particular, attachment avoidance thwarts the abilities of individuals to initiate and maintain ties and makes them more likely to dissolve existing relationships across various types of social networks. Our two sets of studies provide consistent results to support these associations. These patterns of network management are consistent with avoidant individuals' overall tendencies to avoid intimacy and closeness (Mikulincer and Shaver 2007a). They are also in line with the deactivating strategies thought to be enacted by avoidant people. According to Mikulincer and Shaver, these strategies are expressed in the downplaying of their emotions, suppressing of their attachment needs, and avoiding extensive contact with others. Feeney and colleagues (e.g., Feeney et al. 1994; Karantzas et al. 2010) also note that avoidant individuals excessive self-reliance and tendency to place relationship goals as secondary to personal goals further hinders their abilities to foster relationships with others.

General Implications and Implications for the Formation of Attachment Bonds

Kadushin (2012) in his recent extensive review of the networks literature argues that researchers should place greater emphasis on personality dimensions and individual differences in their social networks research. In line with Antonucci (e.g., Antonucci et al. 2004), our studies suggest that not only is attachment theory a useful framework to study networks, but that attachment style is an important predictor of both network characteristics and networks management skills. Furthermore, our studies highlight how a 'social networks' perspective may reflect underlying associations between the attachment and affiliation behavioral systems, thus providing insights into initiation, maintenance, and dissolution of attachment-related ties.

Attachment and Density Our work to date has focused on the way attachment style is associated with individuals' perceptions regarding the tightness of the connections amongst people in their network. What are the possible implications of knowing that an individual difference variable, such as attachment style, can influence such perceptions? What does it mean if someone does not feel their network is tight-knit and that this is a function of attachment style? Antonucci and colleagues (e.g., Antonucci et al. 2004; Caldwell and Antonucci 1997) believe that the myriad of people's social relations, which she refers to as "social convoys", are important in that they support the individual as they develop across the lifespan. "It takes a village to raise a child" (p. 230) claim Caldwell and Antonucci (1997), suggesting that convoys are especially important for individuals when coping with challenges, such as the transition to college and coping with illness. A dense network means that network members are more likely to communicate with one another as well as be inclusive of one another. Communication and inclusivity encourage social network members to maintain a vested interest in others. This, in turn, can ensure the wellbeing of others in the network. Insecure people's perceptions of their networks as less dense, is consistent with their belief that people are not as close and as inclusive as they would like. These perceptions may represent accurate realities of insecurely attached individuals' social networks. That is, by the very nature of their past relationship experiences these individuals develop networks that are less inclusive and in which network members are less connected to one another and responsive to each other's needs. Alternatively, these perceptions may represent cognitive distortions such that anxiously and avoidantly attached individuals have the "illusion" that network members are less connected to one another and less amenable to taking an interest in each other's lives. These distortions, which are documented in other aspects of close relationships (for reviews see Bretherton and Munholland 2008; Collins and Allard 2001), are likely to reflect their insecure past relationship histories with significant others who were either: (1) disengaged or (2) highly preoccupied with themselves, such that attending to the others' needs became secondary (Ainsworth et al. 1978; Mikulincer and Shaver 2007a).

From a therapeutic standpoint, it may be important for practitioners to explore how insecurely attached individuals representations are reflected in their network perceptions. In the event that these perceptions represent biases in their appraisal of their network, then practitioners may need to support insecurely attached individuals in relying on their network members to a greater extent (as in the case of avoidantly attached individuals), or encourage insecure people to deepen existing ties rather than initiating more a more ties (as is the case among anxiously attached people).

Attachment and Multiplexity Our findings extend on previous research in two important ways. Firstly, we expand on the types of functions examined in attachment research—functions that go beyond those specifically associated with the fulfillment of attachment needs. Secondly, we extend the implications of attachment style to the study of social networks more broadly—an extension that moves attachment research beyond the traditional study of attachment networks.

Our research suggests that attachment style is an important factor in determining perceptions of social network multiplexity. This finding is significant in that it highlights that the utility of attachment style is not confined to network members who fulfill attachment needs. Rather, attachment style also influences the extent to which individuals turn to network members for other social functions including: instrumental and financial support and the sharing of positive life events and mutual interests. Thus, attachment style filters/biases the perceptions of our network members in fulfilling a multitude of social functions. In particular, our findings point to attachment avoidance as the key dimension associated with network multiplexity. Across different studies and different contexts attachment avoidance was found to be consistently negatively associated with multiplexity. In interpreting this finding we draw on the characteristics, which to a large extent, define avoidantly attached individuals. As noted previously in this chapter, avoidant individual are characterized by their excessive self-reliance, discomfort with closeness and view of relationships as secondary to other life domains (Brennan et al. 1998; Karantzas et al. 2010). We therefore believe that as means of safeguarding against getting too close, or becoming too reliant on network members, avoidant individuals try to avoid having each network member fulfill a number of social functions. Moreover, the less functions that individuals fulfill, the less value they may entail for an avoidant person, and as a consequence, the easier it may be for avoidant individuals to disentangle these people from their social network.

Attachment and Networks' Management Drawing on our newly found associations between attachment and management skills, our research has also provided new ways to look at the links between attachment and the way people manage their social relationships. Examining the association between attachment style and network management across different samples, in different countries, cultures, and contexts, revealed a consistent pattern. Specifically, attachment insecurity, and especially avoidance, was associated with poorer management skills.

Our findings suggest that for people who are dealing with stressful events such as the transition to college or chronic illness, enhancing their social networks management skills may improve their coping and related outcomes. This is especially important for insecurely attached people who are more likely to experience difficulties dealing with stressful situations—a finding documented across numerous studies (e.g., Mikulincer and Florian 2001; Obegi and Berant 2009; Selcuk and Gillath 2009). However, our findings suggest that one should take into account attachment style as well when teaching such management skills to people—especially insecurely attached people. For instance, avoidant individuals may demonstrate resistance to overt attempts at teaching network management skills, perceiving such attempts as threats to self-reliance and lack of social competence on their behalf. Moreover, avoidant people are likely to perceive their network as less trustworthy and less likely to provide them support—in which case working on network management skills may be deemed a futile and misguided endeavor. Avoidant individuals' perceptions of their networks as less trustworthy and supportive is in line with theories of self-consistency and behavioral confirmation (Snyder and Swann 1978) suggesting that people engage in behaviors driven by their self-fulfilling beliefs and attitudes. If one believes that others will not be supportive they are more likely to engage in behaviors that confirm these views—by potentially encouraging others to behave in ways consistent with these views.

Thus when trying to teach avoidant individuals these important management skills, one should approach the task in a manner that does not compromise an avoidant person's sense of independence, while assuring them that the development of these skills does not make them more dependent on others, but rather empowers them to make more effective choices in managing their social network. At the same time, to ensure that network management skills are enhanced and maintained, therapeutic work is likely to require cognitive-based approaches that work on recalibrating avoidant individuals' perceptions of their social networks. Recalibrating the erroneous perceptions of network members being untrustworthy and unreliable is likely to make avoidant individuals more open to adopting network management skills that foster the initiation and maintenance of social network ties. From a therapeutic perspective, such recalibration of perceptions can be pursued through various clinical approaches such as Intergrative Cognitive Behavioral Therapy (Jacobson and Christensen 1996), Emotion-Focused therapy (Johnson 2004), or mindfulness-based therapeutic methods (Carson et al. 2004).

Attachment and Affiliation A final implication of our research has to do more broadly with understanding the interplay between two behavioral systems—the attachment and affiliation system—an interplay that is relatively understudied in the relationships literature (Bemporad 1984; Mikulincer and Selinger 2001). If we regard the development of multiple social ties as the manifestation of the workings of the affiliation system, then our research into attachment and social networks provide some insight into the association between the attachment and affiliation behavioral systems. In examining our results through this lens, we note that the findings between attachment avoidance and affiliation (conceptualized as the management of social networks) bear resemblance to the findings of the much studied interplay between the attachment and—the caregiving system (for a review see Canterberry and Gillath 2012). Similar to the attachment-caregiving interplay, attachment avoidance seems to be the primary dimension associated with affiliation. As in caregiving, attachment avoidance mitigates against the initiation and maintenance of new ties. This may be because avoidant individuals, similarly to the situation when they are faced with the need to provide care, are highly self-focused rather than shift their views to acknowledge others (Obegi and Berant 2009). As a result, avoidant individuals may be less likely to affiliate with others. Furthermore, the inability to trust others, as well as experiences of consistent rejection in the past, are likely to hamper any desires they may have to develop new bonds, even in situations where they should do so. Our results suggest that the network management tendencies of avoidant individuals reflect a deactivation of the affiliation system.

The lack of findings regarding attachment anxiety and network management resembles findings by Mikulincer and colleagues on the associations between the attachment and caregiving systems (Mikulincer et al. 2005; but see work by Feeney and Collins, for example, Feeney and Collins 2001). Specifically, Mikulincer and colleagues found that attachment anxiety was not associated with the tendency to help or provide care per se, but rather with the reason associated with the provision (or lack thereof) of caregiving. Perhaps future studies focusing on the associations between attachment and affiliation should focus on examining people's reasons for initiating, maintaining and dissolving social network ties. Focusing on the reasoning behind the use of these network management skills rather than the behaviors themselves may reveal a similar association to that found between attachment anxiety and reasons for providing care.

Future Questions and Directions

Our research agenda to date has provided some important insights into the study of attachment and social networks. However, many questions remain unanswered. For instance, how do network characteristics, network management skills, and the configuration of networks change over time, and is this change associated with attachment style? Relatedly, do reciprocal associations exist between attachment style, network characteristics, and management skills, such that at a given point in time, attachment may influence network characteristics and management, while at other time-points the opposite may occur? In answering these questions, future studies would need to study stability and change in social networks as well as reciprocal associations between attachment and networks from a longitudinal perspective (e.g., Wrzus et al. 2012). Presently, we are extending our research using longitudinal designs to tackle these issues. By answering these questions, we will also gain insight into issues of directionality and causality between attachment style, network characteristics, and network management.

A further means of examining the issue of causality would be to integrate priming techniques as part of experimental studies on social networks. To date studies on security priming have revealed that enhancing people's sense of security is associated with many positive outcomes (e.g., Gillath et al. 2008; Mikulincer and Shaver 2007b). For example priming security has been found to promote prosocial behaviors even among avoidant individuals (Mikulincer et al. 2005). We anticipate a similar pattern of results to ensue when applying priming to the study of social networks. Preliminary support for this contention comes from pilot data collected in our laboratories demonstrating that subliminal security priming, when compared to a neutral prime condition, results in lowered tendencies to dissolve existing social ties among avoidantly attached individuals.

Another goal for future research is to compare people's perceptions of density (subjective density) with more objective assessment of density via sociometric methods that capture data on "complete networks" (i.e., all network members report on their degree of closeness to all other members, van Duijn and Vermunt 2006). Data collection to gather information on complete networks is commonly used in social network research and can ensure that the characteristics of a given network are determined by the connections reported by *all members* of a bounded network (van Duijn and Vermunt 2006). In this respect, sociometric methods regarding complete networks yield self-report assessments from more than one individual thus combating many of the limitations of single self-report study designs (Wasserman and Faust 1994).

Conclusion

In this chapter, we have provided theoretical and empirical insights into how a 'social networks' perspective can shed light on the way social ties may develop into attachment bonds. In doing so, we proposed that various characteristics of social networks and their management may represent manifestations of the affiliation behavioral system, and that this in turn is interrelated with individual differences in attachment style. As part of this chapter we provided an overview of our research linking attachment style to social network characteristics and network management skills. We believe that our research focus helps to broaden attachment researchers', relationship researchers' and counselors' views of how attachment processes shape people's broad network of social ties. In line with the aims of this text, our research also provides insight into how the attachment dimensions influence the formation, maintenance and dissolution of social affiliations within people's social networks.

In adopting a social networks perspective for the study of attachment, we brought some of the methods and metrics used in social network analysis squarely into the field of relationship research, and more specifically, attachment research. In doing so, we have tried to fill an important gap in the close relationships literature. Aside from a notable few studies (e.g., Kenny and La Voie 1984; Milardo et al. 1983) much of the close relationships research into social networks has been conducted devoid of a social network analysis framework (Milardo 1988). Likewise, many social network researchers conduct studies on relationships devoid of theories about relationships. Therefore, our research examining social networks from an attachment theory perspective—a theory that has significantly advanced the understanding of relationships—is of value to both fields. On the basis of our reviewed work, we propose that the value of attachment theory extends well beyond the levels of the individual, dyad, or attachment network. Rather it informs us about how we navigate and organize the network of our social relations—a context that significantly shapes our development and wellbeing (Cohen and Pressman 2006).

References

Ainsworth, M. D. S., Blehar, M. C., Waters, E., & Wall, S. (1978). *Patterns of attachment: A psychological study of the strange situation*. Oxford: Lawrence Erlbaum.

Allan, G. (2006). Social networks and personal communities. In A. L. Vangelisti & D. Perlman (Eds.), *Cambridge handbook of personal relationships* (pp. 657–671). Cambridge: Cambridge University Press.

Antonucci, T. C., & Akiyama, H. (1987). Social networks in adult life and a preliminary examination of the convoy model. *Journal of Gerontology, 42,* 519–527. doi:10.1093/geronj/42.5.519.

Antonucci, T. C., & Akiyama, H. (1994). Convoys of attachment and social relations in children, adolescents, and adults. In F. Nestmann & K. Hurrelmann (Eds.), *Social networks and social support in childhood and adolescence* (pp. 37–52). Oxford: Walter De Gruyter.

Antonucci, T. C., & Akiyama, H., & Takahashi, K. (2004). Attachment and close relationships across the life span. *Attachment & Human Development, 6,* 353–370.

Baker, W. E., & Faulkner, R. R. (1993). The social organization of conspiracy: Illegal networks in the heavy electrical equipment industry. *American Sociological Review, 58,* 837–860.

Baron, M. J. (1993). Fear, attachment and affiliation: The interaction of functional systems in 8- and 12-month-old infants. *Early Development and Parenting, 2,* 121–130.

Bartholomew, K., & Horowitz, L. M. (1991). Attachment styles among young adults: A test of a four-category model. *Journal of Personality and Social Psychology, 61,* 226–244. doi:10.1037/0022-3514.61.2.226.

Baumeister, R. F., & Leary, M. R. (1995). The need to belong: Desire for interpersonal attachments as a fundamental human motivation. *Psychological Bulletin, 117,* 497–529. doi:http://dx.doi.org/10.1037/0033-2909.117.3.497.

Bell, B. (1991). Loneliness and values. *Journal of Social Behavior & Personality, 6,* 771–778.

Bemporad, J. R. (1984). From Attachment to Affiliation. *American Journal of Psychoanalysis, 44,* 79–92.

Berg, J. H., & McQuinn, R. D. (1989). Loneliness and aspects of social support networks. *Journal of Social and Personal Relationships, 6,* 359–372. doi:10.1177/0265407589063008.

Berkman, L. F. (1995). The role of social relations in health promotion. *Psychosomatic Medicine, 57,* 245–254.

Bippus, A., & Rollin, E. (2003). Attachment style differences in relational maintenance and conflict behaviors: Friends' perceptions. *Communication Reports, 16,* 113–123.

Boissevain, J. (1974). *Friends of friends: Networks, manipulators and coalitions*. Oxford: Basil Blackwell.

Bowlby, J. (1979). *The making and breaking of affectional bonds*. London: Tavistock.

Bowlby, J. (1982). *Attachment and loss: Vol. 1. Attachment* (2nd ed.). New York: Basic Books. (Orig. ed. 1969).

Brennan, K. A., Clark, C. L., & Shaver, P. R. (1998). Self-report measurement of adult attachment: An integrative overview. In J. A. Simpson & W. S. Rholes (Eds.), *Attachment theory and close relationships* (pp. 46–76). New York: Guilford.

Bretherton, I. (1985). A sampler of parent-child relations. *PsycCRITIQUES, 30,* 637–638. doi:http://dx.doi.org/10.1037/024000.

Bretherton, I., & Munholland, K. A. (2008). Internal working models in attachment relationships: Elaborating a central construct in attachment theory. In J. A. Cassidy & P. R. Shaver (Eds.), *Handbook of adult attachment: Theory, research and clinical applications* (2nd ed., pp. 102–127). New York: Guilford.

Burt, R. S. (1984). Network items and the general social survey. *Social Networks, 6,* 293–339.

Cacioppo, J. T., & Patrick, W. (2008). *Loneliness: Human nature and the need for social connection*. New York: Norton.

Cacioppo, J. T., Fowler, J. H., & Christakis, N. A. (2009). Alone in the crowd: The structure and spread of loneliness in a large social network. *Journal of Personality and Social Psychology, 97,* 977–991. doi:10.1037/a0016076.

Caldwell, C. H., & Antonucci, T. C. (1997). Child bearing during adolescence: Mental health risks and opportunities. In J. Schulenberg, J. L. Maggs, & K. Hurrelmann (Eds.), *Health risks and developmental transitions during adolescence* (pp. 220–245). New York: Cambridge University Press.

Campa, M. I., Hazan, C., & Wolfe, J. E. (2008). The form and function of attachment behavior in the daily lives of young adults. *Social Development, 18,* 288–304.

Campbell, K. E., Marsden, P. V., & Hurlbert, J. S. (1986). Social resources and socioeconomic status. *Social Networks, 8,* 97–117.

Canterberry, M., & Gillath, O. (2012). Attachment and caregiving: Functions, interactions, and implications. In G. C. Karantzas & P. Noller (Eds.), *Handbook of intimate and family relationships: Bridging research, policy, and practice* (pp. 207–220). New York: Wiley-Blackwell.

Carson, J. W., Carson, K. M., Gil, K. M., & Baucom, D. H. (2004). Mindfulness-based relationship enhancement. *Behavioral Therapy, 35,* 471–494.

Cassidy, J. (2008). The nature of a child's ties. In J. Cassidy & P. R. Shaver (Eds.), *Handbook of attachment: Theory, research, and clinical applications* (2nd ed., pp. 2–20). New York: Guilford.

Cassidy, J., & Shaver, P. (Eds.). (2008). *Handbook of attachment: Theory, research, and clinical applications* (2nd ed.). New York: Guilford.

Cicchetti, D., & Serafica, F. C. (1981). Interplay among behavioral systems: Illustrations from the study of attachment, affiliation, and wariness in young children with Down's syndrome. *Developmental Psychology, 17,* 36–49. doi:10.1037/0012-1649.17.1.36.

Cohen, S., & Pressman, S. D. (2006). Positive affect and health. *Current Directions in Psychological Science, 15,* 122–125. doi:10.1111/j.0963-7214.2006.00420.x.

Collins, N. L., & Allard, L. M. (2001). Cognitive representations of attachment: The content and function of working models. In G. J. O. Fletcher & M. S. Clark (Eds.), *Blackwell handbook of social psychology: Vol. 2. Interpersonal processes* (pp. 60–85). UK: Blackwell.

Collins, N. L., & Feeney, B. C. (2004). Working models of attachment shape perceptions of social support: Evidence from experimental and observational studies. *Journal of Personality and Social Psychology, 87,* 363–383.

Crittenden, P. M. (1995). Attachment and psychopathology. In S. Goldberg, R. Muir, & J. Kerr (Eds.), *Attachment theory: Social, developmental, and clinical perspectives* (pp. 367–406). Hillsdale: Analytic.

Doherty, N. A., & Feeney, J. A. (2004). The composition of attachment networks throughout the adult years. *Personal Relationships, 11,* 469–488. doi:10.1111/j.1475-6811.2004.00093.x.

Dykstra, P. A., Van Tilburg, T., & De Jong Gierveld, J. (2005). Changes in older adult loneliness. *Research on Aging, 27,* 725–747.

Fagundes, C. P., & Schindler, I. (2012). Making of romantic attachment bonds: Longitudinal trajectories and implications for relationship stability. *Personal Relationships, 19,* 723–742. http://dx.doi.org/10.1111/j.1467-9507.2008.00466.x.

Feeney, J. A. (2008). Adult romantic attachment: Developments in the study of couple relationships. In J. Cassidy & P. R. Shaver (Eds.), *Handbook of attachment: Theory, research, and clinical applications* (2nd ed., pp. 456–481). New York: Guilford.

Feeney, B. C., & Collins, N. L. (2001). Predictors of caregiving in adult intimate relationships: An attachment theoretical perspective. *Journal of Personality and Social Psychology, 80,* 972–994. doi:10.1037/0022-3514.80.6.972.

Feeney, J. A., Noller, P., & Hanrahan, M. (1994). Assessing adult attachment. In M. B. Sperling & W. H. Berman (Eds.), *Attachment in adults: Clinical and developmental perspectives* (pp. 128–152). New York: Guilford.

Florian, V., Mikulincer, M., & Bucholtz, I. (1995). Effects of adult attachment style on the perception and search for social support. *Journal of Psychology: Interdisciplinary and Applied, 129,* 665–676.

Fraley, R. C., & Davis, K. E. (1997). Attachment formation and transfer in young adults' close friendships and romantic relationships. *Personal Relationships, 4,* 131–144.

Fredrickson, B. L. (2001). The role of positive emotions in positive psychology: The broaden-and-build theory of positive emotions. *American Psychologist, 56,* 218–226.

Gillath, O., Shaver, P. R., Mikulincer, M., Nitzberg, R. E., Erez, A., & Van Ijzendoorn, M. H. (2005). Attachment, caregiving, and volunteering: Placing volunteerism in an attachment-theoretical framework. *Personal Relationships, 12,* 425–446. doi:http://dx.doi.org/10.1111/j.1475-6811.2005.00124.x.

Gillath, O., Selcuk, E., & Shaver, P. R. (2008). Moving toward a secure attachment style: Can repeated security priming help? *Social and Personality Psychology Compass, 2/4,* 1651–1666.

Gillath, O., Johnson, D. K., Selcuk, E., & Teel, C. (2011). Comparing old and young adults as they cope with life transitions: The links between social network management skills and attachment style to depression. *Clinical Gerontologist: The Journal of Aging and Mental Health, 34,* 251–265. doi:10.1080/07317115.2011.554345.

Gillath, O., Karantzas, G., & Selcuk, E. (2012). *Attachment and perceptions of friendship networks in young adulthood.* Paper submitted for publication.

Gottman, J. M., & Graziano, W. G. (1983). *How children become friends. Monographs of the society for research in child development* (Vol. 48, pp. 1–86). New York: Wiley. http://www.jstor.org/stable/1165860. Accessed Jan 2014.

Granovetter, M. S. (1973). The strength of weak ties. *American Journal of Sociology, 73,* 1361–1380.
Havighurst, R. J. (1972). *Developmental tasks and education.* New York: Longman.
Hays, R. B. (1985). A longitudinal study of friendship development. *Journal of Personality and Social Psychology, 48,* 909–924. doi:10.1037/0022-3514.48.4.909.
Hazan, C., & Zeifman, D. (1994). Sex and the psychological tether. In K. Bartholomew & D. Perlman (Eds.), *Advances in personal relationships: Attachment processes in adulthood* (Vol. 5, pp. 151–177). London: Jessica Kingsley.
Hazan, C., Gur-Yaish, N., & Campa, M. (2004). What does it mean to be attached? In W. S. Rholes & J. A. Simpson (Eds.), *Adult attachment: Theory, research, and clinical implications* (pp. 55–85). New York: Guilford.
Henderson, S. (1977). The social network support neurosis. The function of attachment in adult life. *British Journal of Psychiatry, 131,* 185–191.
Jacobson, N. S., & Christensen, A. (1996). *Integrative couple therapy: Promoting acceptance and change.* New York: Norton.
Jang, S. A., Smith, S. W., & Levine, T. R. (2002). To stay or to leave? the role of attachment styles in communication patterns and potential termination of romantic relationships following discovery of deception. *Communication Monographs, 69,* 236–252. doi:10.1080/03637750216543.
Johnson, S. M. (2004). *The practice of emotionally focused couple therapy: Creating connection* (2nd ed.). New York: Brunner-Routledge.
Kadushin, C. (2012). *Understanding social networks: Theories, concepts, and findings.* New York: Oxford University Press.
Karantzas, G. C., & Gillath, O. (2012). *Attachment style and the management of social networks during the transition to college.* Manuscript submitted for publication.
Karantzas, G. C., Feeney, J. A., & Wilkinson, R. (2010). Is less more? confirmatory factor analysis of the attachment style questionnaires. *Journal of Social and Personal Relationships, 27,* 749–780. doi:10.1177/0265407510373756.
Karantzas, G. C., Gillath, O., McCabe, M. P., & Cole, S. F. (2012). *The management of social networks and chronic illness: An attachment perspective.* Manuscript submitted for publication.
Kavadas, V., & Karantzas, G. C. (2012). *Co-worker network functions: The role of attachment and leadership style.* Unpublished manuscript.
Kenny, D. A., & La Voie, L. (1984). The social relations model. In L. Berkowitz (Ed.), *Advances in experimental social psychology* (Vol. 18, pp. 142–182). Orlando: Academic.
Kirkpatrick, L. A., & Davis, K. E. (1994). Attachment style, gender, and relationship stability: A longitudinal analysis. *Journal of Personality and Social Psychology, 66,* 502–512. doi:10.1037/0022-3514.66.3.502.
Kirkpatrick, L. A., & Shaver, P. R. (1992). An attachment-theoretical approach to romantic love and religious belief. *Personality and Social Psychology Bulletin, 18,* 266–275. doi:http://dx.doi.org/10.1177/0146167292183002.
Knapp, M. L. (1984). *Interpersonal communication and human relationships* (3rd ed.). Boston: Allyn and Bacon.
Knoke, D., & Kuklinski, J. H. (1982). *Network analysis.* Beverly Hills: Sage.
Kobak, R., Rosenthal, N. L., Zajac, K., & Madsen, S. D. (2007). Adolescent attachment hierarchies and the search for an adult pair-bond. *New Directions for Child and Adolescent Development, 117,* 57–72. doi:10.1002/cd.194.
Kosfeld, M., Heinrichs, M., Zak, P. J., Fischbacher, U., & Fehr, E. (2005). Oxytocin increases trust in humans. *Nature, 435*(7042), 673–676. doi:http://dx.doi.org/10.1038/nature03701.
Kruglanski, A. W., Shah, J. Y., Fishbach, A., Friedman, R. S., Chun, W. Y., & Sleeth- Keppler, D. (2002). A theory of goal systems: Implications for social cognition, affect, and action. In M. Zanna (Ed.), *Advances in experimental social psychology* (Vol. 34, pp. 331–376). New York: Academic.
Lang, F. R., & Carstensen, L. L. (1994). Close emotional relationships in late life: Further support for proactive aging in the social domain. *Psychology and Aging, 9,* 315–324. doi:10.1037/0882-7974.9.2.315.

Levitt, M. J. (1980). Contingent feedback, familiarization, and infant affect: How a stranger becomes a friend. *Developmental Psychology, 16,* 425–432.

Levitt, M. J. (1991). Attachment and close relationships: A life span perspective. In J. L. Gewirtz & W. M. Kurtines (Eds.), *Intersections with attachment* (pp. 183–205). Hillsdale: Erlbaum.

Levitt, M. J. (2005). Social relations in childhood and adolescence: The convoy model perspective. *Human Development, 48,* 28–47. doi:10.1159/000083214.

Levitt, M. J., Coffman, S., Guacci-Franco, N., & Loveless, S. C. (1994). Attachment relations and life transitions: An expectancy model. In M. B. Sperling & W. H. Berman (Eds.), *Attachment in adults: Clinical and developmental perspectives* (pp. 232–255). New York: Guilford.

Lewin, K. (1935). *A dynamic theory of personality*. New York: McGraw Hill.

McPherson, M., Smith-Lovin, L., & Cook, J. M. (2001). Birds of a Feather: Homophily in. *Social Networks. Annual Review of Sociology, 27,* 415–444.

Mead, N. L., Baumeister, R. F., Stillman, T. F., Rawn, C. D., & Vohs, K. D. (2011). Social exclusion causes people to spend and consume strategically in the service of affiliation. *Journal of Consumer Research, 37,* 902–919. doi:http://dx.doi.org/10.1086/656667.

Mesch, G., & Talmud, I. (2006). The quality of online and offline relationships, the role of multiplexity and duration. *The Information Society, 22,* 137–149.

Mikulincer, M. (1998). Attachment working models and the sense of trust: An exploration of interaction goals and affect regulation. *Journal of Personality and Social Psychology, 74,* 1209–1224.

Mikulincer, M., & Florian, V. (2001). Attachment style and affect regulation—Implications for coping with stress and mental health. In G. Fletcher & M. Clark (Eds.), *Blackwell handbook of social psychology: Interpersonal processes* (pp. 537–557). Oxford: Blackwell.

Mikulincer, M., & Selinger, M. (2001). The interplay between attachment and affiliation systems in adolescents' same-sex friendships: The role of attachment style. *Journal of Social and Personal Relationships, 18,* 81–106. doi:10.1177/0265407501181004.

Mikulincer, M., & Shaver, P. R. (2007a). *Attachment patterns in adulthood: Structure, dynamics, and change*. New York: Guilford.

Mikulincer, M., & Shaver, P. R. (2007b). Boosting attachment security to promote mental health, prosocial values, and inter-group tolerance. *Psychological Inquiry, 18,* 139–156.

Mikulincer, M., Gillath, O., & Shaver, P. R. (2002). Activation of the attachment system in adulthood: Threat-related primes increase the accessibility of mental representations of attachment figures. *Journal of Personality and Social Psychology, 83,* 881–895.

Mikulincer, M., Shaver, P. R., Gillath, O., & Nitzberg, R. A. (2005). Attachment, caregiving, and altruism: Boosting attachment security increases compassion and helping. *Journal of Personality and Social Psychology, 89,* 817–839. doi:10.1037/0022-3514.89.5.817.

Milardo, R. M. (1982). Friendship networks in developing relationships: Converging and diverging social environments. *Social Psychology Quarterly, 45,* 162–172.

Milardo, R. M. (Ed.). (1988). *Families and social networks. New perspectives on family*. Thousand Oaks: Sage.

Milardo, R. M., & Allan, G. (1997). Social networks and marital relationships. In S. Duck (Ed.), *Handbook of personal relationships* (2nd ed., pp. 505–522). Chichester: Wiley.

Milardo, R. M., Johnson, M. P., & Huston, T. L. (1983). Developing close relationships: Changing patterns of interaction between pair members and social networks. *Journal of Personality and Social Psychology, 44,* 964–976. doi:10.1037/0022-3514.44.5.964.

Mischel, W. (2011). In "*The many faces of network analysis*". Daily Observations. http://www.psychologicalscience.org/index.php/publications/observer/obsonline/network-analysis-a-better-way-to-represent-data.html. Accessed Jan 2014.

Murray, H. A. (1953). *Explorations in personality*. New York: Oxford Hill.

Obegi, J. H., & Berant, E. (2009). Introduction. In J. H. Obegi & E. Berant (Eds.), *Attachment theory and research in clinical work with adults*. (pp. 1–14). New York: Guilford.

Parker, J. G., Low, C. M., Walker, A. R., & Gamm, B. K. (2005). Friendship jealousy in young adolescents: Individual differences and links to sex, self-esteem, aggression, and social adjustment. *Developmental Psychology, 41,* 235–250. doi:http://dx.doi.org/10.1037/0012-1649.41.1.235.

Pitkow, L. J., Sharer, C. A., Ren, X., Insel, T. R., Terwilliger, E. F., & Young, L. J. (2001). Facilitation of affiliation and pair-bond formation by vasopressin receptor gene transfer into the ventral forebrain of a monogamous vole. *The Journal of Neuroscience, 21,* 7392–7396.

Reis, H. T., & Shaver, P. R. (1988). Intimacy as an interpersonal process. In S. Duck (Ed.), *Handbook of research in personal relationships* (pp. 367–389). London: Wiley.

Roberts, S. G. B., & Dunbar, R. I. M. (2011). Communication in social networks: Effects of kinship, network size, and emotional closeness. *Personal Relationships, 18,* 439–452. doi:http://dx.doi.org/10.1111/j.1475-6811.2010.01310.x.

Rowe, A. C., & Carnelley, K. B. (2005). Preliminary support for the use of a hierarchical mapping technique to examine attachment networks. *Personal Relationships, 12,* 499–519. doi:10.1111/j.1475-6811.2005.00128.x.

Schultheiss, O. C. (2008). Implicit motives. In O. P. John, R. W. Robins, & L. A. Pervin (Eds.), *Handbook of personality: Theory and research* (3rd ed., pp. 603–633). New York: Guilford.

Schwartz, J. P., Lindley, L. D., & Buboltz, W. C. (2007). Adult attachment orientations: Relation to affiliation motivation. *Counseling Psychology Quarterly, 20,* 253–265. doi:http://dx.doi.org/10.1080/09515070701308480.

Selcuk, E., & Gillath, O. (2009). Attachment and depression. In R. Ingram (Ed.), *Encyclopedia of depression* (pp. 32–37). New York: Springer.

Shaver, P. R., Schachner, D. A., & Mikulincer, M. (2005). Attachment style, excessive reassurance seeking, relationship processes, and depression. *Personality and Social Psychology Bulletin, 31,* 343–359.

Sheldon, A. E., & West, M. (1989). The functional discrimination of attachment and affiliation. Theory and empirical demonstration. *British Journal of Psychiatry, 155,* 18–23.

Simpson, J. A. (1990). Influence of attachment styles on romantic relationships. *Journal of Personality and Social Psychology, 59,* 971–980.

Simpson, J. A., Rholes, W. S., & Nelligan, J. S. (1992). Support seeking and support giving within couples in an anxiety-provoking situation: The role of attachment styles. *Journal of Personality and Social Psychology, 62,* 434–446.

Snyder, M., & Swann, W. B. Jr. (1978). Hypothesis testing process in social interactions. *Journal of Personality and Social Psychology, 36,* 1202–1212.

Snyder, M., Gangestad, S., & Simpson, J. (1983). Choosing friends as activity partners: The role of self-monitoring. *Journal of Personality and Social Psychology, 45,* 1061–1072. doi:10.1037/0022-3514.45.5.1061.

Sprecher, S. (2011). The influence of social networks on romantic relationships: Through the lens of the social network. *Personal Relationships, 18,* 630–644.

Stoller, E. P., Miller, B., & Guo, S. (2001). Shared ethnicity and relationship multiplexity within the informal networks of retired European American sunbelt migrants. *Research on Aging, 23,* 304–325. doi:10.1177/0164027501233002.

Tesch, S. A. (1983). Review of friendship development across the life span. *Human Development, 26,* 266–276. doi:10.1159/000272888.

Trinke, S. J., & Bartholomew, K. (1997). Hierarchies of attachment relationships in young adulthood. *Journal of Social and Personal Relationships, 14,* 603–625. doi:10.1177/0265407597145002.

Uchino, B. N. (2009). Understanding the links between social support and physical health: A life-spa perspective with emphasis on the separability of perceived and received support. *Perspectives on Psychological Science, 4,* 236–255.

van Duijn, M. A., & Vermunt. J. K. (2006). What is special about social network analysis? *Methodology, 2,* 2–6.

Wallace, J. L., & Vaux, A. (1993). Social support network orientation: The role of adult attachment style. *Journal of Social and Clinical Psychology, 12,* 354–365. doi:10.1521/jscp.1993.12.3.354.

Wasserman, S., & Faust, K. (1994). *Social network analysis: Methods and applications*. New York: Cambridge University.

Watson, J. S. (1972). Smiling, cooing, and 'the game'. *Merrill-Palmer Quarterly, 18,* 323–341.

Watt, S. E., & Badger, A. J. (2009). Effects of social belonging on homesickness: An application of the belongingness hypothesis. *Personality and Social Psychology Bulletin, 35,* 516–530. doi:10.1177/0146167208329695.

Weiss, R. S. (1998). A taxonomy of relationships. *Journal of Social and Personal Relationships, 15,* 671–683.

Wellman, B., & Wellman, B. (1992). Domestic affairs and network relations. *Journal of Social and Personal Relationships, 9,* 385–409.

Wrzus, C., Hänel, M., Wagner, J., & Neyer, F. J. (2012). Social network changes and life events across the lifespan: A meta-analysis. *Psychological Bulletin*. doi:10.1037/a0028601.

Zajonc, R. B. (1968). Attitudinal effects of mere exposure. *Journal of Personality and Social Psychology, 9,* 1–27. doi:10.1037/h0025848.

Zeifman, D., & Hazan, C. (1997). Attachment: The bond in pair-bonds. In J. A. Simpson & D. T. Kenrick (Eds.), *Evolutionary social psychology* (pp. 237–263). Hillsdale: Lawrence Erlbaum Associates.

Chapter 8
From an Unknown Other to an Attachment Figure: How Do Mental Representations Change as Attachments Form?

Vivian Zayas, Gül Günaydin and Yuichi Shoda

In adulthood, long-term pair bonds confer a number of beneficial psychological and physical benefits. Irrespective of the level of relationship satisfaction, partners are capable of regulating each other's physiological systems, daily mood, and affective states, as well as eating and sleeping patterns (Selcuk et al. 2010). Most important, partners in long-term pair-bonds are capable of alleviating physiological and psychological distress and promoting feelings of security in each other—such emotion regulation benefits is one of the defining features of attachment bonds.

A key and well-supported assumption in the literature is that these observable manifestations of adult pair bonds reflect the functioning of *mental representations*, or *internal working models*. Mental representations are the residue of past experiences with the particular partner, as well as experiences from other past and present relationships experienced directly or indirectly, stored in memory. Mental representations are powerful because they implicitly affect perceptions and expectations about likely events (e.g., if I seek help, then I will be supported), which in turn guide behaviors. Their influence extends beyond the relationship with the partner to interactions with friends, colleagues, acquaintances, and unknown others, and even to behaviors in seemingly asocial settings (e.g., when at work or alone), and may do so even without one's awareness (Günaydin et al. 2012).

Interestingly, although the field of adult attachment has uncovered much about the structure, content, functioning, and ontology of the mental representations underlying attachment relationships, little is known about the processes by which mental representations form, develop, and are maintained in *adult* pair-bonds. That is, how do mental representations change as a relationship develops from one between two strangers to one between two acquaintances and casual friends to a dating

V. Zayas (✉)
Department of Psychology, Cornell University, 238 Uris Hall, Ithaca, NY, 14853-7601, USA
e-mail: vz29@cornell.edu

G. Günaydin
Department of Psychology, Bilkent University, Ankara, Turkey

Y. Shoda
Department of Psychology, University of Washington, Seattle, USA

V. Zayas, C. Hazan (eds.), *Bases of Adult Attachment*,
DOI 10.1007/978-1-4614-9622-9_8

relationship characterized by romantic and sexual interest to a full-fledged attachment bond capable of regulating various psychological and physiological systems?

In the present chapter, we explore the metamorphosis that two individuals undergo as they form a pair bond. We describe a social cognitive framework for beginning to understand the changes that unfold at the level of *mental representations* as individuals go from two strangers whose lives and "minds" are relatively asynchronous and independent to two individuals in a full-fledged attachment relationship whose lives and minds are intertwined and synchronized. We propose that the positive psychological and physical outcomes, as well as the emotion regulatory effects, observed in pair bonds occur as a result of the two individuals developing elaborated mental representations of one another and extensive associations between the representation of the self and that of the partner. Moreover, as a result of having extensive experiences with the other person, frequently encountered interactions (*If I'm upset, then my partner will comfort me*) eventually become automatic and no longer require the actual person for the psychological and physical benefits to be realized. In a sense, through the elaboration of partner (and self) mental representations, the two people begin to form a linked or "coupled" cognitive system.

To describe our social cognitive approach to normative development of mental representations of adult attachment relationships, the present chapter is organized into four sections: First, we provide a brief review of what is known about the processes by which adult romantic attachments form. Second, we describe a social cognitive framework, personality-in-context (PiC) approach (Zayas et al. 2002), for conceptualizing developmental processes of change necessary for adult attachment formation. Our model draws from research on relationship *turning points* (e.g., first kiss, exclusivity; Baxter and Erbert 1999; Bolton 1961), which are events associated with changes (i.e., subsequent increases or decreases in commitment) in relationship trajectories, and how they may provide fertile ground for the evolution of the mental representations underlying the relationship. Third, we review and integrate existing empirical work, from diverse fields, on what is known about mental representations at various stages of attachment formation into this framework. We end by raising unanswered questions and discussing fruitful avenues for future empirical work on adult attachment formation and development processes.

Attachment Formation in Adult Attachment Relationships

Perhaps the best starting point to thinking about the development of adult attachment bonds is theorizing on the development of infant-caregiver bonds (Bowlby 1982; Hazan et al. 2004; Hazan and Zeifman 1994; Zeifman and Hazan 1997). In infant/caregiver relationships, attachment bonds are believed to form through four stages. In the *preattachment phase* (0–2 months), the infant is open to accepting care from anyone. In the *attachment-in-the-making phase* (2–6 months), the infant begins to discriminate among caregivers by differentially directing various social signals and selectively responding to certain caregivers. In the *clear-cut attachment phase* (after 6–7 months), the infant displays all four behaviors that define a full-fledged attachment bond. These are proximity-seeking, safe haven, separation distress, and secure base. And finally, in the *goal-corrected partnership phase* (after 36 months), as a consequence of cognitive maturation and the construction of a mental representation of the caregiver, the infant experiences less stress from temporary separations and a relative decline in proximity-seeking behaviors because she or he understands that the caregiver will eventually return.

Drawing from the infant attachment literature, Hazan and colleagues (Hazan et al. 2004; Zeifman and Hazan 1997) have proposed an analogous four-stage developmental framework to the formation of attachment bonds between two adults. In the *preattachment phase*, individuals get to know and seek proximity to potential romantic partners by what is colloquially referred to as "flirting," but critically in this stage, attachment behaviors are not directed exclusively to specific individuals. In the *attachment-in-the-making phase*, individuals preferentially seek proximity to a specific romantic partner and engage in various behaviors promoting attachment formation (e.g., self-disclosures, physical contact, mutual gazing, kissing, sex). In the *clear-cut attachment phase*, all behaviors that define an attachment bond are organized around the romantic partner. Now, the partner helps alleviate stress even when he or she is not physically present, and separations from the partner cause distress as well as disrupting regulation of affect and physiology. In the *goal-corrected partnership phase*, the representation of the partner becomes further elaborated and has a greater influence on person perception and stress alleviation.

Theoretical Framework

Personality-in-Context (PiC) Approach

The stages of attachment development identified by Hazan and colleagues provide an organizing framework for delineating how attachment bonds form and develop over time. Less is known, however, about how this development occurs at the level of *mental representations* of attachment figures. To address this central question, we draw on the PiC approach (Mischel and Shoda 1995; Shoda and Mischel 1998; Zayas et al. 2002). PiC is a social-cognitive metatheory that provides a framework for understanding how two individuals go from being strangers—a stage in which their lives and minds are independent and asynchronous—to a full-fledged pair bond—a stage in which the lives and minds of both individuals are intricately intertwined. In this section, we aim to describe basic concepts of the PiC approach (for a detailed description see Zayas et al. 2002) and extend them towards developing a normative model of adult attachment relationships.

Each Person's CAPs Network. To illustrate key principles, Fig. 8.1 provides a schematic of highly simplified CAPS networks of two individuals, referred to as Sam and Terry. The PiC approach conceptualizes each person's "mind" as a

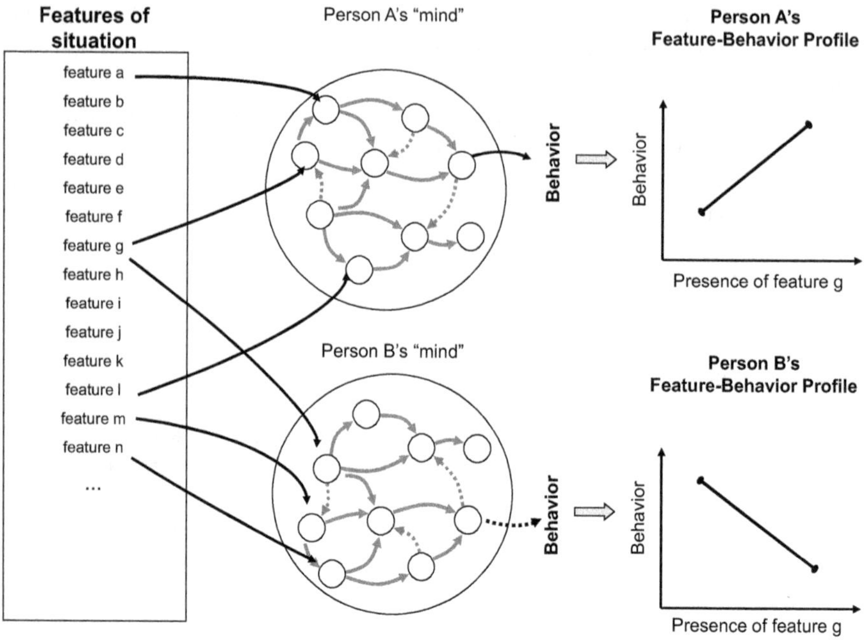

Fig. 8.1. Schematic representation of the cognitive-affective processing system (CAPS) for two hypothetical individuals (i.e., Person *A, Sam,* and Person *B, Terry*). Each person's mind is conceptualized by a stable network of interconnected cognitions and affects that mediates the effect of the situational features on behavior. *Solid lines* within and outside of the network represent excitatory associations (e.g., activation of one cognition automatically activates associated cognitions). *Dotted lines* within and outside of the network represent inhibitory associations (e.g., activation of one cognition makes it more difficult to activate associated cognitions). In the above illustration, each person encounters the same situation that consists of a common set of features (e.g., *a* through *n*). Because not all the features are meaningful for all people, Person *A* and Person *B* differ in the specific situational features that activate (or inhibit) certain cognitions and affects within each person's network, which in turn lean to a behavioral response. Figure reproduced from Zayas et al. (2008)

distinctive and *stable* system of interconnected cognitions and affects (also referred to as *cognitive-affective processing system* or *CAPS network).* These cognitions and affects, which are sometimes referred to as cognitive-affective units or CAUs, are essentially another term for mental representations. Thus, for the purpose of this chapter, change in mental representations is synonymous with change in a person's CAPs network, and vice versa. CAUs represent affective reactions (basic evaluations of goodness or badness to full-blown feelings and emotions), encodings (schemas and categories of self, others, events, and objects), expectations and beliefs (about the world and likely outcomes in particular situations), abstract goals (desired and undesired outcomes, goals and life projects), and competencies and self-regulatory plans (behavioral scripts that organize action).

Such social cognitive associationist approaches are not new to attachment theory. For decades, they have been fruitfully applied to understanding the complexity of the mechanisms of attachment working models (see Bartz et al., this volume). These frameworks draw on social cognitive ideas, such as *availability* and *temporary* and *chronic accessibility* (e.g., Bruner 1957; Higgins and King 1981), to understand *interindividual* or *attachment style* differences—why different people experience attachment relationships so differently—as well as *intraindividual* variability in experiences—why a given individual may feel secure in one relationship or at one moment in time, but not in another relationship or at a different moment in time. A key assumption of social cognitive approaches is that, each person's unique network of cognitions and affects mediates how he or she perceives, reacts, and behaves to particular situations. It is assumed that, the presence of a situational cue either external (in the environment) or internal (generated by one's own thoughts) activates a *subset* of cognitions and affects within the person's network. For example, if Sam has an upsetting encounter with a work colleague, this situation might activate a subset of encoding units within Sam's CAPS network (e.g., fear of disapproval, being excluded), which then via principles of spreading activation activates other associated cognitions and affects (e.g., feelings of insecurity and incompetence), which, in turn, gives rise to Sam's behaviors (e.g., defensiveness and anger). However, if Sam is instead enjoying the company of friends, this situation might activate a different subset of encoding units within Sam's network, which will in turn lead to a different subjective experience and behaviors.

Accounting for attachment style (interindividual) differences. Each person's network is distinct, as illustrated by comparing Terry's and Sam's network in Fig. 8.1. The networks differ in (i) the *availability* of the particular cognitions and affects within each person's network, as well as (ii) the *accessibility* of available cognitions and affects determined by the pattern and strengths of their interconnections. Individual differences are assumed to arise as a result of differences in the *pattern* of interconnections among available cognitions and affects.

To illustrate, imagine that Sam has had a couple of significant romantic relationships, both of which have been characterized by supportiveness and responsiveness, whereas Terry has had a string of difficult relationships in which there was little trust with previous partners. For both individuals, the residue of these past experiences becomes crystalized in memory and leads to changes in their networks. For Sam, the mental representation of past romantic partners is likely to be strongly connected to other CAUs encoding experiences of supportiveness, whereas for Terry the mental representation of past romantic partners is likely connected to other CAUs encoding untrustworthiness. Differences in both the patterning and strength of associations among CAUs characterizing the two people's networks contribute to the ease with which certain thoughts and feelings and behavioral repertoires become activated in particular situations. For Sam, attributions that a current partner is behaving in a supportive manner are likely to become spontaneously activated even in ambiguous situations, whereas such attributions might require much more effort for Terry who has less positive experiences. These differences in networks are expected to account for differences in the *chronic accessibility* of certain cognitions and affects (e.g., characteristic ways of encoding a situation), which in turn produce predictable differences between people in their behavioral responses and patterns.

Accounting for intraindividual variability across situations and across relationships. The functioning of the network is able to account for variability *within* a given person's ongoing behavior, such as, why Sam might be anxious when having a confrontation with a colleague, but relaxed when spending an evening with friends. At least in the short term, the internal organization of each person's cognitive-affective processing *system* itself remains relatively stable and invariant, even though the *particular* thoughts and affects activated at a given moment change, depending on the situational input that activates them.

If ... then ... situation ... behavior patterns: Behavioral Signatures. To the extent that a person encounters situations with similar features, the same CAPS subnetwork will become activated in those situations, generating similar behavioral responses. Although the underlying network is difficult to assess directly, the observable manifestations of the network dynamics are distinctive and stable *if... then... situation...behavior...*relationships between features of situations (i.e., *ifs*), on one hand, and behavioral responses (i.e., *thens*), on the other. These *if...then...* situation–behavior relationships are assumed to uniquely describe the consistency within a person's behavioral variability across situations. For example, if Sam has a conflict with a colleague, then she feels anxious. And, this *if...then... profile* is expected to be stable and characterize Sam's behaviors over time.

This point is particularly relevant to the present chapter on how an attachment bond develops. If the observable *if...then... situation–behavior* relationships of a person change, then presumably the underlying network has changed also. Thus, changes in behavioral signatures with regards to behavioral dynamics of two individuals may provide behavioral markers that their networks (i.e., partner and self representations) are also changing.

Conceptualizing the situation, or "ifs," as one's partner

Past social cognitive approaches to the attachment dynamics have conceptualized the situation or *ifs* in terms of the presence (or absence) of an interpersonal threat that activates (or deactivates) the attachment behavioral system (Mikulincer et al 2002), or as a particular relationship partner that affects the specific working models active in a given moment (Baldwin et al. 1996). Building on this tradition, the PiC approach assumes that the most significant aspects of the *situation*, that is, the "*ifs*,"—both metaphorically and literally speaking—are one's partner and her behaviors.

The PiC approach assumes that in close relationships, particularly those that involve romantic partners, the thoughts, feelings, and behaviors of one partner come to matter more, and a large and integral part of one partner's environment is the behavior of the other partner. For example, fast forward and imagine that Sam and Terry are now in a full-fledged pair bond. As shown in Fig. 8.2, once a dyad is formed, the behavior of one partner, Sam (B_1), emerges from the interaction between her "mind" or network (P_1) and the situational input provided primarily by her partner's behavior, Terry (B_2), hence $B_1 = f(P_1, B_2)$. Similarly, the behavior of the other partner in the dyad, Terry (B_2), can be conceptualized as a function of the interaction between his "mind" or network (P_2) and the situational information provided by his partner's behavior, Sam (B_1), hence $B_2 = f(P_2, B_1)$.

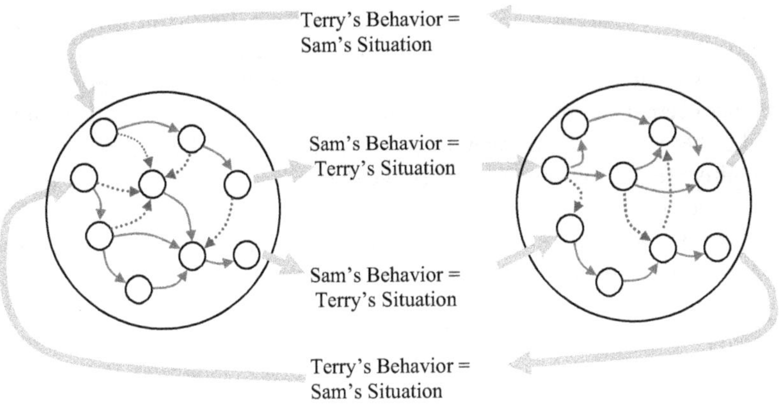

Fig. 8.2. The "interlocking" of the CAPS networks of two members of a dyad. As individuals develop a relationship, the CAPS networks of each partner become "interlocked" so that the significant part of the situations encountered by one partner consists of the behaviors of the partner, and vice versa. In the hypothetical scenario, Sam and Terry have begun to form a relationship. The resulting dyadic system which consists of Sam's and Terry's CAPS networks begins to become interconnected in such a way that the behavioral output from Sam's CAPS network becomes Terry's situation. This situation, in turn, is the input that activates a particular cognitive-affective dynamic in Terry, leading to Terry's behavior. Similarly, the behavioral output from Terry's CAPS network becomes Sam's situation, which in turn, activates in Sam a particular cognitive-affective dynamic, leading to her behavior. In this manner, a dyadic interpersonal system starts to develop, and once formed may account for consistency and stability within interpersonal relationships. Figure adapted from Zayas et al. (2002)

Interlocking of Two CAPS Networks: The Dyadic System

How does such a dyadic system, as represented in Fig. 8.2, develop? Two assumptions are central for understanding how dyadic systems emerge. First is the idea that situations with similar features tend to activate the same CAPS subnetworks, which in turn are expected to generate similar behavioral responses and second is the assumption that in close relationships the behavior of one partner is the situational input for the other. In combination, these two assumptions suggest that if one partner's behavior is relatively consistent over time (e.g., one's partner is sensitive and responsive especially when the other is distressed), then, in effect, the other partner is repeatedly exposed to situations that involve similar features (a responsive and sensitive partner), which in turn will repeatedly activate a specific subset of cognitions and affects in her CAPS network (e.g., comfort and alleviation of distress). Over time of repeatedly encountering these situations, the particular cognitive-affective dynamics that become activated in one partner in response to the other partner's specific behaviors may become increasingly more accessible and in future interactions might start to become activated with minimal behavioral input.

Returning to Sam and Terry, in the early phase of the relationship, if Sam experiences distress as a result of the confrontation with a colleague, she may need to obtain concrete physical and verbal comfort from Terry to experience relief. However, if over time, Sam repeatedly experiences relief from distress as a result of the behavior of Terry, then an association between the mental representation of her partner (Terry) and relief becomes encoded in memory. Eventually, simply the thought of her partner is sufficient to experience distress-relieving benefits. In social cognitive terms, the cognitive-affective dynamics characterizing distress-relief have become *chronically accessible*.

Furthermore, as a relationship develops, each partner is learning (implicitly or explicitly) about how her partner behaves in different situations and in a sense, begins to develop a mental representation of the partner. For example, early on in the relationship, Sam may have to explicitly communicate to Terry that she is upset and why. At this point, Terry may not yet be able to read her subtle cues of distress (e.g., Sam tends to be less talkative when upset). However, as the relationship develops and with repeated interactions, Sam may no longer have to explicitly express when she is upset. Now, Terry may be much attuned to any subtle changes in her verbal and nonverbal cues that signal distress and can provide comfort even without any explicit communication. He may even become particularly adept at knowing exactly what she needs depending on the source and nature of the distress.

Once the mental representation of each partner is formed, an individual may be more likely to engage in top-down, schema-driven processing (rather than bottom-up, stimulus-driven processing) and consequently, may interpret the behaviors of her partner as consistent with the schema. Over time, we expect that two individuals will form a dynamic dyadic system that generates stable and predictable patterns of behavior (see Fig. 8.2). The resulting dyadic system is dynamic in the sense that the specific cognitions and affects that become activated within the CAPS network of each person of the dyad, as well as the observable behaviors that each CAPS network produces, are not constant, but vary from moment-to-moment depending on the situational input (i.e., partner's behaviors).

A Model of Adult Attachment Formation

The PiC approach begins to provide a conceptual framework for understanding how a dyadic relationship forms. However, many questions remain about the processes contributing to the formation of a dyadic system in general and the formation of an attachment bond specifically. To develop a process model of adult attachment formation, we not only draw on PiC, but also bring together two distinct lines of work. We draw upon the relationship literature on *turning points* (Bolton 1961). These are relationship events that are important because they are associated with subsequent increases and decreases in the dyad's commitment level. We also draw upon the learning and memory literature that speaks to how novel information becomes stored in long-term memory.

1. Turning Points The manner in which two individuals solve the challenges posed by particular turning points has implications for the linking of the two systems.

Work on relationship development has shown that couples go through key *turning points* in their relationships (e.g., first kiss, exclusivity, etc.) that are associated with increases (and in some cases decreases) in relationship commitment (Baxter and Bullis 1986). Each type of turning point, such as spending time together, is associated with particular cues (e.g., partner scent, mannerisms, personal history) and interactions (e.g., comfort, sexual arousal) that may elicit certain psychological, behavioral, and physical changes in the person him or herself.

Moreover, turning points are associated with psychological themes. At each turning point, couples experience increased tension between competing interpersonal motives and goals (e.g., independence versus connectedness; Baxter and Erbert 1999). How two individuals resolve these conflicts undoubtedly has implications for the linking of the two systems, via overlapping partner and self representations, and thus profoundly affects the formation of the attachment bond, as well as its quality (promoting security or insecurity). For example, siding towards greater connectedness should go hand in hand with greater interconnectedness of the partner and self mental representations in each person's mind. Conversely, if conflicts engendered by turning points lead to siding towards greater independence, then the partner and self mental representations will remain separate and distinct within the mind of both individuals.

Thus, the set of cues associated with a particular turning point is large, including all the sensory information about the partner and changes to the self, as well as implicit learning about the partner's behaviors and the self, and any meta-cognitions (e.g., thoughts and feelings about the meaning of particular events) that arise from the resolution of conflicting motives. We propose that the turning points (either a singular event or events reoccurring over a period of time) are times during which significant learning about the relationship partner, the self, and the self-in-relation-to-partner occurs. This learning is reflected in enduring changes in the mental representations of the individuals in the dyad (i.e., changes in each person's CAPs networks) and the resulting representation leads to changes at the level of affect, thought, and behavior within the relationship.

2. Learning process from co-occurrence in short-term memory to permanent changes in representations in long-term memory. We suggest that these turning points are fertile ground for each partner undergoing significant changes in their mental representations—i.e., changes in each person's CAPs network. In turn, these changes in the minds of the individuals naturally give rise to changes in the subsequent functioning of the two individuals.

The idea that learning, particularly associative learning, is involved in the formation of attachment bonds is not new. The role of associative conditioning in attachment has long been discussed in both the human (see also Acevedo, Bartz et al., and Beckes and Coan, this volume) and animal literature (Cairns 1966; Hofer 1994). Extrapolating from these literatures, it is assumed that through the course of a relationship, partners become conditioned to various features of one another, and that these cues regulate distinct physiological, affective, cognitive, and behavioral systems.

Here we extend theory and research on learning processes to the *development of adult attachment relationships*. Specifically, we extend past work by proposing that *what* is learned is contingent on the various external cues (e.g., partner's scent, verbal and nonverbal behaviors) and internal cues (e.g., one's own internal motivations and states) during key turning points in the relationship. Drawing from the memory literature (Atkinson and Shiffrin 1968; Hebb 1969; Tulving 1972), we suggest that the mental representation of the partner, the self-in-relation-to-partner, and the relationship itself builds over time in two-phases. First, the set of cues present during turning points simply co-occur with the activation of the existing mental representation of the partner in short-term memory, which has a fairly limited capacity. We hypothesize that the coactivation of the partner representation with the various cues elicited by the turning point first occurs in short term memory. The more one is exposed to the cues, or the more that one uses cue-relevant information, the greater likelihood that the information will become stored in long-term memory. Because the turning point, by definition, provides novel cues (or novel constellation of cues) not previously encountered, the set of cues are highly salient, which further contributes to their encoding and storage in memory.

Second, information about the partner is gradually transferred from short-term memory into long-term memory. With repeated exposure to cues present during turning points, or single exposure if the cues are highly potent, the cues increasingly become associated with mental representations and are expected to leave a permanent trace in long-term memory, thus resulting in stable and enduring changes in mental representations. Moreover, unlike short-term memory with limited capacity and rapid decay, long-term memory can store unlimited amounts of information indefinitely. Thus, the resultant mental representation of the partner is expected to exert its influence on behaviors within and outside of the relationship.

Through this learning process, we expect that the mental representations that characterize each individual at different points in the relationship undergo significant change in their structure. They are elaborated and increasingly linked with the self-representation, and thus lead to mental representations that characterize a different stage in the relationship.

3. What Are the Key Turning Points at Each Stage of Adult Attachment Formation? Is it possible to identify a finite set of turning points that predictably shape the course of adult attachment formation? This is a daunting task. The literature suggests that relational development is quite diverse (Huston et al. 1981). Moreover, although most people report experiencing turning points in their relationships, members of the same dyad rarely report the same key events and may experience the same event in drastically different ways (Sillars and Scot 1983; see also Christensen and Nies 1980; Jacobson and Moore 1981). Such variability in the events that play a significant role in relationship development is even greater *across* relationships. For example, of 80 participants (40 couples), only 10 participants listed the "first kiss" as a turning point in the relationship, and only 23 participants listed "first sex" as a turning point (Baxter and Bullis 1986).

Nonetheless, based on the extant research on turning points and work on adult attachment, there are a few natural candidates. Work by Baxter and colleagues has identified 26 turning points, which were further subdivided into 14 supratypes. Although turning points with respect to commitment levels is not the same as turning points with respect to an attachment bond, this list provides a reasonable empirically based starting point from which to identify events in relationship development that might foster, or hinder, the formation of an attachment bond. Among the turning points identified, not surprisingly, there were a few key attachment-related turning points, such as, get to know time (first meeting), quality time, physical separation, reunion, provision of support, and serious commitment, which we consider in this chapter.

The PiC Approach in Action: Revisiting the Story of Sam and Terry

To illustrate the basic ideas of the PiC approach to adult attachment formation, let's return to the story of Sam and Terry. They first met at a party hosted by a mutual friend. They remained acquaintances for a few months, seeing each other at social gatherings. At this point, the mental representation that each person had of the other was based primarily on their previous experiences with others, such as partners, parents, and friends, as well as broader social categories about what one knows about different types of people. All these experiences are encoded in memory and are all used in the service of making sense of newly encountered others.

However, based on the attraction and relationship literature, a few key ingredients are likely to put the two on a path to forming an attachment bond. One is attraction, whether dispositionally the two are drawn to each other based on each other's physical and psychological characteristics or situationally given the particular events in their life situation. In the story of Sam and Terry, each finds the other attractive. Sam is immediately smitten by Terry's dry wit, and Terry is captivated by Sam's appearance. They also share a few common interests, which fans the initial spark. However, perhaps equally as important, situational factors push them together as well. They both have recovered from their most recent relationship and are in a time in their lives in which they are interested in dating with the possibility of more. Everyone in their social circle thinks they are perfect for one another. And, each of their families is ready for them to settle down.

With forces of attraction drawing the two together, over time, Sam and Terry increasingly spend more time together. They try out the latest restaurants, spend the evening listening to live music, and walk through the farmer's market on weekends. Not surprisingly, their initial attraction and time together increases the likelihood of experiencing more emotionally and physically intimate events (first kiss, first sexual encounter, deciding to be exclusive), which provide opportunities for Sam and Terry to learn about each other and to develop a representation of themselves in relation to one another. Turning points provide novel cues or constellation of cues, that when presented repeatedly over time build up the mental representation of the partner. The mental representation of the partner is expected to become increasingly complex in terms of shear amount of information, its interconnection with existing representations, and particularly its interconnections with representations of the self.

These turning points also provide opportunities for each person to meet the needs of the other. The safe haven provision is one of the defining features of adult attachment relationships. The first time that Terry is distressed and comforted by Sam sets the stage for learning, explicitly and implicitly, that Sam can be counted on for support in the future, and perhaps more importantly, that her behaviors or even mere presence and sound of her voice are soothing. For a full-fledged attachment bond to form, these types of interactions in which the safe haven provision is met, must be encountered repeatedly.

Over time, these experiences are expected to become crystalized in the minds of both individuals. From a PiC approach, this process of changing mental representations is conceptualized as enduring changes in the networks (pattern and strength of existing associations) of the two individuals. These changes are reflected in greater associations between the partner mental representation and the self representation, as well as how these are associated with various cognitive, affective, and behavioral responses. The new pattern of associations affects encoding of the partner's behavior, and the cognitive and affective reactions that the encoding activates. Thus, as a result of learning that occurs in the early stages of a relationship as individuals encounter key events, the networks of the two individuals become increasingly attuned to each other, which in turn contributes to synchronization of the two individuals' affective, cognitive, physiological, and behavioral responses.

In addition, because the behavioral manifestations of each person's network are the stable *if (situation)…then (behavior)…* patterns, as the networks of the two individuals change so too should we expect to see changes in their *if…then…* patterns. For example, in the early stage of their relationship, if Sam happened to arrive at a party upset from the day's events, Terry's presence might only provide minimal relief and would be incapable of regulating affective and physiological systems. However, in a full-fledged pair bond, even a simple reminder of Terry (e.g., thinking of him, seeing his photograph, receiving a text message) is capable of inducing feelings of calm. Similarly, whereas separations from Terry early on would not disrupt basic physiological and psychological functioning, critically, these systems would be severely affected by separation in a full-fledged pair bond.

Reviewing and Integrating Existing Literature Within this Framework

How does one go from being unattached to attached? More specifically, what are the changes that occur at the level of the mental representation as an attachment bond develops? To date, there is little empirical longitudinal evidence documenting these changes. Instead, there is research on mental representations at various stages of relationship development, starting from a rich body of social cognition research on mental representations of unknown others and acquaintances, which is the state that most individuals start out at, to the extensive work in the area of adult and child attachment on the deep influences of attachment representations. Here we summarize literature from diverse fields, including social and cognitive psychology and neuropsychology, for clues to the possible changes in representations as individuals form an attachment bond in adulthood. We also highlight how particular turning points in the relationship may promote changes in the mental representation at each stage and possible areas for future inquiry. Although we are not proposing that these turning points can only occur in specific stages, based on the literature, we identify the stages in which they are likely to occur in order to illustrate the PiC approach to adult attachment formation.

We divide this section into three parts reflecting the stages of attachment development that have been identified in previous work (e.g., Zeifman and Hazan 1997). Preattachment, attachment-in-the-making, and clear-cut attachment/goal-corrected partnership. Towards the end, we illustrate how the PiC approach can be used to inform adult attachment formation by continuing with our hypothetical scenario of Sam and Terry.

Preattachment

A defining feature of the preattachment stage is that attachment behaviors are not exclusively directed to the future partner. Indeed, in this initial stage, when two individuals first meet, they have very little information about one another. However, even so, research suggests that instead of possessing *no* mental representation of one another, or possessing some sort of "blank slate" on which experiences with the person are etched, individuals come into these situations making a number of inferences about one another (e.g., Andersen and Baum 1994; Goodwin et al. 2002), even based on minimal nonverbal and verbal cues (e.g., for a review see Macrae and Quadflieg 2010). These initial impressions and inferences (e.g., whether the other person is attractive, funny, or competent) are important because they strongly affect the extent to which the two individuals are drawn towards each other and likely to encounter various key events or turning points that further pull them towards (or away from) one another. In a sense, inferences, albeit not necessarily conscious, can serve to either highlight some individuals as potential partners, or eliminate them from contention.

1. Initial Impressions: *When the Past Affects the Present.* The objective characteristics of each person (e.g., physical attractiveness) are important factors in these initial impressions, and people possessing certain characteristics (e.g., symmetrical faces) are consensually viewed as more attractive and desirable. Indeed, viewing attractive faces activates dopaminergic regions of the brain implicated in reward processing such as ventral striatum and nucleus accumbens (e.g., Aharon et al. 2001; Kampe et al. 2001). Nonetheless, there is considerable *variability* across people in who and what features and qualities they find attractive. Even seemingly objective cues are evaluated in an idiosyncratic manner and these individual differences have been also shown to activate regions in the brain involved in reward-processing, such as the orbitofrontal cortex (Kim et al. 2007).

The subjective nature of first impressions, and the evidence that "beauty is in the eye of the beholder" (Hönekopp 2006) is not surprising given the assumption that a person's unique network, which reflects a history of life experiences and genetic, temperamental, and biological predispositions, affects how they construe and evaluate any given situation, including potential partners. From an attachment perspective, mental representations of significant others, which is a key CAU in people's networks, are highly chronically accessible and are expected to color, in a spontaneous fashion, evaluations and inferences of novel others, including evaluations of potential mates. Research by Andersen and colleagues, for example, has shown that when a new person shares attributes with a significant other, the existing mental representation is spontaneously activated and used to make sense of the new person—a phenomenon referred to as transference (e.g., Andersen and Chen 2002; Andersen and Baum 1994). In recent work, novel others who bore minimal facial resemblance to women's current romantic partner were evaluated more positively (e.g., intelligent, trustworthy, attractive), even though the participants were not aware of the physical resemblance (Günaydin et al. 2012). Other studies have similarly found that physical resemblance to significant others (e.g., Kraus and Chen 2010; White and Shapiro 1987) have a profound influence on first impressions, and likely play an important role in guiding who one is gravitated towards (or away). In a sea of potential partners, these subtle evaluative responses and inferences occurring outside of conscious awareness begin to shape the likelihood of learning more about the person—the very initial steps in the path towards an attachment bond.

2. Infatuation. Although not identified as a turning point in past work, from an attachment perspective, a pivotal event in the preattachment stage is the state of being infatuated with a potential partner (Günaydin et al. 2013; Tennov 1979). Infatuation manifests itself as constantly thinking about (Marazziti et al. 1999) and longing to be with the person (Aron et al. 2005). Such feelings are typically accompanied by physiological arousal and anxiety (Marazziti and Canale 2004). Infatuation focuses one's attention on one potential partner to the exclusion of all others (Tennov 1979) and thus might speed up one's progression to the next, attachment-in-the-making stage; a proposition needing further experimental investigation.

At the affective and neural level, infatuation in the preattachment stage has been linked to reward-related processing (e.g., Marazziti and Baroni 2012), which in turn may be associated with a heightened positive mental representation of the partner. Work has found that in early stage dating couples, photographs of the partner activate reward-related areas of the brain (Acevedo, this volume; Aron et al. 2005; Bartels and Zeki 2000). Although speculative and in need for empirical testing, animal research suggests the possibility that the heightened positivity may be coupled with inhibition of negative (e.g., Moriceau and Sullivan 2005).

3. If ... Then ... Dyadic Patterns. The turning points in the preattachment phase offer individuals opportunities to get to know one another. As they do, mental representations are updated to reflect the new information acquired through mutual interactions although initial impressions still color representations (e.g., Fiske and Neuberg 1990; Funder 2012). Despite this, the partner has not yet been integrated into the self. Consequently, the CAPS networks of the two individuals are still relatively asynchronous, meaning that the two individuals are still getting to know one another and do not yet have stable patterns of behaving when they are together. Thus, the behavioral signature arising from their interactions is not yet stable, reflecting the fact that they have not yet formed an effective "coupled" dyadic cognitive system.

Attachment-in-the-Making

In the attachment-in-the-making stage, individuals preferentially seek proximity to one another and increasingly engage in behaviors (e.g., self-disclosures, physical contact, mutual gazing, kissing, sex) in which the other person, and the relationship, is the primary focal point of attention. Through these key turning points a number of changes occur at the level of the mental representation. These changes, in turn, promote the emergence of behaviors that collectively signify the making of an attachment bond, namely, proximity maintenance, safe haven, secure base, and separation distress.

1. Building a Robust, Context-Independent, Chronically Accessible Mental Representation of the Partner. Based on a review and synthesis of the extant literature, we believe that a prerequisite for the development of an attachment bond and its behavioral manifestations is the development of a robust, context-independent, and chronically accessible mental representation of the partner. That is, the mental representation of the potential partner must be built up and elaborated. In the preattachment phase, much of the partner representation is based on the perceiver's own past experiences. In the attachment-in-the-making stage, through a variety of mundane and significant interactions, this mental representation becomes updated with more information representing the partner. The development of a robust, context-independent representation allows it to be easily activated in a number of situations and to guide behaviors.

One key turning point identified in previous work is simply spending a greater proportion of time together. Interestingly, previous work has found that the sheer *quantity* of exposure may be more important for relationship development than the *quality* of time spent together (Baxter and Bullis 1986). We hypothesize even in the absence of intimate encounters, exposure allows individuals to learn about the varied cues associated with the partner (e.g., partner's scent, facial and bodily structure and movement, nonverbal behaviors, moods, and behavioral patterns) and encounter them in varied ways (e.g., from different viewpoints, displaying different emotions, under different lighting, speaking with different volume of voice, wearing different clothing, in different settings). With repeated exposure of these visual, auditory, olfactory, and tactile cues, the representation of the partner becomes richer and critically, more context-independent (i.e., view-invariant, robust). One consequence is that it can easily be activated in different contexts.

With greater exposure, the representation of the partner is also activated more frequently. Given that the frequency of construct activation is linearly related to chronic accessibility, spending time together is the first step to making the representation chronically accessible—easily brought to mind in a variety of situations. The idea that greater exposure leads to a mental representation of the partner that is richer, context-independent, and chronically accessible has consequences for affective responding. For example, any cue that is even remotely associated with the partner (e.g., an unknown other who shares a hobby with the partner) would be sufficient to activate the partner representation from memory. Moreover, cues associated with the partner should be processed more fluently and should elicit feelings of familiarity, which have been shown to promote liking (e.g., Reis et al. 2011).

Although initial interactions with potential mates may be superfluous, as past research suggests, they tend to gradually increase in intimacy over time. Accordingly, another turning point identified in the literature, which is a byproduct of proximity maintenance, is getting to know a potential mate. In contrast to the learning that occurs through sheer exposure, this turning point involves higher quality and more intimate interactions in which two people learn about and disclose personal information to each other. Not only do couples report greater commitment following such turning points (e.g., Gonzaga et al. 2001), experimental work shows that self-disclosure increases feelings of intimacy and liking and leads to a sense of mutual trust (Aron et al. 1997; Collins and Miller 1994). Moreover, such activities may lead the two individuals to engage in novel activities together or share humorous experiences, which in turn elicit feelings of reward and further promote intimacy and liking (Aron et al. 2000; Fraley and Aron 2004).

With increased time together and intimacy, both individuals would eventually come to learn about each other's behavioral signatures. Sam may learn that Terry is chronically late when it comes to meeting up with friends but punctual for work-related events. At a more intimate level, it may become clear that when worried, Terry becomes argumentative, but that talking about the worries, has a calming effect. Eventually, they become "experts" about one another's behavioral patterns (*if…then… pattern)* and would even describe the other in these terms (Wright et al. 1988). One benefit is that they can automatically anticipate how their partner would respond to different situations.

2. Conditioning the affective, cognitive, and behavioral responses. A key characteristic of an attachment bond is that the two individuals' affective, cognitive, and behavioral responses become intricately attuned to one another (see Selcuk et al. 2010). In the attachment-in-the-making phase, a number of events transpire that not only involve each person learning relatively abstract information about their partner (e.g., hometown, favorite restaurant, biggest dream), but also involve conditioning each other's affective and physiological responses to the other partner's cues.

A turning point identified in the literature that naturally reflects this preferential treatment of the partner, which may promote the conditioning of one another's responses, is exclusivity in which individuals typically break their involvement with other potential mates and start spending time exclusively with one another. The development of partner representation at this stage is generally influenced by two types of turning points: positive arousing episodes (e.g., sex) and comfort-seeking episodes to cope with negative experiences (e.g., day-to-day stressors). Both types of experiences typically have an arousal phase, which is followed by a calm quiescent state, which, if repeated over time, facilitates the formation of the attachment bond (see Beckes and Coan this volume for a discussion of distress-relief processes in promoting attachment security).

a. Positive Arousing Experiences. Positive arousing experiences that promote attachment formation include intimate self-disclosures, mutual gazing, physical contact, and sex. Simply being with the partner and engaging in these behaviors can elicit feelings of desire, high arousal, and anticipation of reward (e.g., Gonzaga et al. 2006), which have been linked with activation in dopamine-rich areas of the brain—such as the ventral tegmental area, nucleus accumbens, and caudate nucleus (Depue and Morrone-Strupinsky 2005). With repeated interactions with the partner, the partner representation comes to be automatically associated with these feelings of reward and positive affect (Zayas and Shoda 2005). Indeed, in fledgling relationships, activating the representation of one's romantic partner (vs. a close friend or a highly familiar acquaintance) was found to be associated with activity in reward-related areas of the brain—namely, the ventral tegmental area and caudate (Aron et al. 2005; Bartels and Zeki 2000; Xu et al. 2010).

Anticipation of reward characterized by high arousal and desire is thought to be followed by feelings of calm, comfort, and satisfaction if one's desire for intimacy is fulfilled (e.g., Carter 1998; Depue and Morrone-Strupinsky 2005). For example, activation of the HPA axis during sex is followed by oxytocin, vasopressin, and opioid release, which produces a calm state. When one repeatedly experiences feelings of comfort and satisfaction in the presence of the partner, mental representation of this person starts to be associated with these feelings, which in turn facilitates formation of the attachment bond (e.g., Depue and Morrone-Strupinsky 2005; Uvnäs-Moberg 1998). Of course, the attachment bond will be formed even when the partners do not engage in physically intimate behaviors or sex. It is possible however that these behaviors accelerate attachment formation although this possibility is yet to be empirically investigated.

b. Distress-Relief Experiences. In addition to positive arousing experiences, seeking comfort and support from the partner following stressful experiences is another turning point that has a profound influence on attachment formation (see Beckes and Coan, this volume). In times of stress, being comforted by a responsive partner leads to the release of oxytocin and opioids, which were shown to have anxiety-reducing effects (e.g., Chong et al. 2006; Petrovic et al. 2008). For example, soft touch—which is a soothing behavior romantic partners typically engage in—leads to release of opioids, which produces a pleasant affective state (e.g., Löken et al. 2009).

After repeatedly encountering alleviation of negative affect in the presence of the partner, the mental representation of the partner starts to be associated with feelings of comfort and relief, strengthening the attachment bond. The idea that stress relief facilitates attachment formation is also supported by recent experimental work. For example, Beckes, Simpson, and Erikson showed that individuals developed more positive associations with smiling individuals preceded by a distressing stimulus (e.g., a snake) compared with those preceded by a neutral stimulus (e.g., a rolling pin). Von Dawans et al. (2012) found that participants who completed a stressful (vs. non-stressful) task in the lab subsequently tended to display behaviors indicative of trust and liking during economic games. This research suggests that seeking comfort from one's partner following a stressful experience helps associate the partner representation with feelings of relief and trust as well as strengthening the expectation that partner will be supportive and responsive in times of need (e.g., Baldwin et al. 1993).

3. If (situation)...Then (behavior)... Dyadic Patterns. Towards the end of the attachment-in-the-making stage, as the partner becomes more familiar, feelings of arousal and desire associated with the partner representation start to dampen while feelings of comfort, relief, and pleasantness continue to grow. As the two individuals get to know one another more intimately, their CAPS networks start to become interlocked and stable patterns of behaving with one another start to emerge. Yet, the behavioral signature arising from their interactions reflects the fact they have not formed a fully effective "coupled" cognitive system.

Clear-Cut Attachment/Goal-Corrected Partnership

At this stage, a full-fledged attachment bond is formed between the partners. We discuss clear-cut attachment and goal-corrected partnership stages together because as compared with infancy, it is harder to distinguish these two stages in adulthood, especially at the level of the representation. In infancy, the major distinction between the clear-cut attachment stage and the goal-corrected partnership stage is related to the cognitive development of the infant. In the clear-cut attachment stage, the infant reacts to temporary separations from the caregiver by showing overt signs of distress (e.g., crying) whereas in the goal-corrected partnership stage, the infant does not react as strongly to such separations (Hazan and Zeifman 1994). This is partly because the infant becomes cognitively capable of negotiating separations with the caregiver and is able to use the mental representation of the caregiver to derive comfort. Because adults are already capable of doing this in the clear-cut attachment stage, it is hard to make a clear distinction between this stage and goal-corrected partnership. Hence, we will discuss these two stages together in the current chapter.

1. From Passion to Security. The partner representation acquires greater reward value as a clear-cut attachment bond is established. Indeed, individuals in established (vs. fledgling) relationships were found to show greater activation in ventral pallidum, a brain region implicated in reward processing (see Acevedo, this volume). However, as compared with the attachment-in-the-making stage, feelings of passion and high arousal experienced in the presence of the partner decline in the clear-cut attachment stage (e.g., Gonzaga et al. 2006; Sprecher and Regan 1998), along with sexual intimacy (Christopher and Sprecher 2000). Thus, activating the partner representation leads to less arousal but rather feelings of calm, comfort, and pleasantness. For example, activating one's spouse's representation (vs. a highly familiar acquaintance) elicits activation in areas of the brain rich in oxytocin and vasopressin receptors, which are known to induce a state of calm (Acevedo et al. 2012). Moreover, activation in these areas was found to be associated with self-reported friendship-based love, suggesting that feelings of calm and comfort derived from the partner representation is an important feature of clear-cut attachment.

Comfort-seeking is still an important turning point at the clear-cut attachment stage. However, one important difference from the attachment-in-the-making stage is that the partner representation now provides a safe haven even in the physical absence of the partner. For example, Selcuk et al. (2012) demonstrated the affect regulation benefits of activating the partner representation in couples who have been in a romantic relationship for at least a year, when previous work suggests a clear-cut attachment bond is likely to be formed (Zeifman and Hazan 2008). Specifically, viewing the partner's (vs. another participant's partner's) photograph helped participants recover from negative affect resulting from thinking about stressful memories. Importantly, the magnitude of this recovery effect predicted physical and mental health in-day-to-day life, demonstrating the critical role of attachment representations in affect regulation and well-being.

2. Synchronization of Affective, Physiological, and Behavioral Systems. The profound role a full-fledged attachment bond plays in affect regulation is also reflected in temporally coordinated affective and physiological responses of partners—a phenomenon called synchrony or co-regulation (see Sbarra and Hazan 2008). Synchrony is observed for daily affect (Butner et al. 2007) as well as for physiological responses including heart rate (Helmet al., in press) and cortisol response (Saxbe and Repetti 2010). Yet, the exact role mental representations play in development of synchrony is not known. It is possible that a detailed representation of the partner's affective and physiological responses is formed in clear-cut attachment and this representation facilitates synchrony effects. Then, synchrony should be observed even during unshared experiences in which partners cannot directly influence each other's affect and physiology. Butner et al. (2007) found that this was indeed the case. Specifically, synchrony in daily affect was observed even after statistically controlling for couples' shared experiences. Moreover, past work showed that even when probed separately, partners show similar affective responses to various events (e.g., successes, worries), with substantial convergence observed in couples who are together for over a year (Anderson et al. 2003). This suggests that the partner representation contains detailed knowledge about how the partner might feel, think, and act in different situations, which might be implicitly influencing one's physiology and affect even during unshared experiences. An interesting direction for future research is to investigate whether the synchrony effects depend on how detailed the partner representation is.

3. Separation Distress. Another turning point that brings about a host of important consequences is being involuntarily separated from the partner. One might be separated from the partner for a short duration—for example, because of a business trip—or for longer—for example, when the partners work in different cities. A psychological theme associated with separations is missing the partner, which is characterized by feeling sad, daydreaming about the partner, and talking to others about the partner (Le et al. 2008). Although individuals might cope with missing the partner by calling, texting, or emailing him/her, physical cues such as partner's warmth, scent, and touch—which are critical in regulating one's physiology and affect—are not available during separations. That is why, even separations that last only a few days have a host of negative consequences for one's well-being—including disruption of sleep, poor appetite, and increased cortisol response (e.g., Diamond et al. 2008). It is possible that individuals who are better at using the partner representation to recover from negative affect (Selcuk et al. 2012) are less adversely affected from being separated from the partner although this possibility remains to be tested. Some positive feelings toward the partner (e.g., feelings of closeness, appreciation) also decline during separations, but so does criticism and conflict (Diamond et al. 2008). The relative absence of conflict might be one of the reasons why long-distance couples tend to be as satisfied in their relationships as geographically close couples (see Stafford 2010). Another reason might be that long-distance couples tend to have more idealized representations of one another (e.g., Jiang and Hancock 2013).

4. Commitment. Another important turning point marking clear-cut attachment is serious commitment. For example, participants who reported having discussed marriage with their partner expressed greater love and less sexual desire for their partner than those who reported not having discussed marriage (Gonzaga et al. 2006), suggesting that considering serious commitment is a turning point indicative of clear-cut attachment. When two individuals seriously commit to the relationship—for example, get married—they typically experience feelings of reward and happiness (e.g., Clark et al. 2008), which infuses the partner representation with positivity. Whether positive effects of serious commitment on the partner representation are lasting depends on individual differences—for example, the extent to which partners idealize one another (Murray et al. 2011) or engage in constructive strategies to deal with conflict (Finkel et al. 2013).

5. If ... Then ... Dyadic Patterns. In addition to effects of the partner representation on information processing, the CAPS networks of the two individuals are interlocked at the clear-cut attachment stage—that is, stable patterns of behaving with one another are unequivocally observed.

Unanswered Questions and Future Directions

This framework naturally sparks further questions about the process by which two individuals form an attachment bond in adulthood such as: what are the key turning points, do most people experience them, and if so, do they experience them in the same way, at the same time, and in the same order? We attempt to begin addressing a few of these questions below.

Are All Turning Points Alike?

The set of features present in particular turning points are likely to have different effects on how mental representations change. This is a logical assumption given that the process of changing mental representations involves the coactivation in short-term memory of the existing mental representation with the unique set of cues engendered by the particular turning point. It thus stands to reason that, if one turning point (first kiss) is associated with particular set of cues (touch, scent), and a different turning point (deciding to be exclusive or not) is associated with a different set of cues (psychological security and relationship stability), then the coupling of the mental representation with the first turning point will lead to different changes in long-term memory than the coupling of the mental representation with the second turning point.

What About Individual Differences?

The literature suggests that relational development is quite diverse (Huston et al. 1981). And this is perhaps the case now more than ever given the greater flexibility in people's lives. Thus, it is reasonable to assume that individual differences (e.g., adult attachment style) might play an important role in adult attachment formation and development.

Our argument is not that particular turning points will be the same for all individuals, occurring at the same time and experienced in a similar manner, but rather that these turning points are a time of learning and updating mental representations. It is during these key turning points where the mental representations undergo profound changes and the particular cues relevant to the turning points become linked with the representations. Moreover because turning points often involve tensions and themes, for example of self and other, these turning points have implications for representations of self and other.

We identified seemingly logical candidates for affecting attachment development of an average individual. Individual differences in these processes at all stages of attachment formation are inevitable. It is very likely that the turning points encountered are not random events, but that people have preferences towards or away from them (e.g., promiscuity, commitment). We are not arguing that there are no individual differences, but rather that these key events offer opportunities for changes in the mental representation. Future work should uncover how (or whether) the turning points discussed in this chapter and other work affect mental representations and identify whether different types of individuals (e.g., secure, anxious, avoidant) experience turning points differently.

Similarly, future research would need to empirically address whether the same objective event (e.g., first sexual encounter) occurring at a later stage of attachment formation has the same effect on the nature of the mental representation as if it had occurred in an earlier stage. From a social cognitive perspective, it is reasonable to hypothesize that the existing associations with a person's network, which would vary across stages of attachment formation, would affect how the event itself would be construed and, in turn, the effect of the event on the existing representations would be expected to vary. However, this is an empirical question.

Are There Other Turning Points That Influence Attachment Development?

The present chapter is not a comprehensive analysis of all of the turning points identified in previous research (e.g., Baxter and Bullis 1986) but rather a first attempt at identifying critical events that might influence development of an attachment bond based on extant literature on social cognition and relationship formation. Future work should empirically investigate whether turning points other than those described in this chapter might contribute to the development of attachment representations and how.

How Does the Formation of a Romantic Attachment Differ From the Formation of a Platonic Attachment or Other Relationships?

People readily learn information on subject matters that are personally meaningful and for which they already have existing information. So, not surprisingly, people are very efficient learners of social information in general. This process of interlocking is likely to occur for many different types of relationships. However, we expect that it will be most pronounced in a full-fledged attachment bond in which the interlocking occurs at various levels of functioning: behavioral, cognitive, affective, and physiological. What distinguishes more general social learning from attachment learning are the particular cues present during turning points (ventral ventral contact, repeated distress-relief interactions). However, future work might investigate similarities and differences in different types of bonds as a function of turning points experienced.

Concluding Thoughts

In this chapter we have focused on understanding the normative processes by which two adults go from being mere acquaintances to forming a full-fledged adult attachment bond. We propose that turning points, whether they be a single event (the first kiss) or reoccurring events over a specified period of time (spending time together early on in the relationship), are fertile ground for significant changes in the mental representations that guide the behaviors of the two individuals. Initially, the two individuals' "minds," conceptualized as networks, are separate and disconnected from one another. However, at each turning point, the opportunity presents itself for greater integration of the partner in the self concept and for greater learning of the partner. Through processes of learning, the cues that individuals are exposed to during a particular turning point are associated with the mental representation of the partner, and over time with repeated exposure will become part of the enduring mental representation. Not only will the mental representation of the partner be enhanced, elaborated on, and made more chronically accessible, but mental representations of self and partner will become increasingly interconnected. Such integration should contribute to meaningful changes in the behavioral signature of the couple.

References

Acevedo, B. P., Aron, A., Fisher, H. E., & Brown, L. L. (2012). Neural correlates of long-term intense romantic love. *Social Cognitive and Affective Neuroscience, 7,* 145–159.

Aharon, I., Etcoff, N., Ariely, D., Chabris, C. F., O'Connor, E., & Breiter, H. C. (2001). Beautiful faces have variable reward value: fMRI and behavioral evidence. *Neuron, 32,* 537–551.

Andersen, S. M., & Baum, A. (1994). Transference in interpersonal relations: Inferences and affect based on significant-other representations. *Journal of Personality, 62,* 459–497.

Andersen, S. M., & Chen, S. (2002). The relational self: An interpersonal social-cognitive theory. *Psychological Review, 109,* 619–645.

Anderson, C., Keltner, D., & John, O. P. (2003). Emotional convergence between people over time. *Journal of Personality and Social Psychology, 84,* 1054–1068.

Aron, A., Aron, E. N., & Smollan, D. (1992). Inclusion of other in the self scale and the structure of interpersonal closeness. *Journal of Personality and Social Psychology, 63,* 596–612.

Aron, A., Melinat, E., Aron, E. N., Vallone, R. D., & Bator, R. J. (1997). The experimental generation of interpersonal closeness: A procedure and some preliminary findings. *Personality and Social Psychology Bulletin, 23,* 363–377.

Aron, A., Norman, C. C., Aron, E. N., McKenna, C., & Heyman, R. E. (2000). Couples' shared participation in novel and arousing activities and experienced relationship quality. *Journal of Personality and Social Psychology, 78,* 273–284.

Aron, A., Fisher, H., Mashek, D., Strong, G., Li, H., & Brown, L. (2005). Reward, motivation and emotion systems associated with early-stage intense romantic love. *Journal of Neurophysiology, 93,* 327–337.

Atkinson, R. C., & Shiffrin, R. M. (1968). Human memory: A proposed system and its control processes. In K. W. Spence & J. T. Spence (Eds.), *The psychology of learning and motivation: Advances in research and theory* (Vol. II, pp. 89–195). New York: Academic.

Baldwin, M. W., Fehr, B., Keedian, E., Seidel, M., & Thomson, D. W. (1993). An exploration of the relational schemas underlying attachment styles: Self-report and lexical decision approaches. *Personality and Social Psychology Bulletin, 19,* 746–754.

Baldwin, M. W., Keelan, J. P. R., Fehr, B., Enns, V., & Koh-Rangarajoo, E. (1996). Social-cognitive conceptualization of attachment working models: Availability and accessibility effects. *Journal of Personality and Social Psychology, 71,* 94–109.

Bartels, A., & Zeki, S. (2000). The neural basis of romantic love. *Neuroreport, 11,* 3829–3834.

Baxter, L. A., & Bullis, C. (1986). Turning points in developing romantic relationships. *Human Communication Research, 12,* 469–493.

Baxter, L. A., & Erbert, L. A. (1999). Perceptions of dialectical contradictions in turning points of development in heterosexual romantic relationships. *Journal of Social and Personal Relationships, 16,* 547–569.

Beckes, L., Simpson, J. A., & Erickson, A. (2010). Of snakes and succor: Learning secure attachment associations with novel faces via negative stimulus pairings. *Psychological Science, 21,* 721–728.

Bolton, C. D. (1961). Mate selection as the development of a relationship. *Marriage and Family Living, 23,* 234–240.

Bowlby, J. (1982). *Attachment and loss: Vol. 1. Attachment* (2nd ed.). New York: Basic Books.

Bruner, J. S. (1957). On perceptual readiness. *Psychological Review, 64,* 123–152.

Butner, J., Diamond, L. M., & Hicks, A. M. (2007). Attachment style and two forms of affect coregulation between romantic partners. *Personal Relationships, 14,* 431–455.

Cairns, R. B. (1966). Attachment behavior of mammals. *Psychological Review, 73,* 409–426.

Carter, C. S. (1998). Neuroendocrine perspectives on social attachment and love. *Psychoneuroendocrinology, 23,* 779–818.

Chong, R. Y., Oswald, L., Yang, X., Uhart, M., Lin, P. I., & Wand, G. S. (2006). The Micro-opioid receptor polymorphism A118G predicts cortisol responses to naloxone and stress. *Neuropsychopharmacology, 31,* 204–211.

Christensen, A., & Nies, D. C. (1980). The spouse observation checklist: Empirical analysis and critique. *American Journal of Family Therapy, 8,* 69–79.

Christopher, F. S., & Sprecher, S. (2000). Sexuality in marriage, dating, and other relationships: A decade review. *Journal of Marriage and Family, 62,* 999–1017.

Clark, A. E., Diener, E., Georgellis, Y., & Lucas, R. E. (2008). Lags and leads in life satisfaction: A test of the baseline hypothesis. *The Economic Journal, 118,* F222–243.

Collins, N. L., & Miller, L. C. (1994). Self-disclosure and liking: A meta-analytic review. *Psychological Bulletin, 116,* 457–475.

von Dawans, B., Fischbacher, U., Kirschbaum, C., Fehr, E., & Heinrichs, M. (2012). The social dimension of stress reactivity acute stress increases prosocial behavior in humans. *Psychological Science, 23,* 651–660.

Depue, R. A., & Morrone-Strupinsky, J. V. (2005). A neurobiobehavioral model of affiliative bonding: Implications for conceptualizing a human trait of affiliation. *Behavioral and Brain Sciences, 28,* 313–395.

Diamond, L. M., Hicks, A. M., & Otter-Henderson, K. D. (2008). Everytime you go away: Changes in affect, behavior, and physiology associated with travel-related separations from romantic partners. *Journal of Personality and Social Psychology, 95,* 385–403.

Finkel, E. J., Slotter, E. B., Luchies, L. B., Walton, G. M., & Gross, J. J. (2013). A brief intervention to promote conflict reappraisal preserves marital quality over time. *Psychological Science, 24,* 1595–1601.

Fiske, S. T., & Neuberg, S. L. (1990). A continuum of impression formation, from category based to individuating processes: Influences of information and motivation on attention and interpretation. In M. P. Zanna (Ed.), *Advances in experimental social psychology* (Vol. 23, pp. 1–74). San Diego: Academic.

Fraley, B., & Aron, A. (2004). The effect of a shared humorous experience on closeness in initial encounters. *Personal Relationships, 11,* 61–78.

Funder, D. C. (2012). Accurate personality judgment. *Current Directions in Psychological Science, 21,* 177–182.
Gonzaga, G. C., Keltner, D., Londahl, E. A., & Smith, M. D. (2001). Love and the commitment problem in romantic relations and friendship. *Journal of Personality and Social Psychology, 81,* 247–262.
Gonzaga, G. C., Turner, R. A., Keltner, D., Campos, B., & Altemus, M. (2006). Romantic love and sexual desire in close relationships. *Emotion, 6,* 163–179.
Goodwin, S. A., Fiske, S. T., Rosen, L. D., & Rosenthal, A. M. (2002). The eye of the beholder: Romantic goals and impression biases. *Journal of Experimental Social Psychology, 38,* 232–241.
Günaydin, G., Zayas, V., Selcuk, E., & Hazan, C. (2012). I like you but I don't know why: Objective facial resemblance to significant others influences snap judgments. *Journal of Experimental Social Psychology, 48,* 350–353.
Günaydin, G., Selcuk, E., & Hazan, C. (2013). Finding the one: A process model of human mate selection. In C. Hazan & M. Campa (Eds.), *Human bonding* (pp. 103–131). New York: Guilford.
Hazan, C., & Zeifman, D. (1994). Sex and the psychological tether. In K. Bartholomew & D. Perlman (Eds.), *Advances in personal relationships: Attachment processes in adulthood* (Vol. 5, pp. 151–177). London: Jessica Kingsley.
Hazan, C., Gur-Yaish, N., & Campa, M. (2004). What does it mean to be attached? In W. S. Rholes & J. A. Simpson (Eds.), *Adult attachment: New directions and emerging issues* (pp. 55–85). New York: Guilford.
Hebb, D. O. (1969). *The organization of behavior*. Wiley: New York.
Helm, J. L., Sbarra, D., & Ferrer, E. (2012). Assessing cross-partner associations in physiological responses via coupled oscillator models. *Emotion, 12,* 748–762.
Higgins, E. T., & King, G. (1981). Accessibility of social constructs: Information processing consequences of individual and contextual variability. In N. Cantor & J. F. Kihlstrom (Eds.), *Personality, cognition, and social interaction* (pp. 69–121). Hillsdale: Erlbaum.
Hofer, M. A. (1994).Hidden regulators in attachment, separation, and loss. *Monographs of the Society for Research in Child Development, 59,* 250–283.
Hönekopp, J. (2006). Once more: Is beauty in the eye of the beholder? Relative contributions of private and shared taste to judgments of facial attractiveness. *Journal of Experimental Psychology: Human Perception and Performance, 32,* 199–209.
Huston, T. L., Surra, C. A., Fitzgerald, N. M., & Cate, R. M. (1981). From courtship to marriage: Mate selection as an interpersonal process. *Personal Relationships, 2,* 53–88.
Jacobson, N. S., & Moore, D. (1981). Spouses as observers of the events in their relationship. *Journal of Consulting and Clinical Psychology, 49,* 269–277.
Jiang, L. C., & Hancock, J. T. (2013). Absence makes the communication grow fonder: Geographic separation, interpersonal media, and intimacy in dating relationships. *Journal of Communication, 63,* 556–577.
Kampe, K. K., Frith, C. D., Dolan, R. J., & Frith, U. (2001). Reward value of attractiveness and gaze. *Nature, 413,* 589–589.
Kim, H., Adolphs, R., O'Doherty, J. P., & Shimojo, S. (2007). Temporal isolation of neural processes underlying face preference decisions. *Proceedings of the National Academy of Sciences, 104,* 18253–18258.
Kraus, M. W., & Chen, S. (2010). Facial-feature resemblance elicits the transference effect. *Psychological Science, 21,* 518–522.
Le, B., Loving, T. J., Lewandowski, G. W., Feinberg, E. G., Johnson, K. C., Fiorentino, R., & Ing, J. (2008). Missing a romantic partner: A prototype analysis. *Personal Relationships, 15,* 511–532.
Löken, L. S., Wessberg, J., McGlone, F., & Olausson, H. (2009). Coding of pleasant touch by unmyelinated afferents in humans. *Nature Neuroscience, 12,* 547–548.
Macrae, C. N., & Quadflieg, S. (2010). Perceiving people. In S. T. Fiske, D. T. Gilbert, & G. Lindzey (Eds.), *Handbook of social psychology* (Vol. 1, 5th ed., pp. 428–463). New York: Wiley.

Marazziti, D., & Baroni, S. (2012). Romantic love: The mystery of its biological roots. *Clinical Neuropsychiatry, 9,* 14–19.

Marazziti, D., & Canale, D. (2004). Hormonal changes when falling in love. *Psychoneuroendocrinology, 29,* 931–936.

Marazziti, A., Akiskal, H. S., Rossi, A., & Cassano, G. B. (1999). Alteration of the platelet serotonin transporter in romantic love. *Psychological Medicine, 29,* 741–745.

Mikulincer, M., Gillath, O., & Shaver, P. R. (2002). Activation of the attachment system in adulthood: threat-related primes increase the accessibility of mental representations of attachment figures. *Journal of Personality and Social Psychology, 83,* 881–895.

Mischel, W., & Shoda, Y. (1995). A cognitive-affective system theory of personality: Reconceptualizing situations, dispositions, dynamics, and invariance in personality structure. *Psychological Review, 102,* 246–268.

Moriceau, S., & Sullivan, R. M. (2005). Neurobiology of infant attachment. *Developmental Psychobiology, 47,* 230–242.

Murray, S. L., Griffin, D. W., Derrick, J. L., Harris, B., Aloni, M., & Leder, S. (2011). Tempting fate or inviting happiness? Unrealistic idealization prevents the decline of marital satisfaction. *Psychological Science, 22,* 619–626.

Petrovic, P., Kalisch, R., Singer, T., & Dolan, R. J. (2008). Oxytocin attenuates affective evaluations of conditioned faces and amygdale activity. *Journal of Neuroscience, 28,* 6607–6615.

Reis, H. T., Maniaci, M. R., Caprariello, P. A., Eastwick, P. W., & Finkel, E. J. (2011). Familiarity does indeed promote attraction in live interaction. *Journal of Personality and Social Psychology, 101,* 557–570.

Saxbe, D. E., & Repetti, R. L. (2010). For better or worse? Coregulation of couples' cortisol levels and mood states. *Journal of Personality and Social Psychology, 98,* 92–103.

Sbarra, D. A., & Hazan, C. (2008). Coregulation, dysregulation, self-regulation: An integrative analysis and empirical agenda for understanding adult attachment, separation, loss, and recovery. *Personality and Social Psychology Review, 12,* 141–167.

Selcuk, E., Zayas, V., & Hazan, C. (2010). Beyond satisfaction: The role of attachment in marital functioning. *Journal of Family Theory and Review, 2,* 258–279.

Selcuk, E., Zayas, V., Günaydin, G., Hazan, C., & Kross, E. (2012). Mental representations of attachment figures facilitate recovery following upsetting autobiographical memory recall. *Journal of Personality and Social Psychology, 103,* 362–378.

Shoda, Y., & Mischel, W. (1998). Personality as a stable cognitive-affective activation network: Characteristic patterns of behavior variation emerge from a stable personality structure. In S. J. Read & L. C. Miller (Eds.), *Connectionist models of social reasoning and social behavior* (pp. 175–208). NJ: Lawrence Erlbaum.

Sillars, A., & Scott, M. (1983). Interpersonal perception between intimates: An integrative review. *Human Communication Research, 10,* 153–176.

Sprecher, S., & Regan, P. C. (1998). Passionate and companionate love in courting and young married couples. *Sociological Inquiry, 68,* 163–185.

Stafford, L. (2010). Geographic distance and communication during courtship. *Communication Research, 37,* 275–297.

Tennov, D. (1979). *Love and limerence: The experience of being in love*. New York: Stein and Day.

Tulving, E. (1972). Episodic and semantic memory. In E. Tulving & W. Donaldson (Eds.), *Organization of memory* (pp. 382–403). New York: Academic.

Uvnäs-Moberg, K. (1998). Oxytocin may mediate the benefits of positive social interaction and emotions. *Psychoneuroendocrinology, 23,* 819–835.

White, G. L., & Shapiro, D. (1987). Don't I know you? Antecedents and social consequences of perceived familiarity. *Journal of Experimental Social Psychology, 23,* 75–92.

Xu, X., Aron, A., Brown, L., Cao, G., Feng, T., & Weng, X. (2010). Reward and motivation systems: A brain mapping study of early-stage intense romantic love in Chinese participants. *Human Brain Mapping, 32,* 249–257.

Zayas, V., & Shoda, Y. (2005). Do automatic reactions elicited by thoughts of romantic partner, mother, and self relate to adult romantic attachment? *Personality and Social Psychology Bulletin, 31,* 1011–1025.

Zayas, V., Shoda, Y., & Ayduk, O. N. (2002). Personality in context: An interpersonal systems perspective. *Journal of Personality, 70,* 851–898.

Zayas, V., Whitsett, D., Lee, J. J. Y., Wilson, N., & Shoda, Y. (2008). From situation assessment to personality: Building a social-cognitive model of a person. In G. Boyle, G. Matthews, & D. Saklofske (Eds.), *Handbook of personality theory and testing* (Vol. 2, pp. 377–401). Thousand Oaks CA: Sage.

Zeifman, D., & Hazan, C. (1997). Attachment: The bond in pair-bonds. In J. A. Simpson & D. T. Kenrick (Eds.), *Evolutionary social psychology* (pp. 237–263). Mahwah: Erlbaum.

Zeifman, D., & Hazan, C. (2008). Pair bonds as attachments: Reevaluating the evidence. In J. Cassidy & P. R. Shaver (Eds.), *Handbook of attachment: Theory, research, and clinical applications* (2nd ed., pp. 436–455). New York: Guilford.

Chapter 9
Neural Correlates of Human Attachment: Evidence from fMRI Studies of Adult Pair-Bonding

Bianca P. Acevedo

From the cradle to the grave close relationships play a central role in well-being and survival among humans and other species. For example, attachment bonds serve as a secure base for exploration or a safe haven from threat permitting organisms to venture out into world with a sense of felt security that their loved one is available for support (e.g., Ainsworth and Bel 1970). As such, the attachment system is important for coordinating relationship processes and facilitating many functions that enhance human survival and thriving (Bowlby 1977).

Attachment theory was developed by Bowlby's (1969) observations of child-caregiver relationships. Since then researchers have applied attachment theory to adult relationships suggesting that romantic partnerships are the adult instantiation of attachment in childhood (e.g., Ainsworth 1991; Hazan and Shaver 1987; Mikulincer and Shaver 2007). As such, studies examining the neural circuitry underlying romantic love and maternal love provide the opportunity to examine a basic assumption of attachment theory.

In this chapter, I focus on attachment in the context of adult romantic relationships, also known as pair-bonds. The pair-bond, with varying stages and implications for mating, the formation of the family unit, bi-parental care of offspring, and long-term companionship, provides the unique opportunity to examine the physiology underlying the development of attachment in adults. Specifically, I highlight the reward system implicated in motivation and reward learning (e.g., Hare et al. 2008) as being critical for pair-bond formation and maintenance. I also highlight activation of serotonin, vasopressin, and opioid rich regions of the raphe and ventral pallidum (VP), found among newlyweds and individuals in long-term relationships, as reflecting the emergence of attachment in adulthood.

Animal studies with monogamous rodents and primates have also suggested that the reward system is critical for pair-bonding (Aragona et al. 2006; Curtis et al. 2006; Young et al. 2001). More specifically, these studies have shown that concentrations of dopamine in the mesocorticolimbic system and vasopressin in the VP are

---

B. P. Acevedo (✉)
Department of Psychological and Brain Sciences, University of California, Santa Barbara, Santa Barbara, CA 93106, USA
e-mail: bianca.p.acevedo@gmail.com

V. Zayas, C. Hazan (eds.), *Bases of Adult Attachment*,
DOI 10.1007/978-1-4614-9622-9_9

critical for the expression and maintenance of pair-bonds in monogamous rodents and primates (e.g., Bales et al. 2007; Lim and Young 2004). Human studies have also shown significant activation of the reward system for early-stage, newlywed, and long-term pair-bonds (e.g., Aron et al. 2005; Bartels and Zeki 2000; Acevedo et al. under review, 2011). I conceptualize these studies as elucidating the neural circuitry underlying pair-bond initiation, establishment, and maintenance and extrapolate to fMRI studies of maternal love to make reference to "attachment-related" neural activations.

This chapter reviews research on the neural basis of early-stage, newlywed, and long-term relationships to better understand the development of attachment in adulthood. I focus on the reward system and activations found to be unique to newlyweds and long-term pair-bonders suggesting the emergence of attachment. Second, I review a few studies showing associations between partner-related brain activations and relationship length also suggesting the solidification of attachment bonds. Finally, I review three fMRI studies reporting shared neural circuits for pair-bonds and parent-child bonds. I propose that the areas identified across these three studies provide evidence of key neural sites important for attachment in humans.

The Neural Basis of Human Pair-Bonding

Early-Stage Pair-Bonds The first two studies to examine the neural correlates of early-stage romantic love recruited individuals in relationships of about 6 months and 2 years long, respectively (Aron et al. 2005; Bartels and Zeki 2000). Both studies measured the brain activity of participants in response to face images of their partners versus controls for familiarity. Results showed significant partner effects in dopamine-rich regions of the reward system, namely in the ventral tegmental area (VTA) important for reward and motivation, and the caudate implicated in goal-direct action (e.g., O'Doherty et al. 2004; Lauwereyns et al. 2002).

Subsequent studies of early-stage romantic love have built on this work examining other populations such as students in China (Xu et al. 2011), German participants (Stoessel et al. 2011), and same-sex partnerships (Zeki and Romaya 2010). One study implemented a different experimental paradigm, subliminally priming subjects with partner concepts versus friend or life passion concepts (Ortigue et al. 2007). Across studies of early-stage romantic love with different populations and experimental paradigms, group results showed activation of the brain's reward system, specifically in the VTA and the caudate which are involved in motivation, reinforcement learning, and goal-directed behaviors (e.g., Carter et al. 2009; Delgado et al. 2003; O'Doherty et al. 2004).

Newlyweds One study to date has examined the neural circuits underlying newlywed bonds among a sample of young adults transitioning to first-time marriages (Acevedo et al. under review). In this study, 19 newlyweds (11 women) ages 21–32, without children, and in relationships of about 4 years were scanned using fMRI while viewing face images of their partners versus a familiar, neutral acquaintance. Consistent with research on early-stage romantic love, newlyweds showed significant activation of the VTA and caudate replicating results for early-stage romantic love. Newlyweds also showed partner-specific activations in areas reflecting the "liking" of rewards (the globus pallidus), calm and pain suppression (the periacqueductal gray), homeostatic regulation (hypothalamus), and focused attention (the thalamocingulate circuit). All of these activations elucidate characteristics of attachment bonds, which are important for their solidification and maintenance.

Newlyweds also showed activations in serotonin, vasopressin and opioid rich regions of the raphe and ventral pallidum (VP). These regions are involved in mediating states of calmness and reward processes that get translated to actions (e.g., Borg et al. 2003; Smith et al. 2009, Aldridge and Berridge 2010). Interestingly, activation of the raphe and VP were not reported in studies of early-stage romantic love (e.g., Aron et al. 2005). Thus, recruitment of the raphe and VP in newlyweds may indicate the emergence of attachment.

Long-term Pair-Bonds One study to date has examined the neural basis of long-term romantic love. In the study 17 individuals (10 women) about 50 years of age, married an average of 21 years were scanned while viewing face images of a partner versus controls for familiarity and closeness (Acevedo et al. 2011). Long-term pair-bonders displayed similar patterns of brain activation found for early-stage couples and newlyweds in brain areas reflecting "wanting" and "liking" (the VTA and globus pallidus), goal-directed action (the caudate), calm and pain suppression (the periacqueductal gray), homeostatic regulation (hypothalamus), and focused attention (the thalamocingulate circuit). Thus, activation across three distinct relationship stages suggests that these neural circuits may be critical for pair-bond formation, solidification, and maintenance.

Summary Neuroimaging studies of early-stage romantic love, newlywed, and long-term pair-bonds provide the unique opportunity to understand the neural circuitry underlying the development of attachment in adult romantic relationships. Among these three relationship stages common and distinct themes emerged providing biological evidence of some of the basic tenets of attachment theory and theories of love. For example, across studies of early-stage love, newlyweds, and long-term love results showed similar patterns of activation in the mesolimbic, dopamine "reward" system reflecting "wanting", "liking" and the valuing of rewards (e.g., Berridge and Robinson 1998). This is evidence that romantic love may be present and important for new, established, and long-term pair-bonds (e.g., Acevedo and Aron 2009). These results are also consistent with models defining love in romantic relationships as "a state of intense longing for union with the beloved" (Berscheid and Hatfield 1969), and those characterizing love as an intense focus on the partner (Fisher 1998) with approach-related behaviors (Gonzaga et al. 2001). These findings also highlight how the brain's reward system, implicated in reward learning and motivation, mediates behaviors that are important in forming, solidifying, and maintaining close relationships. For example, learning what makes a partner draw closer, laugh, or smile, and how to respond to his or her different emotional states are important aspects of courtship that continue to play a role in relationship satisfaction and love over time (e.g., Acevedo and Aron 2009). The learning, motivation, and enactment of these and many other attachment-related behaviors are orchestrated by the reward system.

Studies of newly in-love, newlywed, and long-term pair-bonded individuals also showed activation of areas involved in attention and focus (the thalamocingulate circuit), calm and pain suppression (the PAG), homeostasis (hypothalamus), and the "liking" of rewards (globus pallidus). These findings suggest how the brain mediates attachment processes (e.g., proximity-seeking, attention, felt security) which are needed to solidify and maintain pair-bonds over time.

Evidence for the Emergence of Attachment Newlyweds and long-term pair-bonders showed activation in areas of the raphe nucleus and the VP which were not found in studies of early-stage romantic love. These activations however were seen in studies of maternal love (Bartels and Zeki 2004) suggesting that they are evoked in the context of established attachment bonds.

Activation of the VP is particularly interesting as it is rich in receptors for vasopressin (AVP), a hormone that has been implicated in monogamous pair-bonding in rodents and primates (e.g., Bales et al. 2007; Lim and Young 2004). The VP is a major site of corticolimbic integration mediating reward and motivation, and translating inputs into movement (e.g., Smith et al. 2010). The VP has also been associated with enhanced "liking", as well as "wanting" of rewards (Smith and Berridge 2005). Thus, activation of the VP for established relationships shows how the brain may mediate processes that are critical for pair-bonding such as "liking", "wanting" and proximity-seeking.

Activation of the raphe is striking as the raphe nuclei account for a majority of the serotonergic neurons in the brainstem. Serotonin-rich regions (such as the raphe) have been implicated in feelings of calm, spiritual experiences, and are centers for treating anxiety and obsessive-compulsive disorder (e.g., Borg et al. 2003; Delorme et al. 2004). These findings support self-report work suggesting that a key distinction between new and established pair-bonds is greater calm associated with the latter (Acevedo and Aron 2009). They also provide evidence of how the brain regulates a sense of "felt security", which is thought to be the set-point of the attachment system (Sroufe and Waters 1977).

Time-related Changes in Pair-bonding Brain Activity

A few studies have investigated associations between partner-related brain activations and relationship length among individuals newly in-love, those in long-term relationships, and even those experiencing a recent break-up. For example, in one study newly in-love individuals (in relationships of about 6 months long) showed stronger activation in the VP the longer they were together (Aron et al. 2005). Somewhat similarly, in a study of individuals recently rejected by a lover results showed less activation of the VP with increasing number of days since the break-up (Fisher et al. 2010). Thus, time-related activations confirmed the commonalities found for newlyweds and long-term pair-bonds suggesting that activation of the VP in romantic relationships may be a marker for increasing (or decreasing) attachment to a partner and solidification (or dissolution) of the pair-bond.

A study with individuals in long-term pair-bonds of about 21 years showed a somewhat different pattern of brain activations (Acevedo et al. 2011). Findings showed greater recruitment of brain regions implicated in reward (the accumbens) and pain regulation (the PAG) in association with number of years married. Activation of the accumbens is consistently cited in studies of addictive substance use, and more specifically it has associated with cocaine-induced "highs" (Risinger et al. 2005). The accumbens has also been implicated in studies of unrequited love (e.g., Fisher et al. 2010; Najib et al. 2004) and grief for a loved one (O'Connor et al. 2008). These results suggest how the brain mediates attachment, including habituation to and the desire for union with the partner.

The PAG—a region rich in oxytocin, vasopressin, and opioid receptors (e.g., Jenkins et al. 1984; Loup et al. 1989; Peckys and Landwehrmeyer 1999)—has been implicated in pain suppression and acquiescence (e.g., Bittar et al. 2005). Its activation in association with longer relationships likely reflects the calm and felt-security that is characteristic of attachment bonds. Activation of the PAG also highlights how the cognitive representation of a loved partner may be sufficient to buffer individuals from pain or stress as shown in previous studies (e.g., Coan et al. 2006).

Neural Circuits Underlying Human Attachment

In this section, I review three studies reporting shared neural circuitry for pair-bonds and parent-child bonds. The first study reporting commonalities for pair-bonds and parent-child bonds compared the results from two separate fMRI studies; one study investigated the neural correlates of early-stage romantic love and the other for maternal love (Bartels and Zeki 2000, 2004). In both studies participants were shown face images of the target (the individual's partner or child) versus an appropriate control for familiarity. Results showed common activations for pair-bonds and maternal bonds in regions implicated in reward (e.g., the caudate, putamen, and globus pallidus), awareness (e.g., the middle insula), and empathy (e.g., the anterior cingulate cortex).

In another fMRI study, newlyweds were scanned while viewing face images of a partner versus a familiar person (Acevedo et al. under review). Researchers searched areas reported in already published studies of maternal attachment (e.g., Bartels and Zeki 2004) revealing common neural activations for pair-bonds and parental bonds in areas reflecting reward "wanting" and "liking" (e.g., caudate, putamen, and globus pallidus), homeostatic regulation (hypothalamus), pain-suppression and calm (e.g., PAG), and attention (e.g., thalamus and anterior cingulate). These findings replicated commonalities found among early-stage pair-bonds and maternal love.

In a third study, activations for long-term pair-bonders were compared with results from numerous studies of maternal attachment (Acevedo et al. 2011). The results showed common activations in brain regions associated with reward (the substantia nigra, caudate, putamen, and globus pallidus), calm and the regulation of stress and pain (e.g., the PAG and dorsal raphe), homeostasis (hypothalamus), awareness and empathy (the mid-insula and the insular cortex), and attention (thalamus and cingulate). These results largely replicated commonalities found among early-stage pair-bonds, newlyweds, and maternal attachment providing solid evidence that these areas are involved in human attachment.

Summary Pair-bonds have been proposed to be the adult instantiation of parent-infant bonds by some researchers (Carter 1998; Fisher 1998). The three studies described above reported common neural circuits for pair-bonds and parent-child bonds in brain areas reflecting reward and motivation (the caudate, putamen, and globus pallidus), homeostatic regulation (the hypothalamus), calm (e.g., the PAG), and attention (the thalamus and cingulate). Below I discuss the function of these brain regions and how they may be involved in attachment processes.

The caudate is involved in goal-directed behaviors and visual information processing (e.g., O'Doherty et al. 2004; Lauwereyns et al. 2002). It is also interesting that increased oxytocin (OT) in the caudate has been associated with trust in humans, even in the face of betrayal (e.g., Baumgartner et al. 2008). Thus, its activation suggests how the brain may mediate behaviors that promote attachment including proximity-seeking, trust, and assigning special meaning to the partner (e.g., Zeki 2007).

Activation of globus pallidus (GP) is interesting in the context of the attachment as it has been implicated in the "liking" of rewards (e.g., Berridge et al. 2010) and coined as a "hedonic hotspot" for rewards (Smith et al. 2009). The GP is a major site for opiate receptors, which are important for the regulation of anxiety and pain, and are targets for the treatment of anxiety, obsessive-compulsive disorder, and depression (Napier and Mitrovic 1999; Olive et al. 1997). Thus, activation of the GP in response to images of a loved one suggests calm and felt security, supporting a central tenet of attachment theory.

The PAG, a region with high-density OT, AVP, and opioid receptors (e.g., Jenkins et al. 1984), has been implicated in pain suppression and acquiescence (Bittar et al. 2005). The hypothalamus coordinates hormonal patterns, homeostatic mechanisms, and important behaviors for parenting and mating (e.g., Ferretti et al. 2005). Taken together, activation of the PAG and hypothalamus among attachment bonds support attachment theory and prior fMRI research suggesting greater calm and "felt security" in attachment relationships (e.g., Acevedo et al. 2011).

The other major pattern of common results for pair-bonds and parent-child bonds showed activation of the thalamocingulate circuit. The thalamocingulate circuit is important for regulating alertness, and serves as a relay for sensory processes (e.g., auditory, visual) between subcortical and cortical nuclei (e.g., Haber 2003). The thalamus and cingulate are also crucial for performance monitoring, detecting errors, and adjusting goal-directed behaviors (Seifert et al. 2011). Thus, activation of the thalamocingulate circuits reflects attention and monitoring with action, which are necessary for adaptive behavior and responsiveness in relationships. These results are consistent with attachment theory's tenets suggesting that proximity-seeking, monitoring, and responsiveness as central in attachment relationships (e.g., Bowlby 1977; Zeki 2007).

Conclusions

Attachment bonds support the survival, evolution, and thriving of humans and other social species. This chapter reviewed research examining the neural correlates of early-stage, newlywed, and long-term relationships highlighting the reward system's involvement in pair-bond formation, establishment, and maintenance. Reward seems to be particularly important for attachment in social species. For example, individuals must learn important associations for relationships to thrive, such as when and how to respond to one another's needs and states. Even when the patterns of associations are learned, individuals must remain motivated and continue to work for their relationships even in the face of challenges (e.g., Acevedo and Aron 2009). These processes are largely orchestrated in complex ways via the brain's reward system.

Another major finding that emerged from this review was activation of the ventral pallidum (VP) in the context of established newlywed and long-term marriages, and also in association with increasing (or decreasing) relationship length (e.g., Acevedo et al. under review; Aron et al. 2005; Fisher et al. 2010). The VP integrates sensory, emotional, and cognitive information and outputs signals for appropriate actions (e.g., Smith et al. 2010). Thus, the VP is centrally placed for modulating adaptive behaviors necessary for pair-bond solidification (or dissolution) and maintenance. It may also be a marker for increasing (or decreasing) attachment to a partner and signal the emergence of attachment in adult romantic relationships.

Finally, I reviewed research showing common neural circuits for pair-bonds and parent-infant bonds as a preliminary analysis of key regions that may be critical for human attachment. The results showed common activations in sites associated with reward processes and goal-directed actions (the caudate, putamen, and globus pallidus), homeostatic regulation (the hypothalamus), pain-suppression and calm (e.g., the PAG), and attention (the thalamocingulate circuit). These results suggest how the brain mediates attachment-related behaviors such as proximity-seeking, felt security, and responsiveness, which are critical for relationship longevity and also contribute to the evolutionary success of humans and other social species.

Acknowledgement Bianca P. Acevedo, Department of Public Health, Weill Cornell Medical College.

Many thanks Lucy L. Brown and Arthur P. Aron for providing generous feedback on original drafts of this chapter, and to Jonathan Vogelman for his assistance in manuscript preparation.

Correspondence concerning this article should be addressed to Bianca P. Acevedo, Weill Department of Psychological and Brain Sciences, University of California, Santa Barbara, Santa Barbara, CA 93106 USA. E mail address: bianca.p.acevedo@gmail.com.

References

Acevedo, B., & Aron, A. (2009). Does a long-term relationship kill romantic love? *Review of General Psychology, 13,* 59–65.

Acevedo, B. P., Aron, A., Fisher, H., & Brown, L. L. (2011). Neural correlates of long-term intense romantic love. *Social Cognitive and Affective Neuroscience Journal.* doi:10.1093/scan/nsq092.

Acevedo, B. P., Collins, N., Xu, X., & Brown, L. L. (under review). "I do: An fMRI study of newlyweds". *Social Cognitive and Affective Neuroscience Journal.*

Ainsworth, M. D. S., & Bell, S. M. (1970). Attachment, exploration, and separation: Illustrated by the behavior of one-year-olds in a strange situation. *Child Development, 41,* 49–67.

Ainsworth, M. D. S. (1991). Attachments and other affectional bonds across the life cycle (pp. 33–51). In C. M. Parkes, J. Stevenson-Hinde, & P. Marris (Eds.), *Attachment across the life cycle.* London: Tavistock Publications.

Aragona, B. J., Liu, Y., Yu, Y. J., Curtis, J. T., Detwiler, J. M., Insel, T. R., & Wang, Z. X. (2006). Nucleus accumbens dopamine differentially mediates the formation and maintenance of monogamous pair bonds. *Nature Neuroscience, 9,* 133–139.

Aron, A., Fisher, H., Mashek, D., Strong, G., Li, H., & Brown, L. (2005). Reward, motivation and emotion systems associated with early-stage intense romantic love. *Journal of Neurophysiology, 93,* 327–337.

Bales, K. L., Mason, W. A., Catana, C., Cherry, S. R., & Mendoza, S. P. (2007). Neural correlates of pair-bonding in a monogamous primate. *Brain Research, 1184,* 245–253.

Bartels, A., & Zeki, S. (2000). The neural basis of romantic love. *NeuroReport, 11*(17), 3829–3834.

Baumgartner T, Heinrichs, M., Vonlanthen, A., Fischbacher, U., Fehr, E. (2008). Oxytocin shapes the neural circuitry of trust and trust adaptation in humans. *Neuron, 8,* 639–650.

Bartels, A., & Zeki, S. (2004). The neural correlates of maternal and romantic love. *NeuroImage, 21*(3), 1155–1166.

Berridge, K. C., & Robinson, T. E. (1998). What is the role of dopamine in reward: hedonic impact, reward learning, or incentive salience? *Brain Research Reviews, 28,* 309–369.

Berridge, K. C., Ho, C. Y., Richard, J. M., & DiFeliceantonio, A. G. (2010). The tempted brain eats: Pleasure and desire circuits in obesity and eating disorders. *Brain Research, 1350,* 43–64.

Berscheid, E., & Hatfield, E. (1969). *Interpersonal attraction.* New York: Addison Wesley.

Bittar, R. G., Otero, S., Carter, H., & Aziz, T. Z. (2005). Deep brain stimulation for phantomlimb pain. *Journal of Clinical Neuroscience, 12,* 399–404.

Borg, J., Bengt, A., Soderstorm, H., & Farde, L. (2003). The serotonin system and spiritual experiences. *The American Journal of Psychiatry, 160,* 1965–1969.

Bowlby, J. (1969). *Attachment and loss (Volume 1): Attachment.* London, England: Hogarth.

Bowlby, J. (1977). The making and breaking of affectional bonds. I: Aetiology and psychopathology in the light of attachment theory, II: Some principles of psychotherapy. *British Journal of Psychiatry, 130,* 201-210 and 421–431.

Carter, C.S. (1998). Neuroendocrine perspectives on social attachment and love. *Psychoneuroendocrinology, 23,* 779–818.

Carter, R. M., MacInnes, J. J., Huettel, S. A., & Adcock, R. A. (2009). Activation in the VTA and nucleus accumbens increases in anticipation of both gains and losses. *Frontiers in Behavioral Neuroscience, 3*(21). doi:10.3389/neuro.08.021.2009.

Coan, J. A., Schaefer, H. S., & Davidson, R. J. (2006). Lending a hand: Social regulation of the neural response to threat. *Psychological Science, 17*(12), 1032–1039.

Curtis, J. T., Liu, Y., Aragona, B. J., & Wang, Z. (2006). Dopamine and monogamy. *Brain Research, 1126*(1), 76–90.

Delgado, M. R., Locke, H. M., Stenger, V. A., & Fiez, J. A. (2003) Dorsal striatum responses to reward and punishment: Effects of valence and magnitude manipulations. *Cognitive Affective & Behavioral Neuroscience, 3,* 27–38.

Delorme, R., Chabane, N., Callebart, J., Falissard, B., Mouren-Siméoni, M. C., Rouillon, F., Launay, J. M., & Leboyer, M. (2004). Platelet Serotonergic predictors of clinical improvement in obsessive compulsive disorder. *Journal of Clinical Psychopharmacology, 24*(1), 18–23.

Fisher, H. E. (1998). Lust, attraction, and attachment in mammalian reproduction. *Human Nature, 9,* 23–52.

Ferretti, A., Caulo, M., Del Gratta, C., Di Matteo, R., & Merla, A. (2005). Dynamics of male sexual arousal: Distinct components of brain activation revealed by fMRI. *NeuroImage, 26,* 1086–1096.

Fisher, H. E., Brown, L. L., Aron, A., Strong, G., & Mashek, D. (2010). Reward, addiction, and emotion regulation systems associated with rejection in love. *Journal of Neurophysiology, 104,* 51–60.

Gonzaga, G. C., Keltner, D., Londahl, E. A., & Smith, M. D. (2001). Love and the commitment problem in romantic relations and friends. *Journal of Personality and Social Psychology, 81,* 247–262.

Haber, S. N. (2003). The primate basal ganglia: parallel and integrative networks. *Journal of Chemical Neuroanatomy, 26,* 317–330.

Hare, T. A., O'Doherty, J., Camerer, C. F., Schultz, W., & Rangel, A. (2008). Dissociating the role of the orbitofrontal cortex and the striatum in the computation of goal values and prediction errors. *Journal of Neuroscience, 28,* 5623–5630.

Hazan, C., & Shaver, P. R. (1987). Romantic love conceptualized as an attachment process. *Journal of Personality and Social Psychology, 52,* 511–524.

Jenkins, J. S., Ang, V. T., Hawthorn, J., Rossor, M. N., & Iversen, L. L. (1984). Vasopressin, oxytocin and neurophysins in the human brain and spinal cord. *Brain Research, 291*(1), 111–117.

Lauwereyns, J., Watanabe, K., Coe, B., & Hikosaka, O. (2002). A neural correlate of response bias in monkey caudate nucleus. *Nature, 418*(7), 413–417.

Lim, M. M., & Young, L. J. (2004) Vasopressin-dependent neural circuits underlying pair bonding in the monogamous prairie vole. *Neuroscience, 125,* 35–45.

Loup, F., Tribollet, E., Dubois-Daughin M., Pizzolato, G., & Dreifuss, J. J. (1989). Localization of oxytocin binding sites in the human brainstem and upper spinal cord: an autoradiographic study. *Brain Research, 500*(1–2), 223–230.

Mikulincer, M., & Shaver, P. R. (2007). *Attachment in adulthood: Structure, dynamics, and change*. New York: The Guilford Press.

Najib, A., Lorberbaum, J. P., Kose, S., Bohning, D. E., & George, M. S. (2004). Regional brain activity in women grieving a romantic relationship breakup. *The American Journal of Psychiatry, 161,* 2245–2256.

Napier, T. C., & Mitrovic, I. (1999). Opiod modulation of ventral pallidal inputs. *Annals of the New York Academy of Sciences, 877,* 176–201.

O'Connor, M.-F., Wellisch, D. K., Stanton, A. L., Eisenberger, N. I., Irwin, M. R., & Lieberman, M. D. (2008) Craving love? Enduring grief activates brain's reward center. *NeuroImage, 42,* 969–972.

O'Doherty, J., Dayan, P., Schultz, J., Deichmann, R., Friston, K., & Dolan, R. J. (2004). Dissociable roles of ventral and dorsal striatum in instrumental conditioning. *Science, 304,* 452–454.

Olive, M. F., Anton, B., Micevych, P., Evans, C. J., & Maidment, N. T. (1997). Presynaptic versus postsynaptic localization of m and d opioid receptors in dorsal and ventral striatopallidal pathways. *Journal of Neuroscience, 17,* 7471–7479.

Ortigue, S., Bianchi-Demicheli, F., Hamilton, A. F., & Grafton, S. T. (2007). The neural basis of love as a subliminal prime: An event-related fMRI study. *Journal of Cognitive Neuroscience, 19,* 1218–1230.

Peckys, D., & Landwehrmeyer, G. B. (1999). Expression of mu, kappa, and delta opioid receptor messenger RNA in the human CNS: a 33P in situhybridization study. *Neuroscience, 88,* 1093–1135.

Risinger, R. C., Salmeron, B. J., Ross, T. J., Amen, S. L., Sanfilipo, M., Hoffmann, R. G., Bloom, A. S., Garavan, H., & Stein, E. A. (2005). Neural correlates of high and craving during cocaine self-administration using BOLD fMRI. *NeuroImage, 26*(4), 1097–1108.

Seifert, S., von Cramon, D. Y., Imperati, D., Tittgemeyer, M., & Ullsperger, M. (2011). Thalamocingulate interactions in performance monitoring. *The Journal of Neuroscience, 3*(19), 3375–3383.

Smith, K. S., & Berridge, K. C. (2005). The ventral pallidum and hedonic reward: Neurochemical maps of sucrose "liking" and food intake. *Journal of Neuroscience, 25,* 8637–8649.

Smith, K. S., Tindell, A. J., Aldridge, J. W., & Berridge, K. C. (2009). Ventral pallidum roles in reward and motivation. *Behavioral Brain Research, 196*(2), 155–167.

Sroufe, L. A., & Waters, E. (1977). Attachment as an organizational construct. *Child Development, 48,* 1184–1199.

Stoessel, C., Stiller, J., Bleich, S., Boensch, D., Doerfler, A., Garcia, M., Richter-Schmidinger, T., Kornhuber, J., Forster, C. (2011). Differences and similarities on neuronal activities of people being happily and unhappily in love: A functional magnetic resonance imaging study. *Neuropsychobiology, 64*(1), 52–60.

Xu, X., Aron, A., Brown, L., Cao, G., Feng, T., & Weng, X. (2011). Reward and motivation systems: A brain mapping study of early-stage intense romantic love in Chinese participants. *Human Brain Mapping, 32*(2), 249–257. doi:10.1002/hbm.21017.

Young, L. J., Lim, M. M., Gingrich, B., & Insel, T. R. (2001). Cellular mechanisms of social attachment. *Hormones and Behavior, 40*(2), 133–138.

Zeki, S. (2007). The neurobiology of love. *FEBS Letters, 581*(14), 2575–2579. doi:10.1016/j.febslet.2007.03.094.

Zeki, S., & Romaya, J. P. (2008). Neural correlates of hate. *PLoS ONE, 3*(10), e3556. doi:10.1371/journal.pone.0003556

Zeki, S., & Romaya, J. P. (2010). The brain reaction to viewing faces of opposite- and same-sex romantic partners. *PLoS ONE, 5*(12), e15802. doi:10.1371/journal.pone.0015802.

Index

V. Zayas, C. Hazan (eds.), *Bases of Adult Attachment*,
DOI 10.1007/978-1-4614-9622-9

www.ingramcontent.com/pod-product-compliance
Lightning Source LLC
Chambersburg PA
CBHW060745150926
51501CB00003B/96
* 9 7 8 1 4 6 1 4 9 6 2 1 2 *